HAYLEY McGREGOR

Teacher's Pet

1 3 5 7 9 10 8 6 4 2

Ebury Press, an imprint of Ebury Publishing
20 Vauxhall Bridge Road
London SW1V 2SA

Penguin
Random House
UK

Ebury Press is part of the Penguin Random House group of companies
whose addresses can be found at global.penguinrandomhouse.com

First published by Ebury Press in 2017

www.penguin.co.uk

A CIP catalogue record for this book is available from the British Library

ISBN 9781785035531

Printed and bound in Great Britain by Clays Ltd, St Ives PLC

Penguin Random House is committed to a sustainable
future for our business, our readers and our planet.
This book is made from Forest Stewardship Council®
certified paper.

To my Leroy. Thank you for being my shining star in the darkness. Thank you being the lighthouse in this storm. I love you.

Contents

Author's Note

In February 2016, my former teacher, Andrew Victor Willson, pleaded guilty to five counts of indecent assault against me. He denied all other charges. Having pleaded guilty, he was convicted of only those five crimes.

I was all over the place at the time, and I didn't care about the sentence or the number of assaults that he chose to confess to. I didn't push for anything more. For me it was never about the prison sentence, it was about him admitting his guilt and taking responsibility, which he eventually did – for those five crimes, at least.

I want this book to be balanced and fair, so I'm telling you now: he only admitted, and was only ever convicted of, those five offences. He confessed that he kissed me *on one occasion* in his office; *on one occasion* in his car. He said that in an affair (or rather, as it should properly be called, an abusive relationship) lasting more than a year we kissed only twice and were intimate on just three occasions.

But that's not how I remember it.

For more than twenty years, I have stayed quiet about all this, shamed into silence by my feelings of guilt and worthlessness. But I will not be a silent victim anymore. So I'm telling my story in the hope that it will help others – perhaps encourage other women and men to come forward to share their own dark secrets, or cause the blinkers to fall from the eyes of other young girls and boys who are currently as besotted with their teacher as I once was. And I'm telling my *full* story, because I think it's important to know how a teacher's smile can segue into a kiss and how – once they've got you used to the kissing – events, step by step, can take a twisting path into an intimacy that gets more and more intense… until there's no way back.

Andrew Willson, according to his pleas in court, doesn't agree with my version of events. He *has* admitted hurting me – but only five times.

That's his side of the story; this is mine.

Prologue

When I was a little girl, my mum used to read me fairy tales.

> *Once upon a time, there was a beautiful young woman with flowing golden hair and beautiful big blue eyes. She was often lonely and sad, and yearned to meet her soulmate.*
>
> *One day, a charming prince – a handsome knight in shining armour – became entranced by her youthful beauty and confessed his undying love. He promised they would be together forever, and the young woman fell head over heels in love. After a passionate kiss, during which the prince completely swept her off her feet, they rode off together into the sunset and lived happily ever after.*

I always thought that was what real life was like. I thought that was how all love affairs played out.

It turns out, I was wrong.

Chapter 1

The First Lesson

The day began like any other. With my mates Nicola and Cari beside me, I boarded the red double-decker school bus and the three of us headed – as we always did – to the back seat on the lower deck, where we formed a little clan, me facing the direction of travel with my feet up on the seat in front. We were the first kids collected on the journey so we had our pick of the seats, but we always chose that corner. It was inconspicuous and out of the way so that, when the older, rowdier students later boarded the bus as it meandered through the Lancashire hills, we didn't draw any unwanted attention to ourselves.

Even though I was in Year 8 – my second year of secondary school – I was still a bit overawed at being at 'big school': a small fish in a very intimidating pond. I wasn't one of those young kids who walked around cockily; in fact, I still got lost on occasion on my way to lessons because the school seemed so sprawling. In a way I had a bit of a split personality: in my spare time I was a dancer (I'd done ballet since I was three years old, as well as tap and contemporary) and I loved nothing more than being in the limelight, but offstage I wouldn't have said boo to a goose – especially to the older students, who had a reputation for being tough. I wasn't a confident girl inside at all, it was only on the surface.

At least I had Nicola and Cari to look out for me. They'd befriended me in the previous September of 1992, as we'd all caught the bus together on my very first day in Year 7. They were both in the year above me and they'd taken me under their wing. Cari was an edgy, funky sort of girl, whereas Nicola was more geeky – though she was also far more quick-witted than either of us. She lived just around the corner from me so we spent a lot of time together in the evenings and at weekends, in our bedrooms listening to our favourite artists, Take That for me and Tracy Chapman for Nicola. A wispy brunette, Nicola was known for her big, beaming smile.

None of us were smiling on that particular morning though. Why would we when all that lay ahead was just another boring day at school? I sighed and shifted awkwardly in my seat, fiddling with my striped school tie; the rebel fashion was to wear it with just a little bit at the front, but I wasn't quite confident enough to break the rules so mine was an unfashionable fat sausage that hung down the chest of my white school shirt. Our uniform colour scheme was grey and maroon, which I thought was just *vile*. We had to wear these maroon jumpers – horrible woollen things that made my thick blonde hair even frizzier than normal when I pulled the starchy sweater over my head. I stared glumly out of the window as the bus drove on, and gave another deep sigh when I caught sight of my reflection.

At twelve years old, I hated the way I looked. For a start, I was only about five foot and was always told I looked really young for my age, not what any imminent teenager wants to hear. I was also quite a chubby girl; it was puppy fat, or so my dance teachers told me. All I was told, over and over, was: 'It's puppy fat, it'll drop off.' All I heard was: 'You're fat, you're fat, you're fat.' When I felt brave enough to do so, I'd sometimes untuck my shirt at school so that it would cover up what I thought of as my big bum. My thick long hair almost reached my bottom, but it didn't quite do the job.

It wasn't only my weight that bothered me. One of the nicknames the boys taunted me with was 'Spot the Dog'. I'd had bad skin, especially in my T-zone, ever since the last year of primary school. Puberty had hit early with me, so as well as the spots I also had to contend with the boobs and the hips that came with it. Being part of the school netball team, I now found it very uncomfortable playing my favourite sport for, despite the old-fashioned sports bras I wore, nothing seemed to help with the soreness of my growing breasts and I hated it if the boys were watching. Yet it wasn't only my boobs they were staring at; another of my nicknames was 'Tree Trunk Legs', because I had stocky, sporty limbs that looked nothing like the models in the teenage magazines. I just thanked God that my dad had allowed me to wear trousers now I was in Year 8 – I felt a teeny bit more confident out of ankle socks and my grey school skirt.

My father, Neil, was a very strict man – and with my being not only his first child but also his only daughter, he took that strictness to a whole new level. I wasn't allowed to wear make-up and I certainly wasn't allowed boyfriends; not that I wanted one anyway. My experience with boys was pretty much non-existent. When we had first moved back up north to Bacup, Lancashire, after a few years living in Hampshire – which had happened when my baby brother was born in 1990 and I was nine years old – the novelty of my slightly southern accent had made me the toast of my primary-school class. All the boys had wanted to be my 'boyfriend'. But I'd turned them all down – until eventually, when I was ten or eleven, I'd been peer-pressured into going out with a boy called Lee, who'd wanted to kiss me. Well, that was *not* happening. I remember saying, 'You can kiss me on the cheek and that's *it*.' And that *was* it.

Being at big school hadn't really changed my attitude, either – though to be honest, even if I'd *wanted* a boyfriend, these days they were hardly lining up. I was definitely not the pretty and popular girl that all the boys fancied. Other than Lee's peck on the cheek in primary school, I'd only ever been kissed once: I'd had my first snog just a few months before, at the end of Year 7, after my mate Krissy – who I hung out with at school – had declared, 'Jeffery Johnson fancies you. He wants to meet you by the bins.'

How could I resist?

The bins were the most private place on the school grounds, where the teachers were slowest to hear what was going on. It was where us kids went to snog – or fight. Why we thought it was a good idea to hang out there, I don't know, because it absolutely stank to high heaven, especially in summer, but it was hidden, I guess, and that trumped any aesthetic concerns.

I can still remember the kiss well, even though – and no offence intended, Jeffery – it was hardly something to write home about. Jeffery was waiting by the dustbins for me as I nervously walked to meet him, trying not to inhale the whiff of rubbish that permeated the air. I stopped several metres away from him, barely making eye contact, and then his mates had pushed him forward and my mates had pushed me forward and eventually we'd ended up close enough to kiss. He was really small – at that age I was far taller than he was – and as I bent down to kiss him I could hear his mates ribbing him about his height. I kept my eyes open the whole way through, and I don't think it was earth-shattering for either of us. We 'went out' for only a week before our budding romance was over, and that was the extent of my experience with boys.

As I watched the male students cavorting about on the bus, snapping the girls' bra straps and laughing like hyenas as they did so, it struck me – not for the first time – that far more attractive than the boys at school was Take That's dishy Mark Owen. Cheeky and pretty – and safely unattainable – he was my absolute favourite. If I'm being honest, I didn't think he had the best singing voice, but I was so in love it didn't matter. My bedroom at home was plastered in Take That posters, ceiling-to-floor – so much so that you could no longer see the walls were painted pink.

All too soon, the bus pulled up outside school and the rabble of riotous students disembarked. Noisily, we all made our way through the big spiky metal gates that marked the entrance to the school grounds. As I waved goodbye to Nicola and Cari and they headed off to their Year 9 form rooms, I put my head down and fell in with the flow of students walking towards the Year 8 classes. Maybe it wouldn't be such a bad day, after all. For a start, I was quite looking forward to seeing my mate Krissy at registration – we always had gossip to catch up on. And there was something else I was looking forward to, too; something I'd seen in my timetable that had given me a little fillip of excitement.

Today, we were having our first-ever drama lesson with a brand-new teacher.

His name was Mr Willson.

'What d'you think he's gonna look like?' I whispered to Krissy as we waited outside the arts theatre, as we'd been taught to do outside every classroom before each lesson began. We always had to wait for the teacher to arrive and let us in.

'I dunno,' she replied, kicking aimlessly at the tiled floor of the corridor while we queued with the rest of our class. Above us, stark white ceiling tiles and strip lighting cast an unflattering brightness on our pimpled faces. I wore my long hair down and tried to use it to shield my spots, but it didn't really work. As it had for me, puberty had come early for Krissy too and the two of us had bonded over our mutual physical awkwardness. Down-to-earth and funny, Krissy was a petite girl with mega-curly chestnut hair. We giggled together a *lot*.

'He's supposed to be well fit,' I told her in a hushed tone. 'That's what *everyone*'s saying.'

And I meant *everyone*. Our school – like most others – was a hotbed of gossip and ever since Mr Willson had joined the staff a few days before the corridors had been all aquiver with the news of the hot young drama teacher. Nor was he the only one setting tongues wagging, for the principal had hired a whole bunch of new teachers that term and – to the delight of us students – they were *all* young. It made for quite a change from the tweed-suited, staid members of staff we were used to. In the new crop, alongside Mr Willson, was Mr Smith, the music teacher; Miss Tarpy, who taught art; and – Krissy's own personal favourite – Mr Careless, the new science tutor.

But if I'm being honest, it wasn't the teacher I was looking forward to the most: it was the lesson itself. I worked hard at school and was pretty much a straight-A student across the board. It didn't come easily to me but I would get my head down and study when I had to. Though occasionally labelled a 'swot', I didn't care – I thought that was better than being thick. Yet the beauty of drama was that it wouldn't be academic, it would be practical – learning actual stagecraft, mastering the art of performance. For a dancer like me the whole idea was heaven. I chose to spend my free time out of school rehearsing and performing, so to get to do it in school hours was a genuine treat. We hadn't even had drama as a formal subject in Year 7; instead, it had simply been annexed onto our English lessons. The teacher had pushed the tables to the side of the classroom and we'd half-heartedly read aloud some scenes from a Shakespeare play. But now the Head had decided that he wanted drama to be fully part of the school syllabus and so, for one hour a week, I would get to study in a proper theatre and *act*. I was beyond excited.

The noise from my classmates grew exponentially as each second passed and we continued to wait for the mysterious Mr Willson to arrive. And then the brown wooden doors in the corridor flew open, as though in a whirlwind, and he was suddenly there.

'Hello, Year 8!' he cried confidently. 'Y'allright? I'm Mr Willson.' And then he grinned, as though we were all his mates and not a class of cocky twelve-year-olds who might have been out for his blood.

I didn't think I'd *ever* seen anyone as confident as him. As I stared at him shyly from behind my curtain of long thick hair, that confidence seemed to radiate from him, warming and welcome as sunshine on a cloudy day. He had a deep, commanding voice and, although it had a northern twang to it, it wasn't the broad Bacup accent I was used to hearing.

He didn't look anything like the teachers I was used to seeing, either. Tall and slim, Mr Willson had a cheeky smile and sparkly eyes and clean-shaven skin, and his hair was cropped in a trendy nineties style with blond highlights brightening its spiky tips. Something about him – perhaps the sweetness of his smile or his evident cheekiness – reminded me a little of my beloved Mark Owen.

Mr Willson was about twenty-five years old, I guessed, and he wore a funky, fitted shirt and black trousers – they might even have been jeans. As he walked past me to open up the arts theatre, this heavenly cloud of scent followed in his wake. And for some reason, almost without realising I was doing it, I breathed in, deeply, as he passed. He smelled so nice. Later, I would learn the name of that aftershave: Eternity for Men. I nudged Krissy subtly, wondering if she was as mesmerised as I was, but she just stared back at me blankly.

As the noise rose behind Mr Willson, the class avidly discussing his arrival and his hair and his non-tweed suit, he turned at the now open door and addressed us once more in that cheery tone of his. 'Quiet, everyone!' he said, but it wasn't like he was telling us off. 'In you go, let's get started!'

We all crowded into the arts theatre, a mass of students dumping bags and coats along the walls of the space. It was a big venue, capable of seating perhaps 250 people on its special tiered seating, which could be pulled out or pushed away depending on what was required that day. Black curtains could be hung along the white walls if needed to create a performance space, but today they weren't in evidence. Dormant, too, was the mini lighting rig that the theatre had. There was no stage as such: we performed on the flat floor when we performed at all – which to date had just meant assemblies. But, of course, all that was about to change.

Mr Willson clapped his hands together and summoned us into a circle.

'Right, I want to get to know you lot,' he said. He was very good at looking around the circle as he spoke, focusing on individuals, making sure everyone felt included. My skin flushed as our eyes met, but it was only very briefly, because a second later he was looking at another classmate, and then another, as he talked us through what he wanted to do in that very first lesson. I felt strangely disappointed when his gaze moved on.

We started with name games, all standing in a circle and doing quirky little things to introduce ourselves to him and to each other. It was really fun. What amazed me was how much Mr Willson got involved. He threw himself into it, encouraging us to do the same; making a fool of himself so that we all felt able to make fools of *our*selves. I'd never seen a teacher do that before. Feeling inspired, when it was my turn I really went for it.

'That's brilliant, Hayley!' he exclaimed, and I felt my cheeks burn with pleasure and pride – he seemed to know my name before anybody else's.

He explained the next exercise we were going to do. As we stayed in a circle, he now placed a bunch of keys in the middle: we each had to go and pick up the keys, then put them down and walk back to our places. We all had to observe each other as we did so, and then we took it in turns to mimic someone. While we were performing, Mr Willson might say, 'You've got to do it really exaggeratedly now' or 'Bring it down now, make it really minimal' and we'd adapt our movements accordingly. We were all just giggling, taking the mickey out of each other, but there was no cruelty to it at all: it was a genuine ice-breaker that made the whole class feel comfortable. I wasn't used to feeling comfortable, but I did in that lesson.

Mr Willson then took it up a notch. 'OK,' he said merrily, 'so you've seen this person walking in an exaggerated way, how might they talk?'

As before, he led by example. I was in awe of the way he could change and switch his voice; how he could use different accents to create a new character. I'd been a mimic since I was a young kid, trying to get various accents down as and when I heard them, and I could tell that he was *really* good at it. He knew how to use his diaphragm, too, in order to project his voice to hit the very back wall of the arts theatre. To me, it was like watching a master at work.

Each time it was my turn, I'd try harder and harder for him. 'Excellent, Hayley McGregor!' he would say. 'Well done!'

He praised me a lot, and every time he did so I felt those sparkly eyes of his on mine. *Is he looking at me more than anybody else?* I wondered hesitantly. He had this way of making me feel *so* special – but, looking around the room, I could see that many other students seemed to be getting just as much attention as me. *No*, I told myself, *don't be so stupid*.

That hour was the brightest hour of my whole day. I wanted it to last forever, but all too soon the school bell rang loudly, signalling the class was over.

I went and picked up my black Head bag, slinging it over my shoulder. As I filed out of the theatre, I heard him call to me.

'Great work today, McGregor,' he said charmingly. He grinned that grin and his eyes glimmered at me mesmerisingly before he broke our gaze and went over to congratulate another student, just as warmly.

But I didn't care about the other students. I felt really *good* coming out of that class. Happy, excited. I couldn't really explain it, the way he'd made me feel.

Perhaps that was why I kept it to myself.

Chapter 2
Crush

From that moment on, drama was my favourite subject and Mr Willson my favourite teacher by far. I relished every moment in his class. That first term he focused on tutoring us in drama skills. We started out doing improvisations – 'All right, Hayley McGregor, you're the mum, David's the son and he's late home. *Go!*' – and then transitioned onto scripts. Mr Willson shared with us various techniques to learn lines; to use our voices; to take on different characters at the flip of a switch. We did hot-seating – where you had to stay in character and answer in character as Mr Willson and the class fired questions at you – and gradually we honed our ability to maintain the illusion created by our acting, no matter what was thrown at us.

I not only loved what I was doing in class, I adored how Mr Willson singled me out for praise, time and time again. 'Brilliant, Hayley McGregor,' he would often say. 'Right, everyone, just stop for a moment and watch Hayley for this bit. Can you see what she's doing? That's what I need from the rest of you. She's trying to get that character; she's taking everything on; she's listening to what I'm saying. I want the rest of you to do that too. *Go!*'

I certainly *was* listening to what he was saying; I hung onto his every word. And what words they were – for Mr Willson was not only a teacher, he was a professional actor too. He told the whole class about his hotshot agent in Manchester and would casually drop into conversation that he had auditions to attend after school. I would listen wide-eyed as he talked about it all. *Wow*, I thought, *an acting agent… He must be* really *good to have representation*. It all sounded so glamorous.

Ever since I was a small girl, it had been my ambition to become a performer when I grew up. Even as a toddler I'd been drawn to the stage. My grandma and grandad used to take me to the local Yorkshire working men's club they frequented and nine times out of ten I'd end up on stage with the 'turn'. 'Oh, hello!' a seasoned singer or comedian would say as this little blonde dot boldly joined them in the spotlight. I would confidently curtsey and bow in response to the glorious ripple of laughter and applause that greeted my appearance. I just loved it all. Every single Pontins holiday I'd enter the talent competitions and even now, aged twelve, I attended my dance school in Rochdale at least three times a week. I was totally committed to my dream. Because dance was what I'd learned since I was small, I'd always thought I'd become a dancer – yet now, as Mr Willson opened my eyes to the realm of drama, I felt something ignite inside me. Maybe I could be an actress, too. Above all, I just wanted to be a professional performer: to have an agent, to spend my life on stage or screen. I felt a little like Cinderella as I listened to Mr Willson talk about his work outside our school, longing to attend the fabulous 'ball' he described: I wanted to join him in that world and live there for ever after.

And Mr Willson gave me the confidence to believe I could do it, too. I was always the one he called on to demonstrate things to the class and I loved feeling his eyes on me as I stepped up to perform. I always felt as though he was looking into my soul – and he seemed to like what he saw there, from the charming smiles he gave me afterwards. It was weird, but it felt as though we had a special connection...

I told myself not to be so silly; that I must be imagining it. But it was hard to dismiss my fantasy when we each seemed to make the other laugh and he seemed to be genuinely interested in me. We'd always have a chat at the end of class. I'd be dawdling a little – Krissy would be telling me to hurry up and I'd wave her away and say swiftly that I'd catch her up – so Mr Willson might come over to help me pack my bag and we'd have a few minutes to talk. Or we might share a bit of banter as he tidied up after the class and I took my own sweet time zipping up my bag and lifting it onto my shoulder.

'What are you doing tonight, then, Hayley McGregor?' he might say. He always called me by my full name, or just said 'McGregor', which I really liked: it felt cheeky and somehow familiar, as though he'd given me a nickname. 'Have you got dancing this evening?'

From those precious chats after class, Mr Willson knew all about my dreams; I felt like I could tell him anything. And our love of theatre wasn't the only thing we shared: we were both Leeds United fans so we had that in common too. Given we were in Lancashire, supporting Leeds wasn't the 'in' thing to do – I constantly got grief about being a fan – so our mutual love of them seemed to bring us closer. We seemed to share so much;

I loved the way our lives aligned. Mirroring was a drama technique that I learned about and it often felt as though Mr Willson and I were engaged in that same symmetry. I'd smile and he'd smile back. His sparkly eyes would twinkle when he looked at me and I'd feel my own blue peepers seem to shine that little bit brighter in response. He'd roar with laughter at a joke I'd cracked and I'd find myself chuckling uproariously too. He had such a cheeky way about him that I was confident enough to be well cheeky back. I just remember smiling, smiling, smiling – both of us smiling, like Siamese twins. It never felt like I was talking to a teacher, it felt like talking to a friend.

I tried to remind myself that that was just the way of Mr Willson, though – whoever he was dealing with. He had a really informal, matey way of teaching that none of us kids was used to – he talked to us all like we were his pals and even swore in front of us at times. Nothing too serious, of course, and never in anger or at us, but when he was bantering with the class he'd sometimes brazenly say things like, 'Oh shut up, you silly cow' or – under his breath – 'I don't give a shit.'

Us Year 8 kids would all gasp in mock horror, but secretly we loved the way he was with us, skirting close to that line of acceptability. It felt thrilling.

'*Sir*!' we'd exclaim as one. And he'd laugh and say, 'Oh give over, you all do it too.' And we'd just laugh with him. We didn't want to tell on him and get him into trouble; we didn't want to grass. That was how he made us feel: *that* was the magic of Mr Willson.

I wanted to be around him so much. Before too long, on the days I didn't have drama in my timetable I found myself wandering the school at lunch or break time and hanging around outside his office, just in case he was there and free and wanted to have a chat. At the time I thought I was doing it all in a well cool way, nonchalant as can be, but with hindsight I must have looked like a doe-eyed little girl. I'm sure he knew why I was there. 'Oh hello, sir, I've just bumped into you... again.' It was hardly credible; my crush must have been as clear as day.

Yet to my delight Mr Willson never seemed to mind me popping by. As time went on, he'd even invite me into his office: 'Hayley McGregor, can you come in here and pick up these books for me, please?' With my straight-A reputation I was often the kid chosen to run errands for the staff and I acquiesced as eagerly as a puppy dog.

Mr Willson's office was located just down the corridor from the arts theatre, on the corner. It was absolutely minuscule: more like a cupboard that somebody had turned into an office than an actual room. A maroon swing door led into it. Carpeted with those wiry square tiles that all schools use – his were made from an industrial fabric patterned with green-and-brown swirls – the room was so tiny that all it held was a big brown desk and some shelving. It had no windows.

Yet he didn't let the size of his space limit his possessions. His office was completely crammed with stuff – scripts and books and boxes and costumes; crisps and sweets secreted in his drawer – and his desk was always a terrible mess. As I spent more time in there, I started to help him tidy it up. It wasn't that I was a particularly neat person myself – my mum would certainly have disputed that from her regular lectures to me about tidying my bedroom at home – but I wanted to sit on his desk as we chatted, and I couldn't do that if it was covered in paperwork.

Being short, I always liked to sit on the tables in school – but I didn't often get away with it. I was told off all the time for that particular misdemeanour: 'Tables are not for sitting on, Hayley, get *down*' or 'Sit on your chair *properly*' were constant refrains from the staff. But Mr Willson never said a word to me about it; he wasn't that kind of teacher.

I loved spending time in his office. He had personal photographs pinned on the wall behind his desk, as well as newspaper clippings about performances he'd done, and it was fascinating to find out more about him. One jaw-dropping discovery – one that made me even more enamoured – was that Mr Willson was in a band: he had a snapshot on display of him and his two bandmates. *How cool is that?* I thought in awe, peering more closely at the picture.

It showed three men in their mid-twenties striking a classic boyband pose. Mr Willson was at the apex of the triangle and the others were to his side, looking over their shoulders at the camera and pouting furiously. All three were dressed in black, like proper rock stars, and their hair was styled within an inch of its life.

'We're doing a gig this weekend,' he told me casually, noting my interest.

Oh my God, that is so amazing! I thought to myself. *I wonder if I can go…*

As though he'd read my mind, he abruptly put an end to my daydreaming by adding, 'It's in a pub.'

A pub: *sigh*! Not much chance of a twelve-year-old being let in there on a Saturday night. I tried not to let my disappointment show, but inside I was gutted. *I can't wait till I get older*, I thought desperately. *Then I'll be able to go and sing along to all his songs; just like I do with Mark Owen.*

I looked again at the picture on the wall. Of the two men I didn't know, one wasn't particularly good-looking – I guess there always has to be one ugly bloke in a boyband – but the other was totally gorgeous. He had luscious, highlighted swooshy hair that swept across his forehead and beautiful Hispanic skin.

'Your mate's well fit,' I said teasingly.

I thought he'd tease me back, so I was really surprised by his reaction. Instead of joking along with me, Mr Willson took a step backwards in mock hurt and said, almost churlishly, 'He's not that good in real life.'

It was weird: it was as though he was *jealous* that I'd singled out his mate. I felt like I'd hurt him.

'I'm only joking, sir,' I said hurriedly, and I quickly knew that I'd said the right thing because he blessed me with one of those amazing smiles of his and then carried on chatting as normal.

Yet Mr Willson wasn't the only one who was jealous. Because pinned up on his wall, right beside the impressive clippings and the boyband snapshots, was a rather different image: Mr Willson and his wife.

I'd known he was married from the very first day. As I'd drunk in the sight of him, I couldn't help but notice the thick platinum wedding band that was wrapped around the third finger of his left hand. So mesmerising had I found him, I'd actually felt a little disappointed when I'd spotted it. After all, he was only twenty-five, just thirteen years older than me, and maybe in a few years he might – just might – have wanted to be with me, but as soon as I saw that wedding ring I'd known he wasn't mine to have. Seeing the photos of him with his wife brought that home.

He had a son, too, who was less than a year old. Even in the photographs it was obvious something wasn't quite right with him. When I asked Mr Willson about it, he told me that his son had severe special needs. Oh, my heart went out to him and his baby. I've always been a really maternal person – I often babysat for my little brother, and my mum told me that I was so caring with him that I was more like a second mum than a sister – so hearing about this poorly child touched me deeply. I really liked that Mr Willson felt able to talk to me about it, though; I knew he wouldn't tell me things if he didn't think I was mature enough to handle them.

But, as it turned out, I didn't need to worry on that score at all – because Mr Willson often told me that I'd got an older, wiser head on my shoulders than anybody else in my year. I really liked that. It made me feel special and grown-up.

As I listened to Mr Willson talk about his son and how he cared for him, he seemed even more of a good person to me. *What a lovely man*, I thought, *not to run away and be scared. He stayed and cared for his disabled son. What a hero; what a great dad.* Though I knew it would never lead to anything, it made him even more attractive in my eyes.

Mr Willson's wife wasn't my only 'rival' for his affection, though, because my favourite teacher was the apple of the eye of almost every other girl in school. Not many were immune to his charms. Krissy was one of the rare few who didn't understand what everybody else saw in him, but my mate Nicola was a firm Mr Willson fan. Perhaps unsurprisingly, once we had each shyly confessed our infatuation, he soon became our very favourite topic of conversation.

'Oh my God, he looked at me *really* intensely today,' I might say to her in a whisper. 'You know that look he does?'

'I know,' Nicola would sigh dreamily, and we'd both fall silent for a few moments, imagining Mr Willson's sparkly eyes.

'I swear, he was looking at me like they do in films,' I'd go on in dead seriousness, and she'd nod eagerly, knowing exactly what I meant.

'He told me I looked pretty today,' she then might say, making my heart sink at her words. 'He said my hair looked nice.'

She'd touch it self-consciously and I'd stare a little enviously at her straight brown hair, which seemed so much more attractive than my own thick blonde locks, which had a natural curl to them that I hated. I envied Nicola's quick-wittedness and her droll sarcasm too; Mr Willson, she said, often told her she was one of the funniest girls he'd *ever* met, something that made a nasty, jealous feeling roil inside my belly. I don't think he knew Nicola and I were friends at that time, because we weren't in the same school year, but every word he said to each of us and every look he gave was dissected at length on the school-bus journey home and then well into the evening.

I'd have to do my chores when I first got in, of course: wash up, vac up and take our Golden Labrador, Tetley (named after the bitter), for a walk. I was usually so hungry when I got home from school that I'd have a bowl of cereal to keep me going before my mum made tea. But after tea, *that*'s when Nicola and I could really analyse everything Mr Willson had said or done. We'd meet up and either wander the streets talking or sit in our rooms with our music on loud and talk very quietly underneath it. For some reason we didn't want anyone else to hear what we were discussing. And we only ever told each other: a secret that never went beyond the borders of our best-friend bond.

One day, I had something *really* exciting to tell Nicola.

'Oh my God, he *touched* me today!' I declared happily.

It had happened that day in drama. Us kids had all been divided into groups and we'd spent the lesson working on a scene, which we were going to perform at the end of class. My group and I were still busy discussing it when Mr Willson had clapped his hands and said, 'Right, everybody, can you take your seats and clear a space for the performances, please!'

There was a big melee of everyone moving about and grabbing seats and so on. My group and I were still chatting, an island of immobility in a sea of movement, and I guess I must have been standing right on the spot where Mr Willson wanted us to perform. But rather than him saying, 'Excuse me, Hayley McGregor, please can you move to one side,' he chose another method instead.

He came up behind me and put his hands firmly on my waist.

Oh my God. His touch literally sent electric shivers all over my body. His hands were big and warm – I'd taken my jumper off in the heat of the lesson and I could feel them through my thin school shirt – but despite their size he was so soft and gentle as he shifted me to the side and moved me out of the way. It was like the whole world stood still for a moment as he did so. Time stood still. And then butterflies began somersaulting in my stomach and the noise of shouting kids and scraping chairs filtered back in and I remembered to breathe once more.

Wow, I thought. I'd never felt anything like it before; I didn't know it was *possible* to feel that way.

I caught his eye as I moved to sit down, and he smiled at me in that special way he always did. *Does he know?* I wondered. *Does he know the way he makes me feel? Can* he *feel those electric pulses inside him, too?*

I didn't know. But it was like he'd lit a fire within me – and I was transfixed by the flames.

I forgot the warnings my mother always said: that children should never, ever play with fire.

Chapter 3
Showtime

It wasn't long before Mr Willson touched me again. He was a very tactile person, so it wasn't unusual for him to put an arm around a student's shoulder or to joke about physically. If I was sat next to him in class, his legs might be crossed so that his foot would tap gently against my calf, or I'd suddenly feel his thigh muscle tensing and twitching beside mine as our legs nestled side by side.

Consequently, after that first time he touched me quite often and my heart thrilled every time he did. The only thing that made me feel glum about it was that I wasn't the only one: he was touchy-feely with everyone he encountered, air-kissing them theatrically and even hugging members of staff. It plainly didn't mean anything to him, the way it did to me. Half the time he touched me so casually that I thought he must be brushing against me accidentally, with no idea I was there, tingling away beneath his touch.

As the school year drew on, an exciting announcement was made: Mr Willson would be running an after-school drama club. The moment he mentioned it to me, I couldn't wait to sign up. Even though it was dark outside in the early evenings after school – more winter than spring, despite the fact the year was moving on –

those sessions we had in the arts theatre seemed as sunny as a summer's day. And they seemed brighter still when Mr Willson told the group that he'd partly organised the club in order to gauge what interest there was in drama as an extra-curricular activity – and as the take-up had been so high, he and Mr Smith, the music teacher, would be organising a full-scale theatrical production later in the year. Though it's hard to remember after all these years, I think we perhaps found out about that around the time of my thirteenth birthday in March 1994 and to me the news was the best birthday present *ever*.

Even after I became a teenager, I still didn't seem to have much luck with boys. Although Mr Willson often complimented me, saying I was pretty and talented, the boys at school didn't seem to agree. When they weren't tripping me up in the corridors or painfully yanking my bra strap, they seemed intent on humiliating me. I was flattered, shortly after my birthday, to be asked out by one of the lads in my year. But in the schoolyard, in front of everyone, his mate told me bluntly that he'd only gone out with me for a bet – and just a £5 one at that. His lips had curled into a nasty sneer as he broke the news and my cheeks burned with mortification when I heard everyone laughing loudly at me, jeering and cackling. The joke was supposedly that this lad was really good-looking and I wasn't, yet I'd actually believed he liked me: ha ha, really funny. I wasn't upset because my heart was broken – though I fancied him because he was the most popular lad in school, I was hardly head over heels in love – but it was incredibly hurtful to be the butt of everyone's joke, especially when the punchline was that I was so ugly no one could possibly want me.

But Mr Willson didn't think I was ugly. In contrast to all the negativity out in the schoolyard, he told me nothing but positive things. I felt safe around him; I felt confident and calm. He was so easy to talk to that I found myself chatting away about anything and everything; he got a load of gossip from me about the other kids that no teacher would normally be privy to. I also told him all about my family and he listened with interest as I described my mum and dad.

I was very proud of my parents. My dad, Neil, was a fireman and I waxed lyrical about that, telling Mr Willson that we lived right next to the fire station in Bacup. I knew he'd like to hear about Dad's footballing career too – my dad had been a professional player for Burnley at the start of his working life, before he got injured – so I burbled away happily about all that, as well as sharing the news that he supported Leeds United, just like Mr Willson himself, which I knew would get my teacher's seal of approval. As for my mum, Andrea, like me she'd been a ballet dancer when she was younger but she never pursued it as a career, perhaps partly because I'd come along when my parents were only twenty years old. I'd once asked her if I'd got in the way of her career, but she said no, the only job she'd ever wanted was to be a mum.

Though my mother was primarily a mum – she worked a bit to bring in some extra cash, but she was in no way a career woman – she was most definitely *not* mumsy. She had a strong, sporty figure and wore stylish clothes, and both she and my dad were lookers. Once, on a Pontins holiday, Dad had been likened to Robert Redford and he'd dined out on that ever since. Both in their early thirties now, they made a striking, handsome couple.

In fact I talked my parents up so much that Mr Willson told me he was more looking forward to meeting my folks at the upcoming parents' evening than he was to doing the parents' evening itself. I can remember clearly the first time they all met. It was one of those events where I had to escort my parents around each of my subject teachers in turn. Both Mum and Dad came along as they were always very keen to know how I was getting on at school; they would have been dead strict with me if ever we'd been told that I needed to pull my socks up. Yet, to date, that had never happened. With a baby brother at home who understandably demanded much of my parents' focus, I had learned to get their attention by being a really, *really* good girl. I was not a rebellious child at all. Consequently, one teacher after another gave glowing reports of my attendance and my work ethic while I sat quietly beside my parents, soaking up the praise like a thirsty sponge.

Soon enough, the time for our appointment with Mr Willson came round and I led my parents over to his table. My heart was pounding, as it always did when he was near. After he shook their hands firmly, we all settled down together; my heart now very much in my mouth as I waited to hear my favourite teacher's verdict on how I was getting on in his class.

'OK, first of all,' Mr Willson began, 'your daughter's *brilliant.*'

I felt a beaming smile crack across my face and sensed my parents relaxing too: another good report. I'd expected Mr Willson to go on, but he just grinned at my folks and said, 'There's nothing else I need to say about her. So, Neil, Leeds United, eh?'

And that was it: laughter, banter, chemistry. It was immediate. They all got on like a house on fire. My dad is everything you'd imagine of a Yorkshireman – proper salt of the earth – and Mr Willson's directness appealed to him. As for Mum, I could see that he was almost flirting with her, charming her. When our five minutes with him came to an end and it was time to move on, he gave my dad a strong handshake and fully embraced my mother, just as he did any other adult woman I saw him with, holding her just a beat longer than other men might.

'Maybe I'll see you at a Leeds match then, Neil,' Mr Willson said in parting. 'We could meet up for a pint?'

With that, a friendship was born. After that evening all my parents did was gush about Mr Willson. I was glad they liked him so much; it seemed to cement my own good impression. Dad thought he was a great guy who had my very best interests at heart. As a result, he had no hesitation in allowing me to try out for the school show when auditions came round later that year.

The production was to be *Smike*, a pop musical adaptation of the novel *Nicholas Nickleby* by Charles Dickens. To be honest, I thought it was a bit naff, but there was no way I wasn't going to be involved. I wanted to spend as much time with Mr Willson as I could so I rocked up eagerly to the auditions, hoping against hope that I would be cast.

It was rather intimidating, I have to say. I'd never had to do an audition before and with this being our school's first-ever theatrical production, it had attracted hopefuls from all across the school. I felt like a minnow as I waited in line next to these giant kids from Year 11, who towered above me – everyone seemed to be older than me.

It was perhaps no surprise that I ended up in the chorus – it was mostly the older kids who landed the main parts – but I was gutted. Nonetheless, I threw myself into rehearsals and in the end I did get picked to do a tiny extra part, a comedic cameo as a washerwoman or a waitress or something like that, and I was really pleased to be rewarded in that way. It was amazing, actually, how much being in *Smike* helped to build my confidence. I'd never been in a proper production before – dance recitals and childhood nativities didn't count – and I adored the whole process: from having nothing and wondering how we were going to learn it all, through the rehearsals to the final fabulous flourish of a finished show. It truly did feel magical: something from nothing.

As I wasn't playing a lead role, I wasn't called for rehearsal that much – which was disappointing, given I'd hoped to spend more time with Mr Willson. But I lived for those rehearsals I did attend, not least because he continued to single me out for praise. I was always being told that I was good and that everybody ought to watch me. I'd come out of rehearsals just buzzing with all these amazing positive feelings. And they weren't all about my teacher, it was the joy of the entire experience. Mr Willson and Mr Smith were brilliant at making the chorus feel integral to the play as a whole and their direction taught me a lot about acting without words; that just because I didn't have any lines, it didn't mean I shouldn't react onstage to what was happening before me. The whole show ignited something in me: I wanted to do this again and again. And as much as I enjoyed being in the chorus, I thought secretly to myself, *I don't want to be in the background next time...*

Maybe the best thing about the rehearsal process – as so many other casts have found throughout time – was how close we all became as a group. Meeting all these kids from other year groups and working with them on the show built up my confidence socially, too, and I started to come out of my shell. As in many theatre groups, there was lots of air-kissing and hugging between us all, and it just seemed natural that Mr Willson, as our leader, might congratulate me on a great performance by squeezing my shoulder or gently touching my arm. The more informal setting of the after-school rehearsals brought us even closer together; made us even closer friends.

All too soon, we performed the finished show to our friends and families and the production came to an end. There was a wrap party on the final night: a buffet with Mr Kipling cakes and a disco in the arts theatre. I agonised over what to wear and eventually settled on a big oversized stripy shirt – chosen mostly because I wasn't confident about my changing body at all and wanted to cover it up as much as I could – paired with jeans and a chunky belt. My dad's ban on make-up still held and I had no clue what to do with my hair other than wear it down, so it wasn't exactly the glamorous 'actress' look I had hoped for, but it would have to do.

Yet, although I didn't think I looked that nice, it seemed I had attracted someone's attention. I was completely mortified when one of the older lads tried to kiss me at the party; I turned my head away in embarrassment and muttered, 'Sorry, I don't want to.' He was a skinny, scruffy boy with glasses and that long nineties hair combed into a parting, and I just didn't fancy him. I felt a bit bad about saying no because he was a lovely lad and we got on well, but for me there was no spark.

In fact, in those days I felt no spark with anyone other than Mr Willson. It was odd, in a way, because even though I knew I didn't stand a chance with my teacher, he was nonetheless at least *part* of the reason I turned that lovely boy down. I was being true to my feelings, because I didn't fancy him, but the real truth was no one could compete with Mr Willson.

As for Mr Willson, he was the life and soul of that party. I remember him dressed in double denim, and snapshots from that night show him with his arms casually draped around us schoolkids.

I've always loved the camera. From day dot, I could be crying and if my mum wanted me to stop sobbing all she had to do was put a lens in front of my face and my tears would instantly dry up; I'd grin madly, ready for my close-up. Even so, unusually for me, I wasn't really aware of the camera that evening as snaps were taken of the festivities. I wasn't aware as someone clicked the shutter and caught me and Mr Willson on film, frozen in time forever.

He was in between me and my mate, his arms around us both. His hand is visible on my friend's shoulder, but you can't see where it ends up behind me. I wonder, now, if that was the first time he did what would become, in time, a favourite thing: to touch me at the very base of my back – gently, intimately, like a lover guiding his girlfriend to her opera seat or to dinner in a fancy restaurant. There is something very personal in that gesture; something that's even, perhaps, a little possessive.

In a heartbeat, the shutter opened and closed and the moment was gone. I didn't even recall it until I saw that same photograph posted on a Facebook wall many, many years later. There were other moments, more important moments, that filled my mind instead.

Such as the time we were alone together in a classroom just at the end of that Year-8 school year. The sun was beating down that day and it was so hot I'd taken off my jumper. I'm not sure why we were in a classroom, because it wasn't his room; sometimes the arts theatre was needed for exams and our drama class was kicked out so maybe that was it, or perhaps he was our cover teacher for some other subject.

The bell rang for the end of class and there was the usual melee as everyone fought to get outside as quickly as possible. On that occasion I had joined them, eager to enjoy the glorious summer sunshine, but just as I was walking out the door I heard: 'Hayley McGregor, can you stay behind, please?'

I let my classmates flow out of the room and turned back to face Mr Willson. He was sat at the front of the classroom in that usual teacher position behind a big wooden desk. Everyone else had gone and the corridors outside had swiftly fallen silent and still. I walked right up to him and put my bag down, leaning forward lazily on his desk as though it was too much effort for me to stand upright. My position made me lower than him, my head near to the desk so that he had to look down at me; our faces were quite close. As a result, perhaps, he spoke to me quietly, because we were almost on top of each other and there was no need to shout.

'How are you, McGregor? Good day?'
'Yes, sir. Thank you, sir.'

'Did you see my mate come into school yesterday?' he asked lightly.

'Yeah,' I replied easily. Then I cracked a smile. 'The rubbish one in the band.'

He smiled back at the insult, sharing the joke. Funnily enough, the bandmate I'd told him I thought was fit never once came into school.

'Well,' he confided, looking deep into my eyes as though to gauge my reaction at his next words, 'he quite fancies you.'

He was lying, I think – an innocent white lie. Yet it had an effect: it normalised the idea that someone Mr Willson's age *could* fancy me.

'Oh no, not *him*, sir!' I groaned at the very idea of his ugly friend. He seemed to like that.

We kept on chatting softly in the classroom, with Mr Willson talking to me and our eyes absolutely locked on one another, as they so often were. And then he seemed to lose his train of thought even as he was talking. He seemed to have to shake himself from a seductive, immobilising trance.

'I'm sorry,' he said to me, 'I'm just getting lost in those eyes of yours...'

Oh! I had no words to say back to him; I simply kept on staring as the butterflies swirled and soared in my soul.

'I need to stop looking in your eyes because they're so sparkly,' he went on, his lines seeming to me to be straight out of a movie – but all this was *real*.

'*Really*?' I whispered the word, not wanting to break the spell. 'Do you really think so, sir?'

'Yeah,' he said, firmly and quietly. We faced each other, only inches apart. 'Beautiful eyes, beautiful smile.'

I couldn't help but grin: to give him that smile that he had so admired. And I kept on grinning all the way home, all night long, and even all the way through the summer holidays.

When those holidays were over, for once I couldn't wait to get back to school. I was Year 9 now, aged thirteen – *and* a half – and I had this feeling that the coming year would be one that I would never, ever forget.

Chapter 4

Back to School

Such was the power of Mr Willson's compliments that I actually felt confident walking into school on the first morning of Year 9 – because I knew he was going to be there. I didn't really understand why I felt so happy around him; I had all these feelings inside me but I didn't quite know what they were, having never felt this way about anyone before. All I knew was that every day was better when he was around; and when he wasn't, I was sad.

I hadn't spent the whole summer pining for him, though. I was a very busy girl, with dance exams, ballet summer school and babysitting my brother to keep me occupied, so, although I'd missed him, I hadn't been heartbroken that we were apart. Nicola and I had kept up our chats over the summer anyway, fuelled by the memory of that special scene in the classroom just before the end of term, so in some ways he'd been a vivid presence to us both in those long hot days away from school. We'd spent a lot of time giggling about him, wondering what he was doing and indulging in flights of fancy with our own made-up scenarios of what might happen next. Nicola was a naturally inquisitive girl so she always asked me lots of questions about how he'd made me feel. Sometimes I simply had to say 'I don't know' in response to her questions because I couldn't get my head around my feelings – or, sometimes, I didn't even know what she meant; that extra year she had on me made a big difference at our age. But the one thing I did know was that I was really excited to see him again now the new term had begun.

I wondered if he'd notice a difference in me. I was a tiny bit taller, though still short; I would never grow taller than five foot two. My family and I had spent two weeks in Menorca for our holidays that year, sunning ourselves in a villa with its own private pool, so I had a really nice tan, which I was proud of; I thought it looked much better than my usual pasty white skin. Perhaps the biggest difference for me personally was that my boobs no longer ached – they seemed to have stopped growing, at last, and had settled at a comfortable 34B. By now I was becoming slightly more confident with my body so I'd chosen a new school shirt that was a little more fitted; I'd also ditched my trousers in favour of thick black tights and a charcoal grey skirt. That 'charcoal grey' was very important because it basically looked like black, which I thought was much more slimming than the horrid, standard grey they wanted us to wear. Of course, I hadn't walked five paces into school grounds before I was called on it.

'Why are you wearing a black skirt, Hayley?' the teacher on the gates asked me wearily.

'It's *charcoal* grey, sir,' I retorted, and showed him the label before flouncing off into school. And there was nothing he could say about it: it *was* a shade of grey, after all.

The moment I saw Mr Willson, it was like we'd never been apart.

'Good summer, McGregor?'

'Yes, sir! Thank you, sir. How about you, sir?'

Our conversation flowed as fluidly as the suntan lotion had on my skin beside the pool in Menorca. We soon fell back into our pattern of my loitering by his office most days of the week; I can still remember the crushing disappointment if ever he wasn't there when I stopped by. I just loved being around him and thrived on the positive way he made my feel, as he dished out compliments like candy: about my talent, my lovely blonde hair, my sparkly blue eyes, my beautiful smile… I used to go home and stare in the mirror, trying to see myself through his eyes, because I couldn't appreciate the beauty he told me I had; I saw only a million faults. But as I stared critically at my reflection, I'd think of my eyes, *Well, they are quite a nice blue, I suppose*. I'd run over his words in my mind and I'd think, *Well, he likes them, so they must be OK*. He made me feel so much better about myself; it was a really addictive high.

A rumour started that Oliver in our year had a massive crush on me. Apparently, he'd liked me since Year 7. A small lad, he had rosy cheeks, black hair and round glasses; he reminded me of Penfold from the cartoon *Danger Mouse*. I didn't fancy him one bit so, sadly for him, his love went unrequited. Just as I had the year before, I basically ignored all the boys my own age because Mr Willson was there.

One day, towards the end of the autumn term, Mr Willson and I were left alone at the end of drama. As usual, I'd told Krissy to go on and I'd catch her up.

'I've been meaning to talk to you about the next show, McGregor,' he said once we were alone.

After the success of *Smike*, I knew that Mr Willson and Mr Smith were keen to stage another production. Rumour had it that the show was to be Willy Russell's *Blood Brothers* and auditions would be held after Christmas. I was really excited by the whole idea.

'You know I think you're very talented,' my teacher went on. I nodded modestly, feeling simultaneously awkward and thrilled by his praise. 'I hope you're going to audition? I can't guarantee any main part, of course, but there will definitely be something for you.'

Because I could talk to Mr Willson about anything, I confessed that I was really nervous. I remembered all too well the intimidating auditions for *Smike* the year before and I knew that – even though I was now in Year 9 and a little bit older – I'd still be competing against the more mature kids from Years 10 and 11. Plus, *Blood Brothers* was a *proper* musical. I was a very experienced dancer, and thanks to Mr Willson I felt confident in my acting skills, but singing was a whole different ball game.

'Well, Mr Smith says you've been doing really well in your music lessons,' Mr Willson said encouragingly once he'd listened patiently to my fears. He held my gaze with those sparkly eyes of his. 'Will you please give it a go?'

Well, when he looked at me like that, I'd have given him *anything*. 'OK, yeah, all right, sir,' I said shyly, and I couldn't help smiling at him when I saw that my words had provoked that same expression on his face. 'Thank you, sir.'

It wasn't long after our chat that the school broke up for Christmas. I spent the holidays researching the show: listening to the music, watching Barbara Dickson on video playing the lead role, Mrs Johnstone, and slowly learning the songs. I totally fell in love with *Blood Brothers*. My family were massive fans of musical theatre but it hadn't been a show that was on my radar before – we'd been to see blockbuster productions like *Les Misérables* and *The Phantom of the Opera* and all the Andrew Lloyd Webber ones. As I practised and practised and practised, I indulged in a little daydream that I'd be given a main part and then Mr Willson and I would… Well, I was never really sure exactly *what* Mr Willson and I would do, but it would be full of flowers and happiness and sunshine, that was for sure.

When we returned to school after Christmas, we had to sign up if we wanted to audition. The school noticeboard hung in the main building, right next to the stairs leading up to languages. When I got to the board, some five or six people had already scribbled their names down. I took a deep breath, feeling those nerves trembling in my belly, but Nicola encouraged me to go for it; she wasn't a performer herself but she was to stage-manage the show. So I pressed my pen to the sign-up sheet and very, very neatly wrote my name. Then, because I knew he would be reading it, I put a little kiss beneath, too.

The next time I saw him, we were passing each other in the corridor.

'Hayley McGregor, how are you?' he cried.

'Yeah, good, sir. I put my name down!'

'Good girl!'

I loved it when he called me that.

The auditions were held one lunchtime in early February 1995. Excruciatingly, they weren't closed, so other kids who weren't auditioning were allowed to sit in the arts theatre and eat their packed lunch while they watched us try out for the show. It was horrifically public; as if I wasn't nervous enough already!

Mr Smith had wheeled the school's grand piano into the room and it was bang in the middle of the performance area. Mr Smith was like an adult Penfold: he had jet-black hair and wore spectacles. Unlike Mr Willson, he was always suited and booted and wore a sober tie. He was proper strict, which was why the pair worked so well together: they were each other's yin and yang. Mr Smith was a tiny, wispy man who was an absolutely phenomenal classical pianist. He was really inspiring; in fact, they both were.

'All right, let's get started!' Mr Willson called out. He was running the auditions, while Mr Smith sat behind the piano and accompanied us. 'If I call your name, please come down to the stage.'

We would be auditioning in groups of five. Mr Willson called out the first few names – I wasn't among them – and the kids shuffled in front of the piano. At least he had arranged the auditionees so they were facing him and Mr Smith and not the rabble of our eagerly watching peers, but that was about the only bright spot.

We hadn't had to prepare an audition piece. Despite all my hard work learning the *Blood Brothers* songs over the holidays, we weren't asked to sing a song from the show, either. Instead, they requested we sang 'Any Dream Will Do' from *Joseph and the Amazing Technicolor Dreamcoat* and then we would do a bit of cold reading from the *Blood Brothers* script.

'Right, next group!' Mr Willson called out once the first group had finished. And then I heard my name: 'Hayley McGregor!'

I stood up and walked out to meet him. Perhaps I was hoping he might reassure me, but there was no special smile for me today: he was very professional, maybe because Mr Smith was there. Mr Willson handed out the lyric sheet and addressed us all.

'I'm going to count you in and I want you to sing together,' he told us. 'Then when I point at you individually, it'll be just that person singing. I'll go down the line so you'll all get a chance to sing solo. OK? A-one, a-two, a-one, two, three, four…'

I couldn't look at him as I sang; I fixed my gaze on a point above Mr Smith's head so I was looking at no one. I was one of the later soloists he pointed to, maybe third in our group; I think I had to sing the chorus. And I sounded *awful*. It was the first time I appreciated how much nerves can affect you. For the voice I sang with was not the voice from my bedroom, where I'd been happily belting out *Blood Brothers* numbers from dawn to dusk. Instead, it was as though my nerves were literally strangling my talent; I could barely hold a tune.

I was very, very upset afterwards; I didn't think it had gone well at all. Somehow I managed to get through the acting part of the audition and then I slunk back to my seat to watch the rest of the hopefuls be put through their paces. But that made me feel even worse. *There's not a chance in hell I'm going to be cast*, I thought miserably. There was a girl in my year called Thea – another blonde-haired, blue-eyed drama lover – who did a fantastic audition. But it was the older kids who really stabbed the final nail in my coffin: Lindsay Davies and Jodie D'Eath, who were both in Nicola's year, had the most phenomenal singing voices *and* they were gorgeous. Jodie was a slim, well-to-do brunette with big gorgeous eyes and a lovely smile; she looked like a ballerina. Lindsay, meanwhile, was completely stunning: one of those girls who could get caught in a downpour and still look picture-perfect. She had olive skin, jet-black hair and dark eyes: a tiny little thing with a massive voice. As I heard their voices confidently fill the theatre, sounding awesome, I just wanted to curl up and die. *They've got this*, I told myself. I could actually taste my disappointment.

Eventually, my purgatory ended and Mr Willson wrapped things up. Dejected, I was one of the last to leave the room; I just felt so embarrassed. Mr Willson had gone on and on about how talented I was and I considered my audition to be a total disaster. As I clomped down the steps of the tiered seating with my head bowed low, I was having to hold my tears in.

'All right, McGregor?' I heard him ask.

'Not really, sir,' I said flatly. He could tell at once I was in a mood.

'Don't worry,' he assured me. 'You did fine, you'll be OK.'

I just rolled my eyes at him sardonically.

'Look, you'll find out in the next few days.' He could see that his words were having no effect, so he reached out a hand and touched me on the arm as though to emphasise his point. 'It's *OK*, McGregor.'

Oddly enough, that touch and his words *did* make me feel better. His hand always sent an electric current through me and I let myself warm my broken heart on those feelings that day. Naturally, I still went home and sobbed into my pillow, hugging my favourite teddy – a worn blue Bedtime Bear from the Care Bears range – as close as I could. But his encouragement gave me strength enough to attend the casting announcement a few days later, even though I knew my case was absolutely hopeless.

Everyone who'd auditioned was called into the arts theatre at lunchtime to hear the news; I had Nicola with me for moral support. The tiers of the tiered seating were out, but with no chairs on them: we ranged about on the large wooden steps as they do on the bleachers in *Grease*. Nicola sat on the step behind me and we listened intently as the names were called out by Mr Willson: he was going from the smallest named characters up to the main lead roles. I'd recovered my equilibrium a little and wondered if I'd maybe get cast as one of the Johnstone kids, but as Mr Willson continued to read out the names I switched off because my name wasn't being called. I decided I was going to end up in the chorus again. *Oh well*, I thought, giving up, and turned around to gossip with Nicola.

'Hayley McGregor!' I heard Mr Willson say.

I started guiltily; the good girl's response to being caught not listening to the teacher. There was a weird atmosphere in the room – as I glanced about I saw Jodie D'Eath was giving me daggers while everyone else was looking at me and smiling broadly.

'W-what, sir?' I stuttered. 'Sorry, sir?'

'Did you not hear what I just said?' he asked sternly.

I shook my head, my cheeks flaming with embarrassment. 'No, sir. Sorry.'

He cleared his throat and spoke again. 'And the part of Mrs Johnstone goes to Hayley McGregor.'

Oh my God! I just screamed. Nicola screamed. The arts theatre rang with the sound of applause and I was hugging everyone and crying.

'Are you serious?' I called to Mr Willson over the hullabaloo. 'Is this a joke?'

'No, you're right for the part,' he told me firmly, smiling. 'Mr Smith and I both agree.'

Jodie had been cast as Mrs Lyons, which suited her down to the ground because she herself was a very elegant girl and Mrs Lyons is the upper-class role. But I think it's fair to say, especially because she was older than me, she'd been hoping for the lead. Stunning Lindsay Davies was cast as the twins' love interest, Linda, while my doppelgänger, Thea, was named the narrator. Two boys named Adam and Matt would play my sons, Mickey and Eddie.

I felt totally overwhelmed; on top of the world. I made my way down from the wooden tiers as everyone started heading off for afternoon lessons, chattering away about who was playing whom. Mr Smith gave me a quick hug to say well done and then Mr Willson wrapped me up in his arms and did the same.

Wow. Our bodies were pressed close together and – unlike with Mr Smith – it wasn't a perfunctory hold and then release: he properly squeezed me. As I'd seen him do with my mum and other women, his hug seemed to last that extra bit longer than normal. And was it my imagination or was this hug *even* longer than the ones I'd seen him give to other women? It certainly felt that way; it felt special. *I* felt special.

I couldn't help myself: I closed my eyes. He was so close, I could smell him: smell that Eternity for Men aftershave that followed him everywhere he went. It was so potent that even later that night, at home, I would still be able to smell him on my skin. I inhaled – I hoped subtly – as he held me tightly in his arms. That hug felt so safe and warm and exciting and, yes, a little confusing too. But I pushed the confusing feelings to one side. There was no room for that, not when I was so very, very excited.

I had the lead role in a play I adored. I was to be directed in that part by Mr Willson. He had already warned us that rehearsals were going to be very intense because it was a quick turnaround for such a complex production – so all that lay ahead for me was hour after hour after hour in his presence.

I couldn't wait for rehearsals to begin.

Chapter 5

Crossing the Line

Mr Willson hadn't been wrong: rehearsals *were* intense. They happened at lunchtimes as well as after school and there was an awful lot to learn. Despite my hopes that I'd be spending countless hours working closely with Mr Willson, in fact I spent more time with Mr Smith as he got me up to speed on the songs. He and I would gather round the piano in the arts theatre while Mr Willson worked with the chorus on the other side of the room, occasionally borrowing me to fit me into a group number. But there were also times, of course, when Mr Willson would direct me and I felt a lot of special attention from him, though maybe that was simply because I was his leading lady.

As time drew on, though, I started to doubt that. It wasn't just the way he'd pay me attention in rehearsal and give me one of his special hugs when I did something well, it was the way he treated me all the time: in class, in the corridor, at the Valentine's school disco. I was dead proud at that February disco of 1995 to don this green bowler hat that was my pride and joy – I'm a real hat girl and I thought I looked well cool in it – and Mr Willson, teasingly, kept stealing it, putting it on and running off; a real joker, goading me to chase after him. I loved the way we could rib each other but still be friends; the way our eyes were somehow saying something completely different even as we dissed each other and playfully sparred. It was my first experience of flirting, I guess.

That evening at the school disco, as the evening drew to a close, a slow mushy song came over the sound system as me and my mates were milling about with Mr Willson and the other chaperones.

'How about it then, McGregor?' he asked me, in full earshot of everyone, suggesting we share a slow dance together.

I tossed my hair over my shoulder. 'In your dreams, sir,' I retorted – acting as though it wasn't the kind of thing I myself dreamed about every single night. I instinctively knew that I couldn't say yes – and that he didn't want me to say yes either. We both enjoyed the game.

'Give over,' he said, his eyes twinkling at me. 'I know what you want, Hayley McGregor.'

'Nah, you're all right, Mr Willson,' I replied nonchalantly. 'You're not all that, sir.'

He smiled at me and I smiled back as the group laughed out loud at our banter. It was all just a great big laugh, but beneath it there was a serious undertow – and I do mean undertow: something unexpected and serious that threatened to pull us under the sunny surface into a murky underwater world. At the time, though, in my innocence, I probably thought that world would see me starring as the happy-go-lucky Little Mermaid.

As it happened, that February my parents were going through some dark times. The very day I'd been cast in *Blood Brothers* my grandad – my dad's dad – had passed away, and they had been very busy organising the funeral and coping with their grief. It was a chaotic time as they juggled not only that but also caring for my little brother, now aged four, and the three-days-on, three-days-off nature of Dad's shift work as a fireman, which sometimes saw him working nights. They supported me as much as they could, of course, but there came a day when it was impossible for them to pick me up after a late rehearsal so my dad told me I'd have to miss it. As the school buses stopped running long before my rehearsal was due to end, and Mum wasn't a confident driver in the dark, there was no way for me to get home safely.

I broke the bad news to Mr Willson a couple of days beforehand.

'My dad's told me to tell you I can't make rehearsal because I can't get safely home,' I told him bluntly. I was really gutted about it and I thought Mr Willson would be too, but he didn't look sad. In fact, he didn't miss a beat.

'Tell your dad I can bring you home,' he said smoothly.

'*Really*, sir?' I asked brightly, scarcely daring to hope that he meant it.

'Yeah, of course.' He smiled. 'You live by the fire station, don't you?' I nodded, pleased he had remembered. 'Well, it's on my way back. I live in Rochdale. I'll happily give you a lift, Hayley McGregor.'

That night I almost skipped home and couldn't wait to tell Dad the good news that a solution had been found.

'Brilliant!' my father exclaimed. 'Tell him thank you very much, that's a massive help.'

It was that easy for him. With him and my dad footie mates as well, he trusted my teacher 100 per cent.

I'm not sure I've ever felt as privileged and special as I did the day I first slid into Mr Willson's car at the end of rehearsal. Everyone saw me get in; I knew the other girls who fancied him would be dead jealous. And not only was he driving me home – I got to sit in the front passenger seat! I felt like one of those girls who had an older boyfriend: a boy-racer with his own automobile. I felt all grown-up.

The impression of being with a boy-racer didn't fade as I took in my surroundings. Other than the child car seat in the back, the interior of Mr Willson's motor had all the hallmarks of a teenager's runaround. Like his office, it was in a right mess, with sweets and mints strewn across it; it was really scruffy. A green magic tree hung from the rear-view mirror.

As Mr Willson swung himself into the driver's seat and started the engine, I felt suddenly and inexplicably nervous. I was glad it was dark, so that he couldn't see the blush spreading on my cheeks or notice my hands fiddling with the edge of my skirt as I sat self-consciously in my school uniform on the seat beside him. It was odd: in the past few weeks, as we'd been rehearsing *Blood Brothers*, we'd grown closer than ever – he'd often hugged me or we'd sat with our legs touching in class, so that I'd almost grown used to his touch (though I would never, ever grow used to that electric spark he gave me every time). Sitting next to him in his car, however, in that enclosed and private space, he felt somehow closer to me than ever before.

I swallowed anxiously as he manoeuvred out of the school car park and turned onto the main road. The setting felt so different from all the other places we'd been together; I was suddenly nowhere near as confident as I'd been when we were in school. I'm sure he must have noticed my nerves because I think I was acting differently: my smart mouth had shut up and the mousey Hayley who wouldn't say boo to a goose had returned.

I was acutely aware of myself and of my body; of where my leg was, and his hand too. He kept it on the gear stick all the time, just a few inches from me, and as he started up a conversation, maybe to relax me, he'd occasionally tap my leg affectionately in a joky sort of way, so that he always seemed to have a part of him touching me. I was used to that after the past few weeks. There'd been a really natural, organic development to the way we had become so used to each other's bodies that I now thought nothing of it when his hand brushed casually against my knee.

We chatted all the way back about the rehearsal, which had gone really well. I always remember us laughing; he used to make me laugh a lot. At one point he mimicked Mr Smith and that had me in stitches; he took the mickey out of him and it felt a bit naughty because they were supposed to be on the same side, but instead it was me and Mr Willson.

As it always did, our conversation felt like I was chatting to a mate. I felt like he was my age or that I was his age: the actual thirteen-year age difference was completely imperceptible. And even though I was nervous, I didn't feel awkward. In fact, as the journey went on and we continued to laugh together and that lovely hand of his changed gear just inches from my thigh, my thoughts started circling on a single track.

Is something going to happen? Do I want something to happen? What do I do if it does?

Way too soon, we neared my house. My family lived in a cul-de-sac and most people giving me a lift home turned left into it from the main road, so that they could drop me right by my door. But Mr Willson didn't do that. Instead, he kept on the main road and only pulled up on the other side of this big square field that lay in front of my house; I'd have to walk across this large grassy area to get home now.

'Are you OK if I drop you here?' he asked nonchalantly.

'Oh yeah, that's fine, sir. Thank you.'

I was confused as to why he'd stopped there, but it didn't make much difference to me so I didn't question it. It was dark where he'd pulled up, with no streetlights near us, though the lights from the main road and from the front of the fire station nevertheless cast a dim orangey glow on his face when I glanced at him. As it was slightly misty outside, with dew on the grass, the quiet, warm car felt very secluded and safe in comparison.

I was struck by the expression on his face when I looked at him: it was incredibly intense. His gaze dropped to my lips for a second, and then pulled back up to my eyes. A bit puzzled, I went to take my seatbelt off – and as I did so he put one hand on my knee and the other on my shoulder and he pulled me into him for a kiss.

Oh my… It was a proper full-on snog, but the softest, most beautiful kiss I had *ever* experienced in my entire life. Our tongues twirled and both my mind and my heart were racing. I'd only ever kissed Jeffery Johnson by the bins before so I didn't really know what I was doing, I just hoped and prayed it was going to be all right and that Mr Willson would like it. It went on for a long, long time – not dead passionate and octopus-like, but a couple of really gentle snogs and then the softest, most loving kiss on the lips at the end. He was stroking my face all the while he was kissing me and I felt butterflies and goosebumps all over me. Mr Willson had really nice hands. My dad's hands were a fireman's hands – rough and weathered with nasty nails – but Mr Willson had hands that hadn't done any manual work and they were really smooth as he caressed my cheeks. They felt warm and incredibly sensual.

Eventually, we broke apart. In the immediate instant of opening my eyes after our kiss I felt a bit weirded out, because my whole world had turned upside-down inside – but just across from where we were parked I could see my house and the fire station, looking as ordinary and as suburban as they did every day when I got in from school. I didn't look at my parents' house after that, I looked at Mr Willson instead.

'You have no idea how long I've been wanting to do that,' he told me in a throaty voice.

'Was it all right, sir?' I asked nervously. After all, Jeffery had dated me for only a week after we'd kissed; perhaps I was the worst snog in the whole wide world.

'It was amazing,' he told me. 'You've got such lovely soft lips. It was everything I'd dreamed of, Hayley McGregor.'

My heart pounded even harder at his words; I felt like multi-coloured fireworks were going off inside me. Perhaps my face flushed, because he asked me: 'Are you OK?'

'Oh yeah!' I said, maybe a touch too eagerly. 'That was amazing, sir.' I looked at him shyly. 'I didn't think you liked me as much as I like you.'

He touched my face again as he gazed at me seriously. 'I've been fighting it,' he said. 'It's so difficult for me. I fight it every single day.'

Yet if he'd lost his fight that evening, I felt like I'd won. I was grinning idiotically and could well have stayed that way forever if he hadn't cleared his throat and broken the spell.

'You have a good night, Hayley McGregor. I'll see you tomorrow.'

'OK, sir. Good night, Mr Willson.'

I opened the car door and stepped out. As I walked across the dewy grass towards home, I thanked God for the cool February air that surrounded me: I felt flushed and I wanted to look at least halfway normal before I let myself into the house. I suspected that what had happened was written all over my face.

But my mum didn't say anything to me when I got in; perhaps because I didn't give her a chance. Instead, I launched straight into my usual exuberant monologue about my day at school, the words tumbling out of me as I told her all about rehearsals and how fabulous Mr Willson was. It was Mr Willson this, and Mr Willson that, and I guess I was gushing a little bit. At any rate, it didn't take long before I caught Mum smiling to herself.

'What?' I asked, pausing in my speech for a second at the amused expression on her face.

She gave me what I thought was a really patronising look. 'I remember that I had a crush on my art teacher at school,' she said knowingly.

I bristled. 'I haven't got a crush,' I snapped at her.

'Oh no,' she said airily, in that irritating know-it-all way grown-ups have. 'I'm not saying *you* have, I'm just telling you about *my* crush.'

Of course, there was no way she could ever have guessed what had just happened. Teachers simply did not kiss their pupils. Yet I knew she was pointing it at me. 'OK, well, I'm going to go and do my homework then,' I announced huffily and flounced off to my bedroom. I knew she'd be entertaining herself downstairs about my so-called crush, though, and it made me mad.

You're so stupid, I thought as I threw my bag to the floor and cleared a space for myself among the large collection of teddy bears on my bed. *You may have had a crush on* your *teacher – but he didn't fancy you and I bet your teacher didn't kiss you. But mine* has. *This isn't a crush, Mother dear, this is* love.

Chapter 6
Demons

I was happy for about an hour after I got home: totally elated and running on the biggest adrenaline rush I'd ever felt in my life.

Then the demons started.

He's just using you.

He'll regret it in the morning.

What if people find out? You're going to be in so much trouble…

He's married, Hayley McGregor. It's wrong. You're such a bad girl for kissing a married man: he'll forget all about you and go back to his wife and it will serve you right.

I was in a very strange place and I didn't like it; I felt weird. My brain couldn't fathom what had happened. I didn't know what to think, what to believe, and in the end I even started to doubt whether the kiss had taken place. With our rehearsal having gone on well into the evening, it was too late to call Nicola or to meet her face-to-face for one of our in-depth analyses of Mr Willson's every move, so I was completely on my own in trying to figure out this unexpected new development. My brain and my heart hurt every time I even attempted to do so.

I soon gave up trying to do my homework and got ready for bed instead. As I climbed beneath my pink eiderdown I shifted my enormous collection of teddy bears – I had *loads* – up to the top of the mattress; I had so many I could almost make a headboard with them. But my favourite blue Care Bear, whom I'd had since I was tiny and who was so well loved he had only one arm and rather ragged fur, always slept in my arms. That night, he was a poor substitute for Mr Willson.

I barely slept a wink, tossing and turning all night long. Every time I woke up, it was him I was thinking of. I could remember where he'd touched me – on my knee, on my shoulder, on my face – and the way his lips had felt on mine. Each time I stirred, I'd fall asleep again hugging Bedtime Bear, wishing it was him instead and wanting him there in my arms. I dreamed of Mr Willson so much that, by the time dawn broke the following morning, the night before itself felt like a dream. Had it *really* happened? In the cold light of day, it suddenly seemed unlikely. Was it all just a dream?

I dragged myself out of bed, trying to shake myself awake and back into real life. I was always the first one up in my household so I tiptoed quietly downstairs and started sorting breakfast out for me and Tetley. The dog gambolled around my feet as I fixed his food, and once we'd both eaten we had a cuddle. Tetley knew – and kept – all the deepest secrets of my heart. That morning I lifted his floppy golden ear and whispered to him: 'Tetley, how lucky am I? I got kissed last night!'

I still felt all over the place but I forced myself to dress with care and I definitely made more of an effort with my hair than I normally did. Memories of the boy in Year 8 who'd only gone out with me for a bet kept ricocheting around in my head; I knew Mr Willson was way too mature to have done something like that, but I'd already been dumped once in my short life for being ugly and I didn't want it to happen twice. Yet there's only so much you can do to glamorise yourself when you're not allowed to wear make-up and your wardrobe consists of a charcoal-grey-and-maroon school uniform. Despite my best efforts, I still didn't feel all that confident in the way I looked when I heard the doorbell go: Nicola and Cari had arrived to collect me for school.

Cari was still mates with us, but over the past year or so she'd grown apart from me and Nicola – I guess two really is company and three's a crowd. Nicola and I never spoke to Cari about Mr Willson, it was our little secret. She had never mentioned that she thought he was fit, anyway; she was dating a lad in her year and was besotted with him. She'd also started smoking, which wasn't really mine and Nicola's scene, so gradually we'd become a little separated.

That day, I waited until Cari was busy chatting to her boyfriend and the noise on the bus had risen to its usual riotous level before I beckoned Nicola forward discreetly with my hand. We were sitting at the back as normal: me on the back seat and Nicola on the chair in front, facing towards me. She looked at me quizzically, but leaned forward so that I could whisper in her ear: 'Last night Mr Willson kissed me in his car.'

'WHAT?!' she exclaimed. Half a dozen of our peers swung their heads around instantly to stare at us, so we tried to act normal. Nicola merely mouthed her next words: 'Oh. My. God.'

She wanted to know all the details, of course.

'I'll tell you later,' I told her blithely.

'You better!' She nearly killed me afterwards because I'd told her on a public bus and she couldn't react as she wanted to.

During the bus journey, with Nicola's excitement at the gossip buoying me up I felt all giddy and excited too, but the instant we went our separate ways at school the demons from the night before started to scuttle out from their hiding places in my brain, ready to torment me all over again.

What if someone spotted us kissing in his car last night?

What if his wife saw through him when he got home and she's thrown him out and it's all my fault?

What if my kiss was rubbish? Maybe I'm an awful kisser and he doesn't want to do it again.

Maybe he does *want to do it again.*

Maybe he hates me for what happened last night.

Most especially, I had this horrible feeling that I might have messed everything up for the both of us, on so many levels, but in particular the way we were together. We'd been getting on so brilliantly; he was the best and most valued person in my life and the thought of being without him was physically painful. I felt a sense of growing dread in my belly that rose higher and higher until it was choking me. In registration I couldn't think, couldn't concentrate; I don't even think I heard my name being called until Krissy nudged me, looking at me with a really concerned expression. God knows what emotions were flitting across my face: I was scared, nervous, in love, in awe, completely and utterly nauseous…

On autopilot, I followed Krissy out of our form room and on to our next lesson. But with all these demon thoughts whirling around in my head I was getting more and more agitated and I couldn't focus on anything. After all the time I'd spent with Mr Willson over the past year, by now I pretty much knew his schedule off by heart – yes, *that's* how much of a crush I had. So I knew he had a free that day, in that first period. *If I could just speak to him*, I thought, *then everything will be OK*. Nobody could reassure me like Mr Willson could.

Before I changed my mind, I raised my hand and invented some reason as to why I needed to be excused. I must have been with a soft teacher because they didn't question me at all as to why I was leaving or why I wanted to; I just made my excuses and left. And after all, I had a good-girl reputation for a reason: I'd never once skived a lesson in my life and there was no reason why my teacher would think I'd suddenly start now.

As soon as the classroom door shut behind me, I scurried off, the school eerily empty with its students all in lessons. I could hear my footfalls echoing in the corridors as I made my way as fast as I could to Mr Willson's office on the ground floor.

Bang, bang, bang! I hammered on his door. Unusually, the maroon swing door didn't fly open at my touch: it was locked. *What?* I thought in growing alarm. I knew his schedule like the back of my hand: he wasn't teaching that period, he was supposed to be *here*. Where was he?

His absence made me feel even more horrible. *He's been found out*, I thought desperately. *He's not come to school*. I was nearly crying; I was absolutely petrified at what was going to happen next. I thought I'd got him into serious trouble. *What if he blames me?* I thought. And then: *What if it IS my fault? What if I've been leading him on and I'm expelled because of it?* I couldn't bear to picture my father's face if that was my fate – I actually felt physically sick.

I took a deep, gulping breath and tried to compose myself. Then I ran to the school office, looking over my shoulder the whole time in case the Principal was about to lay a heavy hand on my shoulder and escort me off the premises for bringing the school into disrepute. I knew they liked me in the office, so I really hoped they could help.

'Excuse me!' I called out to the receptionist brightly, channelling all my best acting skills. 'I'm trying to find Mr Willson but he's not in his office…'

I held my breath as I waited for her to speak – was she about to tell me that he'd been fired or handed in his resignation? But she merely consulted some paperwork before her and then said, matter-of-factly, 'He's covering in technology, Hayley.'

Relief washed over me. I pelted over to the technology block and, without a moment's hesitation, bowled straight into the Year-10 or -11 class that he was covering. I wasn't bothered about what the older kids thought of me and I had no time to give any consideration to how my sudden appearance in their classroom might look: a young girl on the edge, I was too far gone to care.

'Mr Willson, can I have a word, please?' I said breathlessly.

He looked very shocked to see me – and shocked at my tone, too. I hadn't known I was going to talk like that, and I couldn't really help the way my words came out: panicked, but strong and *very* forceful, like *I* was the teacher going in and saying, '*You* need to come out here and talk to *me*.'

'Can it hang on?' he asked me.

'No, not really,' I replied brusquely.

The students in the class were looking at us both with their eyes out on stalks, clearly wondering curiously, *What on earth is going on here?*

'OK, Hayley. It's all right.'

I must look really flustered, I thought. He was clearly trying to calm me down; to do damage control.

'I'll be with you in a minute,' he went on smoothly. Then he turned to the class and gave them some further instructions before pulling me out of the classroom and shutting the door behind us.

The technology block was one of the newer buildings in our school: grey slate with huge windows. It held various classrooms, computer rooms and a library, but Mr Willson instead chose to lead me to a partitioned bit of the corridor where we couldn't really be seen.

I'd hoped being with him would calm me down but if anything my dread, panic and fear had shot up a notch now that I was next to him and could see in his expression that we *had* kissed last night and it *was* all real and I *hadn't* imagined it. I was nearly crying, my stress levels sky-high. I was literally teetering on the edge – so much so that I think, if anyone had walked past at that very moment and asked me what was wrong, I might well have told them and it could all have come out.

I spoke in a rushed whisper, words burbling out of me like an undammed river: 'I was worried because you weren't in your office and you've not been to see me today. I thought you might have made a special effort this morning after… After… After last night, sir.'

I think he could see I was in a dangerous place; his own expression mirrored the panic on mine. He started stroking my arm up and down, up and down, in a really soothing, rhythmic way. 'No, I'm sorry. I'm so, *so* sorry.'

I took a really deep breath. 'Do you regret it, sir? Was it not nice?'

'No, no, it was wonderful,' he reassured me. My dread started to subside – I hadn't ruined our friendship after all. 'It was incredible. It's messed my head up even more.'

'I was worried…' I began.

'I know, but there really is no need to worry.' And then it was like he read my mind and answered the questions that were lurking there. 'It is me and you, and it will happen again, and I *want* it to happen again – but only if you do too?'

I couldn't speak quickly enough. 'Yeah, yeah, yeah, sir, *definitely*,' I said eagerly.

'You know I'm married?' he went on. I nodded glumly. 'Well, I *am* married, but this is like a boyfriend/ girlfriend relationship to me.'

And those were the magic words. As soon as he said that, I was his. There was nobody else for me, it was only ever Mr Willson. As so much of our love affair had done to date, the moment felt like film love; it felt right, that this was meant to happen. My whole life I had adored fairy tales and I knew then that Mr Willson was my Prince Charming. So far he was totally living up to everything I'd read about love or seen in the movies – the way he looked at me, the words he said, the way he touched and kissed me; even the fact that ours was a forbidden romance that had to be fought for. It was magical.

And, as in a magic spell, it was almost as though he'd waved a wand. I forgot all about the things that had worried me that morning; I tried to forget about his wife and child. What mattered was his hand on my arm: hypnotically soothing me, bringing my emotions back into line, coaxing me down from that place of panic into a calm zone where we were Hayley McGregor and Mr Willson and everything was normal... except it wasn't.

We were still stood in the corridor, barely concealed by the partition, when a teacher suddenly walked out of a classroom just a few metres away. Mr Willson dropped his hands from me instantly, as though my skin had suddenly burned him.

And even I was amazed at what happened next. Without missing a beat, I said breezily, in a voice that carried clearly to the teacher walking by, 'OK, sir, that was just a message from Mr Pickup. I'll see you in drama later on!'

The ease with which I slipped into the lie was almost frightening – but then, I had been taught to act so well. All those sessions of hot-seating, where I'd been drilled not to slip out of character, no matter what was thrown at me; all the improvisation lessons where I'd learned to make up lines as I went along. I'd spent more than a year learning how to act, being given the skills that came in handy at this very moment. I'd always been good at switching between characters in a heartbeat and I did it to perfection then. It didn't faze me one bit. I didn't just lie, I lied *convincingly*.

When I looked at Mr Willson, to my eyes he seemed almost proud, as though he might have been thinking, *That's my girl*.

And I was: 100 per cent. I was Mr Willson's girl.

Chapter 7

Getting In Deeper

After that, it was easy. Just really nice and fun and easy. We kept on sharing our little secret looks; carried on with the not-so-innocent brushing by each other in class and those congratulatory hugs that always lasted a beat longer than was necessary. Our *Blood Brothers* rehearsals were really intense – that hadn't been a ruse; we genuinely had a lot to pack into a very short space of time – and I just remember working, working, working.

It was a little while before we had any time alone together in his car again; my dad wasn't a shirker of his parental duties and he was more than happy to ferry me about when he wasn't on shift at the fire station. It would have looked very odd indeed if Mr Willson had offered to drive me home all the time. But on those rare occasions when my parents' schedule made them unable to collect me after rehearsal, he would volunteer to escort me home. Over the next month or so he drove me home perhaps two or three times and, on each occasion that he did, we'd kiss each other good night. It became our little routine.

I started to become a bit more confident in my kissing technique. It was like I learned from him, learned to copy him, so I began to touch his face when we were snogging – feeling his rough adult stubble under my fingertips – and he seemed to enjoy that. Being so inexperienced, I felt a bit apprehensive about being with someone who was so obviously not because – for example – if he put his hand on my knee and raised it higher, I didn't know what to do back. I was always quite aware of myself and of what I was doing; I don't think I ever got lost in the moment. But Mr Willson would reassure me all the time: 'You've got amazing lips,' he might say or 'You know what you're doing with your tongue.' Each time that he pulled up across from my house, parked in the shadows by the field, we turned to each other expectantly and our embraces grew longer and more intense.

Even though Mr Willson was now my boyfriend, he told me it had to stay secret. That wasn't a problem for me: I'd have done anything he asked me to. Nonetheless, I did tell Nicola what was going on – she was the only person I confided in. She listened agog as I described the way he kissed me and the words he used to romance me. 'He must *really* like you, if he's saying that and doing that,' she would say breathlessly. Both of us were completely convinced of his true love for me; we were never in doubt that this was the greatest love affair ever to take place in Bacup.

Mr Willson knew that I'd confided in Nicola, but it didn't seem to be a problem for him. He knew her well, of course, both because she stage-managed the school productions and because, like me, Nicola spent many of her free periods in his office. Nothing physical ever happened between them, but notwithstanding that she and I did sometimes feel in competition for his affection: 'He told me I looked pretty today,' one of us would say; 'Well, he told me *I* had lovely eyes.' It was a case of compliment one-upmanship. If I'm honest – and this is only my opinion – I think he was playing us. My guess, with hindsight, is that he was working out which one of us to go for when he finally made his move; which one of us was the safer option. Nicola was an only child whose parents doted on her; she didn't have a dad who supported Leeds United, with whom he could easily bond; she was also much more of a fire-cracker than me, with a whip-sharp tongue when she needed it. And so he made his choice. He even told me that in as many words.

'I chose you. Aren't you lucky that I chose you?' he'd whisper to me in the car in between our stolen kisses.

And I *was* lucky, I knew I was. I felt like the luckiest girl in the whole wide world.

As the countdown to show week began, behind the scenes on *Blood Brothers* rehearsals stepped up a notch. Now we'd been rehearsing together for weeks, the friendships between us cast members had become tight-knit and affectionate. I really enjoyed the rehearsals I shared with Adam and Matt, who played my sons: the three of us got on like a house on fire and they'd really make me giggle, especially when they were portraying Mickey and Eddie as very young kids. We'd often hug when a rehearsal had gone stonkingly well – 'Well done, mate, that was really good' – or I might perch on one of their knees while we were going through our lines. I didn't think anything of it, but Mr Willson did. He brought up my behaviour with me once we were alone.

'I didn't like it when you sat on Adam's knee today,' he said, looking broodingly like Emily Brontë's Heathcliff. He fixed his eyes on me and I thought I saw a pained, serious expression in them. 'I can tell I'm falling for you, Hayley McGregor, because of how that made me feel.'

The last thing on my mind had been making him feel jealous or hurt; I never, *ever* wanted to hurt him. 'I'm really sorry, sir,' I said contritely.

Even after he became my boyfriend, Mr Willson was always 'sir' or 'Mr Willson' to me. To call him by his first name would just have been weird.

Weird, too, was how flattered and pleased I felt that he was jealous. Yet in my mind it cemented what he'd been saying regarding how he felt about me: it was like he was building a house of cards of his affection and each caring or possessive thing he told me added to that structure, one playing card at a time, as he carefully layered up his love for me.

Time has a funny way of running away from you when you're having fun. Before I knew it, it was show week. I was absolutely petrified heading out on stage as Mrs Johnstone on our opening night: I had to stand on the stage in a spotlight as the show began. As I gripped onto the table next to me for dear life, my heart was pounding as I listened to the overture, then took a breath and sang: 'Tell Me It's Not True…' Yet the feeling I had at the end of that performance was something I knew I wanted for the rest of my life. I may only have been fourteen, but I had found my calling; I felt at home onstage, it was where I was most comfortable, and it filled me with such excitement and joy. Still on cloud nine, I quickly changed out of my costume after the show and headed into the school canteen to meet my parents, who had come to support me on that first night.

Yet they weren't the only significant people in the audience that evening: Mr Willson's wife was there too.

I didn't really want to meet her, but given Mr Willson's blossoming friendship with my parents, he had introduced all the adults before I'd even emerged from the dressing room so my folks were already talking to her by the time I joined their group. Immediately, Mum and Dad gave me massive hugs and congratulated me on my performance while Mrs Willson said 'Well done' too.

I felt so nervous, meeting her; I was worried the guilt was written all over my face. There were so many people there who knew me well enough to see straight into my soul that I tried to overcompensate for my awkwardness by going into typical Hayley mode: very polite and chatty and saying thank you for all the compliments and blah blah blah. As the adults' conversation moved on and the spotlight moved off me, I felt like I'd got away with it and gave a huge sigh of relief. I might even have thought, *Wow, what a wicked actress I am; this* must *be the profession that I should go into...* But it wasn't only my 'talent' at work. After all, why on earth would any of them have been suspicious of a fourteen-year-old girl?

Mr Willson, my mentor, was just as proficient as me at the subterfuge – more so, in fact. He seemed totally relaxed by the whole occasion; not at all fazed by his wife meeting his teenage girlfriend. Then again, he always had this easy way of making me go along with whatever was happening...

The remaining shows were much easier to handle than that uncomfortable encounter. I loved being on stage every night; the only downside to the performances, as far as I could tell, was that show week was actually the worst time for me and Mr Willson to be together for there were teachers everywhere backstage – helping in the dressing room as we all whipped off our costumes in the quick changes, sorting out props or cueing us actors for our next entrance – and Mr Willson even had to keep his office door propped open, so there was no chance of any privacy. Consequently, I was really looking forward to the wrap party on the final night. Not only had my parents granted me permission to stay out late for once, but Mr Willson was to drive me home.

I chose my party outfit carefully, changing into it after the show. The heavenly sound of the last-night applause was still ringing in my ears, giving me an extra-special post-show buzz as I slipped on a pair of white jeans and a navy-blue shirt and then draped a floaty scarf around my neck. As always, my long blonde hair was down, but for a change my face was fully made-up. I was a bit sneaky and kept my stage make-up on for the party, figuring what Dad didn't know wouldn't hurt him. Despite my father's ban, I loved wearing make-up. We'd only done it ourselves so it wasn't very heavy, and I felt so much more grown-up and far more attractive with it on. As I joined the rest of the cast and crew in the arts theatre – the *Blood Brothers* set now struck and put away and the disco lights already flashing – I felt really good about myself.

It was a wonderful night. There was loud nineties pop pounding through the big theatre speakers; we danced and some of the boys had food fights: we all had a really, really good time. Throughout the evening I felt almost as though Mr Willson and I were like the stars and their planets: we seemed magnetically drawn to each other that night. Either I would go to him or he would come to me as the party ebbed and flowed around us. I can remember him standing behind me at one point while I was chatting with some friends – I was seated on one of those plastic school chairs which have a hole in the back and he was stroking me through it. He was touching me in front of all those people, but he was stood so close to me that no one knew but him and me: it was our little secret.

I was so looking forward to our goodnight kiss in his car that I wasn't even that disappointed when the teachers flicked on the main overhead lights and the disco came to a somewhat abrupt end. The two of us slipped into his messy car, as had become our routine, and motored off into the dark night, Mr Willson's hand resting lightly on my thigh as we drove.

He had taken me home enough times by now that I knew I didn't need to give him directions. Instead, I relaxed and enjoyed the treat of being in his presence. Given he knew the route so well, I was surprised when he suddenly pulled up in a secluded spot and cut the engine, even before my house had loomed into view.

'Wait, I don't live here,' I said, my voice burbling with a teasing little laugh running through it, as though he'd stupidly got it wrong.

'I know,' he said. And then: 'Come here.'

I knew what was expected – and what I'd been longing for – so I turned to him and we started kissing. We were kissing, and kissing, and kissing… and then we went much further than I thought we were going to. Unexpectedly, I felt those warm, soft hands of his fully cupping and touching my breasts over my shirt.

I think I tensed up – no one had touched me there before and I personally didn't think I had very nice boobs, so I was really unconfident about him exploring there – but he was murmuring, 'It's all right, McGregor.

Oh my God, your breasts are *so* perfect! So perfectly round, so pert...' and his words relaxed me. I kept kissing him and he kept on fondling me. After a while, he undid the top button on my navy shirt and eased his hand inside my top so that he could feel my breasts over my bra.

It shocked me, but I went with what he was doing and I let him do it. I felt overwhelmed: so much was going on inside me that I didn't understand; now, I know that part of me was becoming aroused, but I didn't know what that feeling was back then. From the moaning noises Mr Willson had started making, he seemed to be feeling something similar. Those panting sounds and his hot breath on my neck made me feel good. Nevertheless, I also felt conflicted: on the one hand I was elated by the effect I was having on him, but on the other I felt really inadequate and not at all confident in that situation.

I didn't know what to do back. I'd always liked it when he'd touched me on my leg, so while he fondled my breasts in their bra I hesitantly reached out a hand and brushed it against his knee. *I'll copy what he's done to me*, I thought, so I pressed my hand firmly against his leg and slowly edged it up towards his groin.

'Yes, *yes*,' he moaned. I knew what that meant: keep going, keep going...

My hand slid higher and higher until I reached his crotch. *Oh my God!* He was hard; I could feel his erection through his trousers. He started rubbing himself against me, writhing on my hand, going faster and faster and faster – until suddenly he pulled away and took a shuddering deep breath.

'OK, we have to stop now,' he announced abruptly. 'We can't do this. We've got to stop now or you're going to get me there.'

We sat in silence for a short while, a silence filled only by his deep breaths as he tried to compose himself. I did up my shirt, my fingers fumbling a little on the buttons in the dark. Then he turned the key in the ignition and we drove off from the random place he'd parked in.

We weren't that far from my house; he dropped me in his usual spot. Despite the unexpectedness of what had just happened, to be honest I wasn't really thinking about that; I was more conscious that I imminently had to walk into my parents' home and I was really worried about how I looked after the passionate fumble we'd just shared. I ran my fingers through my hair and fiddled anxiously with the front of my shirt, where my clothes had been rumpled by his hands.

'Do I look all right?' I asked when the car had come to a halt.

He reached out a hand and stroked my hair. 'Yeah, you're fine,' he told me. He gave me one of those special smiles I loved. 'You look a bit flushed, but you have been at a wrap party.'

I only hoped my parents would think that was all it was as I let myself into the house. I'm not sure exactly what time it was: very late for me to be out at age fourteen, but I'd been given permission because it was such a special occasion, perhaps it was about eleven o'clock or maybe even midnight. My parents were still up, but winding down and about to head to bed.

'Is that you, Hayley?' they called out.

I did what I always did when I got home, and what they indulgently always allowed me to do: I talked at them at a million miles an hour, launching into a long and enthusiastic monologue all about my night: how the show had gone, the specific praise that people had given me afterwards, the songs I'd danced to with my mates at the disco, the food I'd eaten, the food that had been thrown. They wouldn't have known anything was different from any other school disco I'd ever come home from. My secret love affair with Mr Willson didn't suddenly change me into a surly teenager who went straight up to her room with a slam of the door; it didn't cause me to shut them out in a way that might have caused them any concern. In contrast, I was communicative, I was chatty, I was... *lying*. Maybe not outright, but certainly by omission.

It felt horrible. There was definitely a guilt there, tainting my golden evening. Because I *didn't* feel like I was acting with them, the way I perhaps had when I'd fobbed off that teacher in the technology corridor. I felt like I was being deliberately duplicitous.

But I brushed the negative feelings to one side. I told myself they didn't matter – because when I was old enough, in a few years' time, they'd eventually find out that Mr Willson and I were madly in love with each other and then they'd understand. My Prince Charming and I were going to be together forever, of course – that was how all love stories ended – so what did a few white lies matter in the grand scheme of things?

I hated lying to them, though. They looked so happy – so innocent – as they listened to me speak, beaming proudly as I told them all about my latest good-girl achievement. So much so, in fact, that I almost couldn't bear to see that glowing pride in my father's eyes, given what I was doing behind his back.

You'll understand in time, Dad, I told him in my head. *You'll like him – after all, you* already *like him. He's your friend now, but soon he'll be one of the family.*

Chapter 8

An Unexpected Lesson

To my dismay, the highs of the show week of *Blood Brothers* were swiftly followed by the lows of a school holiday. Normally, I'd have been delighted to have some time off from the daily grind, but I'd never wanted to go to school more.

At least I had Nicola to hang out with. And she couldn't believe her ears when I told her what had happened after the wrap party. She was excited – but also concerned. 'How was it?' she asked me eagerly. 'And are you all right?'

'Yeah, yeah,' I replied casually – I was more than all right.

When I told her I'd touched his penis through his jeans she almost choked on her tea. The very idea of me doing that to Mr Willson made us both giggle hysterically.

'How big was it?' she asked jokingly. 'Describe it!'

Nicola was my go-to girl for everything, even though she wasn't very experienced herself. I'd felt so unconfident in the car that I'd decided I wanted to get better at 'it' for him. So I asked Nicola for tips – not that she'd ever really done anything either. Together, we chatted through what we thought might be right and consulted the teen magazines like *Just Seventeen* and

More for advice, poring over the problem pages and the sex guides in the hope that they could help us navigate a path through these uncharted waters.

When I got back to school after the holidays, Mr Willson and I carried on as before. I'd missed him so much and he said he'd missed me too. Any chance we could, we tried to orchestrate being together. I saw him most lunchtimes and we'd always be doing something together whenever we had a free, whether it was talking or reading through a play. With *Blood Brothers* now over, frustratingly we had no valid reason to see each other outside of school, so our rendezvous therefore had to take place within school hours. Every moment was precious: I can remember the way he'd light up when he saw me walking towards his office or even just moving past him in a corridor; he'd wait and hold the door open for me and those snatched few seconds of quasi-intimacy would have to keep us going until the next lunch break or free period.

Of course, unfortunately for us, our timetables had not been arranged so that we were both always free at the same time. But it was Mr Willson who found a way around that particular obstacle.

I was in art the day it first happened. How I hated art! I was attempting to draw a still life of some saucepans, which were all piled up in a heap in front of me, and I was failing miserably. I'd actually given up and started daydreaming about Mr Willson instead – when all of a sudden, as if my thinking about him had magically willed him into being, the man himself strode into the art room and flashed his sparkly smile at me. I almost gasped, his appearance was so unexpected.

Mr Willson walked up to the art teacher and said in a very serious, professional way, 'Sorry to disturb you, sir, but is it possible to have a quick word with Hayley McGregor for five minutes, please?'

My heart started beating faster. *Please let me go with him, please let me go with him*, I begged my art tutor in my head.

The teacher looked over at me and my half-completed drawing. 'Yes, sure, as long as she finishes her work by the end of the lesson.'

'I will, sir, I will,' I promised, already rising out of my chair and following Mr Willson into the corridor.

We closed the door behind us, but we didn't go anywhere: we just stood in the corridor outside the art studio. Mr Willson started stroking me on the arm, just on my elbow, and I felt that feeling of pulsating electricity buzz right through me – a sensation that grew even more intense as he started to speak.

'I've missed you today,' he told me quietly. 'I had to come and find you.' He'd looked up my timetable and tracked me down.

I didn't know what to say back; I just went red. His quest felt so romantic, as though he'd ridden through a thousand-year-old forest to reach me in my saucepan-filled tower. My heart pounded with excitement and pure, undiluted adoration, while my fingers felt all tingly, as though I had pins and needles. Was it me, or had the school corridor suddenly become one hundred degrees warmer?

Though I didn't say anything, I didn't break our eye contact. I knew he liked looking in my eyes – after all, that was how he'd first wooed me in Year 8: 'I'm getting lost in those eyes of yours…' According to him, my perfect blue eyes were why he couldn't fight this anymore, why he couldn't say no: he was mesmerised because there was something about my eyes that made him feel I could see into his soul.

Our one-sided chat only lasted a few minutes, just as Mr Willson had promised my tutor. He did all the talking, I just stood there like a red tomato and then went skipping back into my classroom once our time was up, happy now to draw the pans because I'd had my hit of Mr Willson and that was enough to keep me going until we could meet again.

I wanted to be a good girlfriend; I didn't want our courtship to be all on him. *It's nice for him to visit me unexpectedly, so I might do it too*, I thought. I remembered how easy it had been for me, the day after he'd kissed me, to slip out of a lesson with an invented excuse so I decided to try it again. I never, ever skived a full lesson – I was still a pretty rubbish rebel at heart, and the idea of skiving and my parents finding out scared me witless – but if I was bored in a class and the teacher was a laid-back type, I might take ten or fifteen minutes to 'go to the loo', when in reality I'd spend those illicit minutes with Mr Willson in his office. The teachers never questioned me, even on those rare occasions when I chose not to go back to my lesson at all; I'd just lie to the teacher later and say, 'Oh sorry, sir, Mr Pickup asked me to run this errand for him and there wasn't time to get back to your class.' They didn't check up on me because I was quite honest in their eyes – and that was because, of course, once upon a time, I *had* been honest.

But I didn't skive often – I knew well enough that that would look suspicious – just every now and again, when I couldn't wait another moment longer to feel his arms around me and his lips upon my lips. And we *did* kiss during those snatched, skived minutes. For with the *Blood Brothers* car trips now lost to us, what choice did two star-crossed lovers like me and Mr Willson have? We started kissing in his office, with the door closed and the whole school just beyond that thin wooden barrier: it was all that kept us from discovery.

One day, I bounded happily into his office, having successfully duped yet another soft teacher into letting me out of class for a few minutes: Mr Willson had a free. As had become routine, I plonked myself down on his desk and we immediately started being a bit flirty with one another. Outside in the corridors, everywhere was quiet; you could have heard a pin drop.

It wasn't long before he started stroking and kissing me. From the way we were positioned together, with me sat on his desk, I could feel him growing hard against me, just as he had been in the car on the night of the wrap party.

Without warning, he pulled me off the desk and took my hands to lead me with him. He walked backwards until his back was pressed up against his office door, keeping it firmly closed; I don't think it was actually locked. I stood in front of him; he kissed me again. And then, as we were kissing, I heard a sound.

The sound of his trousers being unzipped.

He gently pushed me down until I was kneeling before him on the floor. I was wearing my school skirt that day and I can remember feeling the tough industrial fibres of those green-and-brown carpet tiles digging uncomfortably into my knees.

Having unzipped himself, Mr Willson got his willy out so that it was right before my eyes. Funnily enough, I wasn't quite sure where to look.

I had never seen his penis before – or, in all honesty, *any* penis at all in a sexual context – and now, suddenly, I was faced with one in all its naked glory. Once again I felt that now familiar yet still horrid feeling of inadequacy, of not really knowing how to navigate this. Kneeling on the floor in Mr Willson's office with his penis before me, I desperately wracked my brains as I tried to remember what I'd read about this situation in the teenage magazines.

Yet I needn't have worried. Mr Willson was on hand to show me the way, and he was keen to prove himself as good a teacher in this new subject as he'd been at mentoring me in drama.

'Put your mouth around the edge,' he urged.

I wanted to please him so I apprised the member before me, and then opened wide.

'That's it…' he moaned.

His willy felt very strange in my mouth, but I'm not going to say it was horrifically bad; I wasn't disgusted by it.

'Rub it with your hand gently,' he instructed, 'as you move your mouth up and down.'

I did as I was told, grateful that he was talking me through. Then I looked up at him as I awaited further instruction and my young blue eyes found that his were locked onto me, drinking in the scene.

He really liked me staring up at him; he told me to. 'Oh yeah, I like that, that's sexy. Now lick underneath…'

Just like the good girl I was, I did exactly as he said.

'Oh, that's right! I'm getting there. Stay there, stay there, stay there…'

His hand was on my head, his fingers tangled in my long blonde hair. He held me in place, but not forcefully, as I felt him thrusting harder and harder into my mouth. The verbal tutorial stopped; I think because I was getting it right now. What struck me was how quiet it was – not only in the corridors beyond Mr Willson's door, but also Mr Willson himself. He was clearly trying to keep his groaning quiet and he was very red in the face.

It didn't take very long, so I think he must have been thinking about it and building himself up for it even before I'd bounced into his office. It was the first time a boy – a man, I should say – had ever come in my presence. I knew that was the end game, of course, and I knew that stuff would come out of his willy and that that stuff made babies, but what it felt like, looked like … all that was new. I didn't actually like the sensation as he ejaculated into my mouth; there was a lot of it as well. It felt weird. Somehow, I just hadn't expected it to be of that consistency and taste. And with him having shot his load into my mouth, I now had another problem: what did I do with it?

Mr Willson, once again, was on hand to assist. When I looked up at him, perhaps in confusion or alarm or just with an obvious 'help!' expression on my face, he just chuckled and said, 'Swallow it, then.'

As before, I did as I was told.

'Urgh, it's not nice, sir!' I exclaimed.

He made some quip in reply; something like, 'No, it's good for you though.'

As I got back onto my feet, Mr Willson put his willy away and zipped himself back up. He was seemingly very happy. I had a drink of water and then he gave me a mint from the collection of sweets that he kept in his desk drawer. And then I went back to class, happy as Larry, skipping through the empty school corridors as though I'd been awarded an A* grade.

Back in my classroom, I slid behind my school desk and turned my attention once again to my studies. No one would ever have guessed what had just happened in Mr Willson's office downstairs; I could barely believe it myself. Yet I wasn't shocked at *what* had happened – it seemed a natural progression in our relationship according to what I'd read in the magazines – but rather by the fact that *I* had done it. Me, Hayley, the golden good girl, had just given Mr Willson a blow job on school premises.

Mr Willson and I kept up our romantic trysts behind his office door. And then one day, as we were snogging in a clinch on his desk, we were rudely interrupted.

Bang, bang, bang!

There was somebody at the door.

Chapter 9

It Must Be Love

I wanted to scream in fright. Panic rose like a tidal wave inside me – this was it, we were going to get caught, it was all going to come out: Mr Willson would be fired, I would be expelled, my parents were going to disown me – and all the negative demons I tried to keep at bay were suddenly yelling at full volume in my brain.

Yet Mr Willson was cool as a cucumber. He pressed a finger to his lips and pointed to the corner. I knew what I had to do: he was going to hide me. The office was so tiny that there was barely enough room for the door to open; when it did, the edge of the door near enough touched the desk. Consequently, when the door was pulled wide it left a small, enclosed square in the corner of the room. Our plan was that I would hide in that square, concealed behind the door as Mr Willson opened it. With no mirrors or windows in the office, as long as I was quiet, nobody would know I was there.

I scrambled off the desk and stood obediently against the wall as Mr Willson composed himself and then swung the door open casually. Though I was dead quiet, I was convinced whoever had disturbed us must be able to hear my heart hammering loudly in my chest.

'How can I help?' Mr Willson said smoothly.

Though *he* could now see who it was, I couldn't. I panicked again, suddenly identifying a flaw in our plan: what if it was a teacher outside and they wanted a private word with Mr Willson? He'd have to invite them in and close the door – and then I'd be revealed like a hapless contestant on *Blind Date*, standing like a muppet behind the door. How could we possibly explain why I was hiding? Would I have to go: 'Boo! I knew it was you, sir!' to the incoming teacher and try to laugh it off? Would they *ever* believe that?

Mr Willson's voice hadn't even trembled as he spoke; I didn't know how he did it. In our very first lesson together, I'd thought he was talented and that I was watching a master at work, but this was something else. The charm and the confidence just oozed out of him; the easy words tripped off his tongue.

Finally, *finally*, the person on the other side of the door spoke – and it was just a kid with a message for Mr Willson. My whole body relaxed, my shoulders slumping in relief. Oh, that had been horrible. Absolutely horrible.

Mr Willson quickly got rid of the kid and shut the door again. When we looked at each other, I could see he hadn't been unsettled by the incident, as I was. Yet that was always his way: I was the one who, when I heard someone walking down the corridor outside when we were snogging in his office, would jump five metres in the air; he never batted an eyelid.

His confidence, in some ways, was catching. We didn't have a big serious talk once the kid had gone about how we had to stop doing this. Instead, we just giggled. We laughed out loud.

'Lucky it wasn't last time…' one of us chuckled, and that set the other one off.

That wasn't the only time someone disturbed us – and sometimes people did come in and find me alone with him in his office. But on those occasions Mr Willson would simply strike up a conversation with me, as though we'd been in the middle of a chat already, and I quickly learned to go along with him, as you have to in drama improvisation games when someone suddenly changes the setting and you've got to keep up.

'OK, sir. Right, sir. Well, I'll come back in half an hour then, sir.'

Mr Willson always seemed at ease. He seemed to have this confidence that we could never get caught, which then gave me that same confidence. Perhaps that was why I now agreed to a new idea of how we could see each other outside of school. I think it was Mr Willson who suggested it: part of me was still that good girl, and my father – as an upstanding member of the community, being a fireman – seemed to know everyone and everything so I would have been too scared to conjure up a new plan for fear we might be found out.

It was a clever idea. Mr Willson lived in Rochdale; my dance school, which I attended several times a week, was also located there. It seemed a happy coincidence, one of those meant-to-be gestures from fate – I guess it seemed rude not to take advantage.

I attended dance on a Saturday as well as in the evenings midweek, often on a Wednesday night. My parents sometimes picked me up after class, but they also trusted me to get the bus back on my own. It became the easiest thing in the world to lie to them that I had an extra-long lesson and had to catch a slightly later bus home. But rather than gain an additional half-hour's tutorial in ballet or tap or jazz, I was in fact receiving a very different type of private lesson from Mr Willson.

He lived about five minutes away from the dance school; we'd meet in the town hall car park, where he'd be waiting for me in his car. We wouldn't go too far, because we were tied by the bus timetable, but he'd drive to a secluded country lane just outside Rochdale so we could spend half an hour or so together. I remember places in the hills, a road coming down towards Healey Dell and another track by a quarry.

I was pleased to have the time alone with him – and not just because I craved his company. Now our relationship had suddenly grown so serious sexually, I wanted to talk to him about his wife.

I felt so guilty about being with a married man. Although I wished I could forget that Mr Willson was married – and often tried to banish it from my mind – it was impossible when he went home to his wife every night and her photo was pinned up on the wall in his office. He'd said we were boyfriend and girlfriend and that he was falling in love with me, but I didn't really feel happy being intimate with him if he was also being intimate with her. I had started to wonder: did he say the same lovely things to her that he did to me? Did he kiss her in the same special way?

One day, I plucked up the courage to ask him: 'Is this what you do with your wife, sir? Do you do all this with her, too?'

I'm not sure he ever answered the question, but he swore to me that I was the only one he loved. I believed him – I *always* believed him – and his behaviour seemed to back it up. After all, he was always so horny for me every single time we were alone and he was never not hard, even with a single touch.

Every time I asked, he insisted that, even though he had a great deal of respect for her as the mother of his child, he wasn't *in* love with her anymore. They had been married for a long time and the spark had gone. All the clichés, you might say, but I was fourteen years old and they didn't sound like clichés to me; I barely knew how to spell that word. I wasn't worldly wise enough yet to recognise the well-worn platitudes he wheeled out. This was Mr Willson, my oracle, who was speaking, and so I swallowed everything he said as the almighty truth.

Once he had confessed that he no longer loved his wife and only had feelings for me, the solution seemed so simple to my young and naive mind.

'You should leave her, sir,' I suggested, my heart breaking for him as he unburdened himself. Why he needed to be with her, I just didn't understand.

But he said he had to stay for his son.

'Well, why can't you leave her and share joint custody?' I suggested reasonably. 'It's all right – I like kids. I'll take your son on and care for him myself.' I'd always wanted children and, with my extensive babysitting experience with my brother, I thought I'd be well able to cope. In my head it was all sorted.

'But I can't do that,' he told me seriously, his eyes grave. 'It would break her. I couldn't break a family apart.'

He told me he couldn't possibly leave his wife at that very moment, yet he offered me an olive branch of hope:

he said he just needed to wait until his son was older and maybe in a special school, and then nothing would stand in our way.

Over the course of our conversations a pattern emerged: he would leave his wife *one day*... maybe when I was eighteen. He would always say he was worried about his son, a refrain that plucked at my heartstrings. I'd sigh dreamily, 'You're such a good dad...' But I'd always reassure him: 'I'm good with kids; I'm not bothered that he's special. I'll look after him and you can be the money man and I'll be the one who stays at home.' It was all planned out: Prince Charming and I – and Prince Charming's son – were all going to live happily ever after.

Mr Willson even used to wonder aloud how my dad, his mate, would take the news of our epic romance.

'How do you think your dad will be?' he'd muse to me thoughtfully.

'He's gonna hate us, he'll disown me,' I'd prophesy, knowing full well how strict my father was. He probably thought I'd never even kissed a boy, yet Mr Willson and I had done way more than that now.

'Nah,' my teacher would retort cockily. 'He'll be happy in the end. After all, I'm a Leeds United fan – what more does he want for his daughter?'

Even though our future was agreed, we both abided by a rule of silence about our plans. Mr Willson would talk about how we would be able to be together publicly in the years to come, but for the time being we needed to keep our relationship under wraps.

'You do understand how much trouble you'd be in if this came out, don't you, Hayley?' he'd say. He wasn't ever threatening when he said those words, they were always light and conversational.

'Yeah, yeah, of course I do, sir.'

'Obviously I'd be in trouble as well, because I'm your teacher, but I just can't help my feelings for you.'

'Oh, I'm the same, Mr Willson!'

'Well, let's just keep it on the down low, then, because it's something we'd both get in trouble for – and neither of us wants that.'

What we wanted was each other. With our drives now restored as a means of being alone, we quickly resumed our intimacy in the front seat of his car. Parked on those quiet country lanes, I was taught what Mr Willson wanted and how to do it well. Now that I understood how to give oral sex, it became expected: all he had to do was unzip himself and present his erection. On some occasions it would be a hand job leading to a blow job, but he seemed to like oral sex and his gestures very much indicated, 'You're going down there…' though never in a nasty or forced way. I loved my teacher so much that I always obliged.

He led what we were doing. Though his regular compliments made me feel much more confident about my sexual abilities, just as a glowing school report might do – 'Your mouth's so good; you're so good with your hands; yeah, that's nice, touch it like that,' he would say – every new development was a whole new world to me and I would never have succeeded at the syllabus without his guidance. He usually started by kissing and touching me and then I'd 'finish him off'.

Over time, his touching of me moved from his gently fondling my breasts, as he'd done on the night of the wrap party, to insistently rubbing at my crotch. If I was wearing trousers, he'd undo the top button and the zip and then slip his hand inside; with a skirt it was even easier for him to slide his hand up my thigh and then circle his fingers over and over on top of my pants.

There came a day when we drove to the country lane that was near the quarry. It was summer now and it was light; I remember feeling quite exposed. Mr Willson had been gently kissing and encouraging me, stroking my breasts, my thighs, my vagina over my pants, when he evidently decided to take things one step further. As he kept on kissing me, he moved his hand right inside my knickers and fingered me for the very first time.

It was quite uncomfortable at first; I didn't even wear tampons so nothing had ever been up there. Mr Willson was panting away: 'That's *amazing*,' he told me, 'you're *so* tight!'

He kept his finger inside me, probing at me. 'Is that good for you?' he asked, breathing heavily.

'Yeah?' I replied, a bit uncertainly. It did feel good, but it also felt awkward, especially because we were in his car. I told myself, *This is what he wants*, and I tried to relax into it.

Notwithstanding my discomfort, I was enjoying discovering myself sexually; it made me feel grown up. I just wished that I was better at it. If I'm honest, I much preferred it when he was simply kissing me and whispering wonderful romantic things in my ear – I liked the loving stuff, I did the other stuff *for* him. But although Mr Willson was moving fast, it didn't necessarily feel *too* fast: in some ways I liked the intensity of it, the way he *had* to have me, no matter what. I only wished I liked it more for him. *If I was older,* I thought, *I would be better at it and everything would be easier.*

But Mr Willson didn't seem to mind. As I relaxed, his moans sped up. 'You're so wet,' he sighed happily. He said he loved the fact that he could only put one finger inside me because I was so very, very tight. It wasn't long on that occasion before he invited me into his lap to suck him off and he came once more in my mouth.

We fell into a routine: we would drive in his car, pull over in a lane and I'd wank him off or give him a blow job. He'd kiss me, fondle me, finger me – done. I would never come, but he would. It wasn't every week we did this, it was only when we could find time to be together, which wasn't all that often – we both had busy lives. Yet when he was able to get away on a Wednesday night or to meet me after dance on a Saturday afternoon, he'd let me know, either in school (after class or in his office) or by telephoning me at home.

It was easy as pie for him to phone me at my parents' house – after all, he was my dad's mate. If ever he phoned at an inconvenient time when my folks were in, he could simply say, 'Is Neil there?' and I'd pass him over. As with most fourteen-year-old girls, I was the phone-answerer in our household and everybody who knew our family knew that well, so it was easy for us to set it up and I could indicate to him instantly if my parents were around.

But most of the time when he called, they weren't. I'd let him know in advance when I was babysitting home alone and what time to call. Bang on the dot, the phone in our hallway would trill and then I'd sit on the stairs with the cable stretched out and chatter away to him. We had some long conversations, just about normal boyfriend/girlfriend stuff. He'd tell me he missed me. I've always been quite shy talking about my feelings – I definitely don't gush – so once again he'd lead the conversation so that I could follow.

'Do you miss me?' he'd ask. 'Do you want to kiss me? What's your favourite part of me?'

As time went on I learned the lesson and was able to praise him without prompting, telling him he'd done this brilliant thing in school today or saying, 'I know so-and-so fancies you too, sir,' or simply commenting on how gorgeous and funny and talented I thought he was.

I could talk to him about anything – and he properly listened. He used to treat me as an adult in our conversations, which was one of my pet gripes about my parents: that they never did. My relationship with my dad was driven by his watchword: 'While you're under my roof, you do as I say.' But I felt Mum and Dad were hypocrites for treating me like a child one minute and then allowing me to babysit my brother the next.

'My dad won't even let me wear make-up!' I wailed to Mr Willson.

'I prefer the natural look,' he told me smoothly, calming me down as he always could.

We often spoke about my future – how I wanted to travel, my acting dreams, that I wanted marriage and babies. He told me I'd make a wonderful wife and a wonderful mum and that whoever got me would be lucky.

'Well, that will be you, sir, won't it?' I'd say contentedly.

As many couples do, we'd reminisce together. Mr Willson even told me how he'd felt the very first time he saw me, queuing up for drama in the corridor outside the arts theatre, when I'd hidden behind my hair like the shy twelve-year-old I then was.

'I just saw these beautiful blonde locks, these blue eyes and that amazing smile and I thought, *Oh dear, I'm in trouble,*' he confessed.

It felt wonderful to hear that: to know our romance had blossomed at exactly the same time. He was always flowery and classically amorous in his words: 'This is the most wonderful thing,' he told me of our affair. 'Why does something so perfect have to have these obstacles? Why can't you be older? Why can't I be younger? Why couldn't we have met at a different time?'

He used to play a Police CD in the car and told me 'our song' was the one called 'Don't Stand So Close To Me', which is about a student/teacher relationship. I was a bit confused by it, because it wasn't the most romantic song in the world – it was hardly 'A Whole New World' from Disney's *Aladdin*, which was perhaps the kind of melody I might have picked out – but nonetheless I was thrilled that we had a special tune that was only ours, because all couples have a song, don't they? I'd never heard it before – I hadn't even been born when the single came out – but the song now became very poignant and special to me.

We listened to all sorts in the car: musical-theatre soundtracks and the radio. And we used to sing along, two luvvies belting it out as only actors know how. I thought we were soulmates – I thought I knew what the word 'soulmate' meant and that he was it for me. And Mr Willson seemed to agree.

'There is no age difference,' he insisted. 'Our souls are the same age.'

And then, that summer, he said the three words that had been destined since the dawn of time to make my belly turn somersaults and fireworks fly high in the sky.

'I love you, Hayley McGregor,' said my teacher, Mr Willson.

Chapter 10

Summer Lovin'

Nicola's mouth dropped open in shock when I told her. This was serious stuff.

'And what did you say?' she whispered on the bus.

'I said I loved him too,' I replied excitedly.

We both squealed and then immediately silenced ourselves as Cari looked at us askance. Thinking ourselves terribly clever, Nicola and I had invented a 'code' whenever we wanted to discuss Mr Willson on the school bus – I think we pretended we were talking about a plot from *The X-Files* or *Friends* or some other TV show; it was hardly top-level espionage. But Cari was getting increasingly annoyed with us because of it; she didn't know what we were actually talking about, but she knew it was made up and that we were keeping something from her. Of course, there was no way on earth that we could let her into the secret.

What surprises me now, looking back, was that no one – not Cari, not the staff and not the other students – ever guessed the truth behind that secret, no matter what Mr Willson did or how brazen he was in front of everyone. As the summer term of Year 9 drew on, he seemed to get more and more confident.

The school was brilliant at organising coach trips to watch different theatre productions: us kids were lucky enough to be taken quite often to shows in Manchester and Bradford and even London's Covent Garden. Mr Willson, being the superb drama teacher that he was, was often at the helm of these events. He seemed to thrive on them, on the informality of the late-night coach journeys, where he could lark about with us kids; from the way he behaved, all joky and chatty, you could tell he thought he was one of us. After he'd got the driver settled at the front he'd make his way up towards the back of the coach where my mates and I would be sitting. He'd squeeze in next to me – there'd always be loads of empty seats on the big coaches they'd ordered, as the theatre trips never sold out – saying breezily, 'All right, what's going on here, then?'

I can remember him actually massaging my elbow on one occasion on a coach: he was sat next to me but simultaneously chatting with the other kids. I barely dared breathe for fear that someone would notice and say something, but Mr Willson maintained the illusion of his casual conversation so well that people looked only at his sparkly eyes and his charismatic face as he talked, and not at his subtle stroking of his student.

I personally loved those theatre trips – and not because of the coach journeys, but because when the lights went down in the auditorium I could pretend that Mr Willson and I were out together on a date. He'd always hand out the tickets in such a way that we'd end up sitting beside one another. Chivalrously, he'd escort me to my seat (though in reality he was getting the whole class settled) and then we'd sit side by side in the dark, our legs and elbows touching. I could kid myself, then, that we were a normal boyfriend and girlfriend and we were out on a normal date.

There is one school trip in particular that I remember. We'd gone to a theatre in Manchester to see some weird contemporary physical-theatre piece; that wasn't my cup of tea back then, when I was only interested in watching frothy musicals with happy endings, but there was no way I wasn't going. Wanting to look cool for Mr Willson, I wore a Dolce & Gabbana black T-shirt and borrowed my mum's leather jacket for the evening. Yet it was nippy in the coach on the way back, so I ended up putting a coat over my legs to keep me warm.

As he had proved so many times before, Mr Willson wasn't one to let an opportunity like that pass him by. Up he came from the front of the coach, chattering away to people, and he eased himself into the seat beside me and then, oh so smoothly, slipped his hand under the coat that lay over my legs. And as he kept up his banter with my schoolmates, that hand started easing its way upwards, rhythmically rubbing at my thigh. He actually got all the way up to my crotch, the intimate position of his hand concealed by the coat, and then kept rubbing as he laughed and chatted with ease.

I felt both embarrassed and excited at the same time. I wasn't aroused by it – there were way too many people around for that – and I actually moved out of his reach after a while because I felt uncomfortable: it was so *bold*. Looking back, I'm not sure what he even got out of it; it was a power trip, I think. He did it just because he could; because he had me in a certain place, and he knew I'd let him do it and he knew he'd get away with it, too.

And he did.

Right at the end of the summer term of Year 9, I received a mysterious message to meet Mr Willson in the arts theatre. I got there all excited, but I wasn't the only one to have been summoned. With me were Nicola, Thea (my doppelgänger who'd played the narrator in *Blood Brothers*), Adam and Matt (who'd played Mickey and Eddie), and also the boy who'd played Sammy Johnstone. We were all looking at each other curiously, wondering what was going on and why Mr Willson had asked us to meet him there. Despite our relationship, he hadn't let me in on whatever it was beforehand. I felt almost aggrieved by that – I was his girlfriend, after all.

It had already been announced that the Year-10 show – which would be staged after the school summer holidays in the autumn term of 1995 – was to be *Grease* so we wondered if it might be to do with that. Already I was worried I was going to be typecast as Sandy because of my blonde hair and blue eyes, but I didn't want to play her because I thought she was boring. In contrast, Rizzo was one of my favourite characters *ever*. I adored Stockard Channing in the movie; I thought she was awesome and all I wanted to do was mimic her. So much so that I had already enthused repeatedly to Mr Willson about how much I wanted to play Rizzo in the upcoming production.

He had chuckled indulgently at my impassioned pleas. 'It's fine,' he'd said easily whenever I'd brought it up. 'Don't worry about it, you're going to get a part.'

Yet *Grease* wasn't the reason for the summons. Mr Willson didn't keep us in the dark for long.

'Mrs Willson and I,' he began, and I felt a jealous twinge inside me at her name, 'would like to invite you round for dinner at our house to say thank you for all your hard work and commitment in *Blood Brothers*.'

What?!

It was such a strange thing to do. *That is going to be weird*, I thought apprehensively. Yet in an odd way I felt excited and intrigued, too. I'd never seen his home; it would provide a further insight into the life of the man I worshipped.

In the week or so leading up to the dinner party, Nicola and I were agog with anticipation: what was the house going to look like; what would we wear; what would we eat? Mr Willson had made me feel so secure in the sincerity of his feelings for me that I wasn't actually too concerned about meeting his wife again: I believed it wasn't her that he cared about because he had properly put it into my head that him and her were fake and – the consequent flipside – he and I were *real*.

When the night came round, it turned out to be a lovely evening, despite the strangeness of the set-up. Of course, as far as everyone else was concerned, it was just a nice opportunity for a reunion with theatre friends. When we arrived, the table was done up beautifully and Mrs Willson served us all a home-cooked three-course meal. Mr Willson was in his element, totally owning the night. The seven of us involved in the production reminisced all night long about *Blood Brothers*, recalling our favourite in-jokes from rehearsals. On reflection, it must have been an incredibly cliquey conversation but at the time I didn't notice; I was just looking at Mr Willson and trying to act as grown up as I possibly could.

Even as we ate dinner, there was stuff going on under the table: footsie, touching… No one else in the room had a clue what was happening. By this stage of our relationship, I wasn't even shocked that he did it in that situation because it was the norm for him always to be touching me, no matter who was there. On occasion, someone might ask me a question and Mr Willson would deliberately choose that moment to caress me under the table as I answered them. I must have a very good poker face because I'm 100 per cent convinced they were totally oblivious. Yet *I* was uncomfortable with him doing it.

The evening wore on and grew a little rowdy as the boys started shouting out their memories of the time that this went wrong onstage or that moment was saved by their brilliant improvising. At the peak of the noisiness, I got a nod from Mr Willson and with the telepathy borne of intense relationships knew exactly what he wanted me to do.

'I'm just going to go and use the toilet,' I announced, folding my napkin neatly and disappearing upstairs.

Mr and Mrs Willson lived in a small house in Rochdale; a two-bedroom cottage. The stairs rose straight up from the living room, so they were visible to all those seated at the dining table, which had been set up in that same room. I went and used the toilet, just as I'd said, and when I came out of the bathroom he was there; he'd followed me upstairs.

Prompted by Mr Willson, we had a very loud conversation on the landing about his son, so that everyone downstairs could hear our 'innocent' chatter.

'Do you want to see him?' Mr Willson asked.

He led me towards the nursery, but before we even got there he grabbed me and passionately kissed me. It took my breath away – in more ways than one, and most of them not good.

'I've been wanting to do that all night,' he told me. He looked down at himself: an erection was visibly pressing against his trousers. 'Look what you've done to me,' he went on, 'I better go and sort myself out.'

He disappeared into the bathroom and I was just left there, gobsmacked. I felt really hot. Even to me, even to my naive and besotted mind, it felt *really* inappropriate. I stood there on my own for a moment while I tried to gather my thoughts; I remember having to shake it off and calm myself down and make sure I felt OK. As I descended the steps, I started to talk very loudly about the child I'd supposedly just seen. 'Oh, isn't he gorgeous when he's sleeping!'

The evening was winding down by then, and before too long we all said our goodbyes and left. Mr Willson drove me home afterwards.

'How exciting was that?' he said when we were alone.

'It was lovely, sir,' I conceded – I always said whatever I thought he wanted me to say – 'but I found it hard. It was quite difficult for me to be there, but I'm glad we got a moment together.'

I was so infatuated that in the end that moment was all that really mattered from that night. Even now, after all these years, all I can really recall about the evening is the footsie under the table and our embrace upstairs – and the fact we had tiramisu for dessert. But our moment of intimacy made all the awkwardness throughout the rest of the night worth it: Mr Willson was worth it.

I had no idea how I was going to survive an entire summer without him.

Nicola was a great help that holiday. The two of us gossiped a lot; we'd go over and over and over the same things – what he might have meant when he said that; what might happen next – and that kept the flame of our romance burning bright. By now she was pretty much over her crush on Mr Willson and fancied a boy in school, so we were trying to get her with him that summer. I went on holiday to the Algarve and had my dance exams to focus on. My mates from dance and I sometimes used to go clothes shopping after our lessons, in Tammy Girl, Topshop and M&S in Rochdale, and during those trips I self-consciously picked out some nicer white bras to wear for school in the coming autumn term; maybe partly chosen for Mr Willson. They weren't sexy or lacy, or anything like that, but they weren't as immature as the ones I'd been wearing in Year 9. I was fourteen and a half, after all: it was time for me to grow up.

On that same note, my mum helped me to select some new outfits in the shops too, and together we tried to get stuff that actually fitted me as opposed to covering me up. That was a relatively new development for me, fashion-wise. Thanks to Mr Willson's constant running commentary for the past few months about my perfect breasts and lips and tummy and my smooth, soft skin, he'd helped me to become a lot more confident with my body. I really couldn't wait to see him again. I felt so much older than I had just the year before; I wondered if he'd notice a difference.

In my memory of that summer, I don't recall being properly heartbroken that we were apart. I suspect, therefore, that I must still have been speaking to him. It was a busy holiday, and I had to slip back into being Hayley the perfect daughter and sister, which meant looking after my little brother. There were no doubt opportunities for Mr Willson to call me when I was home alone.

Yet in all our conversations that summer, he failed to mention one rather important thing. In the end, it was my dad who told me.

'Have you heard the news?' he said to me one day as the holidays were drawing to a close and I had started daydreaming about going back to school.

'What news?' I said, completely clueless.

'Mrs Willson's got a job down in Northampton,' he told me. When I still looked blank, he explained. 'Mr Willson's leaving the school at Christmas. How sad is that?'

Chapter 11

Broken Promises

I couldn't cry; I couldn't show any of my real emotions. I had to hide them, as I had to hide so much from my parents. Even though he wasn't there, Mr Willson's words of warning controlled my behaviour, as though I was a puppet on his strings.

'Oh no!' I tried to say, lightly, swallowing down my hurt and pain and shock. *They know he's my favourite teacher*, I thought, *all I can show them is superficial disappointment because of that*. I took a deep breath and hoped my voice wouldn't wobble: 'Well, we'll miss him!'

Inside, my heart was breaking. As soon as I reasonably could, I made my excuses and quickly went to my bedroom and cried. And I cried and cried, and *cried*. Bedtime Bear was wet through with my tears. I didn't understand: why was *he* leaving? My dad had said Mrs Willson had the new job. And Mr Willson had said it was over with his wife – so wasn't this the perfect opportunity for them to sever their ties? How could he be leaving me to be with her, when he'd assured me that it was *me* he loved?

I felt lied to; I felt worried and sick and scared. And I pushed down the question that loomed its ugly head at me like a monster, stuffing it firmly into a chained-up box deep inside.

Have I been used?

The autumn term started not long after and I returned to school determined to be purposefully aloof. I didn't go looking for him; I didn't skive off a class or go running to his office in the morning break. It wasn't until lunchtime that our paths even crossed.

The canteen was a stone's throw from the arts theatre, so perhaps it was inevitable that that was where we'd meet. I was queuing up with my mates when he pushed in at the front to get his lunch, as most of the teachers did.

My mates and I booed them and gave all the teachers grief. Mr Willson collected his tray full of food and cheekily flaunted it in front of us: 'Mmm, this smells amazing,' he said of the steaming meal, '*so* tasty!' He caught my eye in the queue. 'All right, McGregor?'

It was just the way he said my name... There was that same spark and that same special smile and I just knew: it wasn't over. Whatever was happening in our future didn't even matter in that moment. He was my sun and I his moon and I gravitated towards him helplessly.

I collected my tray and went to join him.

'Nice summer?' he asked me, his eyes twinkling because he knew full well how my summer had been because he'd called me at home during the holidays.

'Yes, sir,' I replied, my eyes eagerly twinkling back at our shared secret. 'Thanks, sir. You?'

It was that easy for us to pick up where we had left off. I did eventually confront him about what my dad had told me, though. Because I knew by now that it was true and that Mr Willson would be leaving at the end of that term: they'd made an announcement in assembly.

I was well off with him after that and I wouldn't go to see him like I normally would; I even played up in his class at times and he had to send me out. I'd think, *How dare you!* (Even though he was right to do it because I was being downright narky and obnoxious.) But I felt he had no right to tell me off: we were equals in my mind, boyfriend and girlfriend. 'How can you treat me like a child one minute in class and then I'm your girlfriend all these other times?' I raged at him. But my anger wasn't really about what had happened that day in class.

The conversation that was inevitably coming finally happened in his car. I even cried in front of him – that's how distraught I felt about his betrayal.

'How could you do this?' I berated him. 'You said you'd be here all the time and we just had to wait until I'd finished school!'

'It's my wife,' he explained meekly. 'She's been offered this job and it's too much money to turn down.' I scoffed at that: what did money matter when we were in love?

He touched my face, making me look at him. 'I don't want to go, McGregor.'

'Don't go then!' I exclaimed, tears staining my cheeks. 'Let *her* go! *You* stay.'

'I can't do that. My son…'

'I can take care of him…'

I tried everything I could to figure out a way to make him stay, to make it possible. I couldn't believe he wasn't fighting this more.

Mr Willson reached out towards me with one of his beautiful thumbs to wipe away my tears. 'Don't worry, McGregor,' he said. 'I'll still see you. Me and your dad are mates, remember? You can come and stay with us. I've got to come up to Manchester for gigs and I'll go to Leeds to see the football – I'll still see you. We can still do this.' He looked me deep in the eye. 'I don't want to lose you.'

He was saying all the wonderful, romantic words and phrases that I'd always fallen for. Hook, line and sinker, I swallowed it.

'In you I've met my soulmate,' he promised me. 'You're everything to me. I have to make this move because of my son, but as soon as he's old enough, then we can be together.'

I think he might even have cried himself; he was easily able to turn on the waterworks, as any actor worth their salt should. But growing up with a father like mine, I'd never seen a grown man cry before. *He must* really *love me*, I thought in wonder. In the end, I think I ended up comforting him.

From that moment on, we knew the clock was ticking down. Every second together was precious. There was just one silver lining: we had one last show to do together that term; one last show that would provide one final easy opportunity for him to regularly drive me home, or to costume stores, or to props outlets. Naturally, such journeys would all involve a little detour to a country lane and the inside of his trousers.

In September 1995, auditions were held for our school production of *Grease*.

I was so, so excited about it. *Grease* was one of my favourite musicals; I knew it inside and out and was well enthusiastic about us staging it. I'd started my campaign early with Mr Willson that Rizzo was the part I wanted and I kept on pouring my heart out to him about how much I really, really wanted it.

'You don't need to keep going on about it!' he'd tell me with a laugh. 'It's sorted.' He added: 'Mr Smith wants it for you anyway.'

Now I was in Year 10, I had started all my GCSE courses and music was one of my subjects. As I didn't play an instrument, my voice was my instrument, so Mr Smith had invested in singing lessons for me and some of the other students. I was really pleased to hear that both teachers were behind me.

The auditions almost seemed like a walk in the park after all the conversations I'd had with Mr Willson about them. I sang 'There Are Worse Things I Could Do' and performed a bit of dialogue. Nervously, I watched the other hopefuls. There were some fantastic performances, but without wanting to sound cocky, I didn't think anyone else was as right for Rizzo as I was. Lots of the girls, of course, were trying out for Sandy; they didn't even want Rizzo, and I hoped that would work in my favour.

This time round, the casting was announced via the noticeboard by the stairs to languages. No actress ever expects to get cast, but on this occasion, from the auditions I'd seen and from Mr Willson's promises, I felt fairly confident that I knew how this was going to shake down. Of course I'd never heard of the 'casting couch' but surely, after everything Mr Willson and I had done together, the part was mine?

I scanned the names on the list, skipping over Sandy and Danny to Rizzo. Mr Willson himself had written the cast list and my heart skipped a beat just to see the familiar scrawl of his handwriting – and then my heartbeat was the only sound I could hear. All the colour drained from my face and I felt sick.

I hadn't been cast as Rizzo.

It may seem a small hurt to anyone who doesn't live for theatre, but for an actress, when you don't get cast in a part you really, really want, it feels absolutely devastating. You feel it so personally. It's a rejection of you: your talent, your looks, your *self*. I didn't even know the girl who'd been given the role, and seeing her name written there in Mr Willson's hand felt like a double betrayal, like he'd stabbed me twice through the heart.

I felt so hurt, but I also felt angry. I would never feel entitled to a role, but Mr Willson had all but promised me Rizzo was mine. Instead, I'd been cast as Frenchy, one of the minor Pink Ladies. I blinked back the tears – I would not cry in front of him this time – and then I did something I've never done before or since: I threw a full-on diva strop.

I went straight to his office and knocked with a hard bang on the door.

But he was ready for me. He swung it open and the smirk was there right away; I wanted to hit him. I was shouting at the top of my voice in the corridor; everyone was looking at us and for once I didn't care.

'How can you give me a part with no singing?'

'Frenchy sings in the group numbers,' he said glibly.

'That's not the point! Rizzo's the part I wanted, I auditioned for it. You know – you *know* – how much I wanted this!' I had told him such personal things, I'd poured my heart out to him and he'd thrown it all back in my face: public humiliation from the man I loved.

'That's just the decision we've come to, McGregor. You're going to have to accept it.'

But I would *not* accept it. I'd seen the auditions; I genuinely couldn't understand why I hadn't been given the part. 'I'm going to go and see Mr Smith then!' I told him.

'Fine,' he said, amused. 'Go and see Mr Smith.'

I went straight to music… and Mr Smith knew nothing about it. 'Come with me, Hayley,' he said, pushing his Penfold glasses up his nose. I walked with him back to Mr Willson's office, my heart still pounding.

'What's all this, Andrew?' he said. 'We discussed the cast list. What are you playing at?'

Mr Willson replied, 'Oh, I thought I'd have a joke with her.'

A joke… This was his idea of a joke. To humiliate me, to break my heart. Ha, ha, really funny. They swapped the casting round after that. The girl I didn't know became Frenchy and I got Rizzo, just as I'd dreamed. But Mr Willson's 'joke' had spoiled it for me.

We had a proper big argument about it. His actions really confused me after everything that had gone on – was *still* going on – between us. It was like he was playing with me; manipulating me. I didn't like the way that made me feel. To this day I don't know why he played that game. I suspect Mr Smith and the other girl were equally foxed by his behaviour, having no inkling of what was going on between the two of us.

I was frosty with him for a little while – a minute, an hour, a day. But I always let it go. He always had the ability to calm me down, to make me forgive him, and there'd be a hug, a rub, a kiss at the end of it. Other times, my frostiness – to my mind – seemed to drive him away: I'd see him chatting animatedly in the corridor with a female staff member, being as tactile as he always was with me, and I'd feel jealousy burn inside me, so acrid I could taste it. I'd ask him about it later, quizzing him like a proper jealous girlfriend – 'What were you talking to her about, sir?' – and he'd smile and say, 'Wouldn't you like to know?' I think he was doing it to wind me up; to put me in my place. I hated how jealous he could make me feel. Some part of me was aware that, despite his declarations of special love for me, he must also have once made similar promises to his wife, I think. In my heart, could I *really* trust him, when he'd already betrayed someone else to be with me?

On the occasion of the *Grease* casting debacle, it wasn't the threat of another woman or an affectionate gesture that made me forgive his hurtful 'game', though. I eventually stopped having a go at him because he was so dismissive and he made me feel silly. He made me feel like I was going to lose him. I didn't want that, and I didn't want to spoil the last few months we had together in the school, so it wasn't long before we were back to normal.

We started rehearsing *Grease* in October and it was due to open on 11 December 1995, which wasn't a long rehearsal period. As with *Blood Brothers*, rehearsals soon became intense. This time I only had two solo songs to learn, but there was a lot to do acting-wise with the accents, the blocking and Rizzo's kissing scenes. The guy playing my boyfriend, Kenickie, had Hispanic skin and jet-black hair that he gelled into those nineties spikes. He smoked, so I wasn't especially looking forward to having to snog him. (Though Mr Willson smoked too, he always kept himself well stocked up with mints and his Eternity for Men so he never reeked of it, the way some do.) Nonetheless, I knew the role required it and stage-kissing would be another skill to learn that would equip me for my future career, so I was apprehensive but professional when the time came to rehearse the scene.

We got to the part in the script where we were supposed to kiss, and as it was our first time reading through it the two of us did the hand thing where we each put up our palms and kissed the backs of our own hands instead of each other's lips.

'Let's pause there a moment,' Mr Willson called from his director's chair. He looked thoughtful. 'I've decided we should cut the Rizzo/Kenickie kiss. It's inappropriate for a school play. There'll be nothing sexual at all.'

What? I was shooting daggers at him, but he ignored me. I had it out with him later, though, in his office.

'What was all that about?' I asked him. 'How can you not show Rizzo necking on? Listen to the song: "There Are Worse Things I Could Do". She thinks she's pregnant!'

'We don't need to show it. You can just put your back to the audience and run your own hands over your back.'

'But that looks naff, sir!'

But Mr Willson put his foot down – and properly. It got serious. 'I'm not having you kiss him,' he said, glowering jealously.

I loved it when he went all possessive and Heathcliff on me. It shocked me, but I also liked it. Perhaps it was a warped way to look at his jealousy, but it made me think, *Oh, he really* does *care.* Because sometimes he could be aloof and distant, or he might not look at me as often, and I'd start to wonder, *Is he going off me?* Declarations like that helped to reassure me – as did the way things were progressing sexually between us.

Our occasional trysts after my dance classes and our *Grease* rehearsals were still happening, and so too were our clinches in his office. That autumn term, we started simulating sex on his desk. I'd be sat on the hard wooden surface and he'd pull my legs around him so that he could start dry-humping me, pressing his erection into my crotch.

To be honest, I was a bit perplexed by it. For a start, it didn't do anything for me – I know, now, that he wasn't putting it in the right place for me to get turned on – but I also hadn't even realised that dry-humping was a thing: it didn't have its own section in the magazines, so I thought you went from what we'd been doing to full-blown sex, with nothing in between. It seemed weird to me, but he seemed to like it: he was always very hard and very panty.

The downside of it was that there was a lot less kissing; it felt less romantic to me, which was not a good thing in my book. He'd even do it up against the door with us both standing up, but I really didn't like that because it hurt my pubic bone at times when he was thrusting too hard and too energetically into me as he pinned me up against the office door. He used to murmur in my ear as he was doing it, and one day he whispered frantically, 'I want to make love to you.'

My stomach flipped.

But, in the next second, he suddenly pulled away from me. 'I can't,' he muttered, 'I can't do that. That's taking it too far.'

That autumn, he seemed to be fighting another battle within himself. On the one hand, he made it very clear that we weren't going to have full penetrative sex because I was only fourteen. On the other, he would tell me that he needed me, craved me, that he knew it would be the most magical experience... He made it sound really romantic – it was always making love, it was never, ever fucking – and I could tell that, whatever he said, he *did* really want it.

And when Mr Willson wanted something, I wanted it too.

'Why do we always have to be together in your office or your car, sir?' I'd say to him. 'Why can't you take me to your house or a hotel?' Now I wanted closeness and cuddles; to feel like a normal couple rather than a dirty secret. I imagined loving embraces with my head resting on his chest, as he gently stroked my hair and kissed my forehead while we lay supported by feather-soft pillows. 'I want to lie in a bed with you, sir,' I said dreamily.

I think he liked that idea too – though probably for different reasons. 'OK, I'll work on it,' he'd say. 'It'll happen.'

But he was resolute about the sex. He kept saying we had to wait until I was sixteen years old. In our detailed future plans for our shared life together, it was age sixteen to lose my virginity; age eighteen to go public about our serious relationship. We discussed my being a virgin and he said he hoped that I would wait for him; I always said I would.

Part of me was very confused by his reticence. I didn't understand why he didn't want to be with me when we were clearly soulmates; I thought making love was what couples did.

'Why don't you want to, sir?' I'd say in bewilderment.

'I *do* want to,' he'd reply. 'My God, I want to! You have no idea how much I want to. When I play with myself, it's you I think about, McGregor. But we just can't.'

It made me feel really rejected; he'd literally pull away from me and almost hold me at arm's length. But then, in the next moment, he'd be telling me how we were soulmates and meant to be together. It was all coming thick and fast and it was really starting to mess my head up. Already I was in love with him but I could feel myself falling harder and harder, and I knew through all of this that he was going to be leaving at the end of term. A lot of our meetings did become fraught, with me getting upset and him having to calm me down.

Yet he wasn't there to calm me when I got upset in my bedroom at home. My mind would run away with itself, knowing he was in his house with his wife, with the two of them about to move together to a town that was over 150 miles away from me and my Bedtime Bear. I'd wonder obsessively what they were doing; I'd go over stuff that he'd said to me, stuff he'd done. I felt like I didn't understand *anything*. I was way out of my depth. I'd just cry in my bedroom, feeling confused and hurt and inexplicably sad – yet how could I be sad when I was Mr Willson's girlfriend? It was all I'd ever wanted. I just wished so much that I was older; I was wishing my life away.

And, like all wishes do in fairy stories, it worked. The time flew by faster and faster. October passed; November. Suddenly I wanted time to slow down, because the closer we got to December, the closer it was to midnight: to the end of the ball when I would abruptly turn back into my former ugly self and Prince Charming would vanish from my life.

I wasn't bothered about anything other than being with him: that was the be-all and end-all. I don't even remember going to lessons that autumn term; I must have done, otherwise I'd have got into a lot of trouble, but that's my memory – of this *need* to be around him. Nothing else mattered. I missed GCSE coursework deadlines and I didn't care – I didn't care about anything but him.

Grease show week was bittersweet: the highs of the performances but the lows of the horrible countdown clock. We snatched every moment we could together. I remember he arranged it so that I would use his office for my quick changes during the show each night. He'd always be there, pottering around, as I hurriedly stripped down to my bra and knickers, throwing off my Pink Lady gear before slipping into a prom gown. My dress was black. Each night Mr Willson would help me with the zip, sliding it in a silken motion up my back as it concealed my naked skin, before he squeezed my shoulders solicitously to let me know he had finished his work. Then he'd usher me out of the room with that familiar hand on the base of my back, as I quickly returned to the stage.

I got sick that week; I could hardly sing on the last night but somehow I managed to find some energy reserves from somewhere. I think now that my illness was caused by stress that he was leaving. There were tears from everybody after the last performance; teachers as well. Loads of people wanted to take photos with him and he was given presents and thank-you cards. So many people were demanding his attention that there were too many people about for us to have a private moment. I have a memory of him rubbing me on the base of my back, but that's it.

I was one of the few people who didn't cry at the wrap party, which was fun but imbued with this feeling of sadness. I couldn't show my true devastation at his departure, of course, and I wasn't going to cry crocodile tears. It actually really annoyed me that everyone else was sobbing and wailing – I didn't think they had the right. Their supposed grief and upset seemed silly and fake, whereas my loss was real and *I* wasn't crying.

In some ways, though, I didn't need to. 'Don't worry, McGregor,' he had said. 'I'll still see you. We can still do this.'

My man had a plan; he'd made me a promise. And this, at least, was one promise that Mr Willson was determined to keep.

Chapter 12
Precious Gifts

'I need to see you,' Mr Willson had told me on one of our last-ever journeys in his car. 'This can't be it, I want you to myself all day.' He revealed he had an 'opportunity' to use a mate's house in Littleborough, a village that was about ten miles from Bacup. 'Are you willing to bunk off school to be with me?' he asked, looking deep into my besotted blue eyes.

Of course I was; I was willing to do anything he asked. Despite my previous pleas for him to arrange such a 'date' for us, though, I felt suddenly nervous now it was actually happening. I was worried about going to a house with him as I didn't know what to expect. Above all else, I felt very apprehensive about him seeing me fully naked, because in his car and his office we'd always kept our clothes on and simply fumbled around them.

It seemed inevitable that we would end up naked. Part of me wondered, too, if his reticence about sleeping with me might waver once he had me alone in a bed with no chance of being interrupted by a knock at the door. I started to imagine what it might be like, making love with Mr Willson. It would be long and loving, I knew that, and maybe we'd have a bath together and there'd be nice smells and candles and clean white sheets, just like in the films. In the magazines it said you needed to be relaxed and with somebody you trusted and loved, so I knew, if it did happen, that I'd be doing it for the right reasons and with the right person, because I loved Mr Willson more than anyone else on the planet. I was excited, yet I was worried, too, because the magazines had warned me that it might hurt when I lost my virginity. But I thought: *I'm in love with him, he's my soulmate; if it happens, it's going to be the most perfect thing in the world.*

As always, I confided in Nicola what was happening: that Mr Willson was going to whisk me away to a hidden love shack in a secluded village. I expected her to be overwhelmed by what I saw as a romantic gesture, in fact she wasn't overly impressed.

'What for?' she said, her forehead furrowed in concern. 'Are you sure you want to do this?'

I was annoyed by her reaction. *Why have I even bothered telling you if you won't support me?* I griped at her in my head as I scowled in silence. *Nicola thinks she knows everything but I know more.* I thought I was so much more worldly wise than her because I was in such a mature relationship with my much-older man.

Nicola didn't like it when I got upset with her. Despite her concern, she agreed that – if she absolutely had to – she'd cover for me when I skived off school.

Yet with Nicola being in the year above me, her covering for me would only save me if my parents asked questions about me not being on the school bus; it couldn't actually get me out of class. Mr Willson and I had to concoct our own little plan for that.

On a crisp, cold winter's day in early January 1996, the appointed date finally arrived.

The weather that day seemed like an omen: it was sunny but chilly, one of those very cold but very bright winter's days that are my absolute favourites. That morning I'd picked out what I thought of as grown-up black underwear – I didn't have nice lacy sets, but I made sure it was matching – to wear beneath my uniform. The plan was that I would leave school during double physics; the subject meant naff all to me so I'd readily proposed it when Mr Willson had suggested I skive. I spent the whole morning on pins, just waiting for the agreed moment.

Double physics for Year 10 was timetabled before lunch; I was hoping to leave school by 11 a.m. Our teacher was quite a sweet man; one of those teachers who never shouted, you'd merely disappoint him. He'd barely got going with the lesson when Mrs Brown, the school receptionist, came bustling into the classroom – just as I'd known she would.

'Hayley McGregor, there's an emergency at home, you need to go,' my teacher announced after speaking briefly with Mrs Brown.

'What is it?' I asked in faux concern as I quickly gathered my stuff and shrugged on my black winter coat.

The receptionist beamed at me reassuringly from across the classroom. 'It's all right, Hayley,' she said kindly, 'it's nothing to worry about.'

I joined her and, as we walked together to the school exit, Mrs Brown relayed to me the message that I myself had invented and that someone else – maybe Mr Willson or a friend of his – had phoned into the school with, pretending to be my dad. Like any lie created by a fourteen-year-old, it was overly complicated: my next-door neighbour was pregnant (which she actually was), and my 'dad' had phoned the school to report that she'd gone into labour but her husband wasn't home so he had to take her to the hospital, but with my mum at work, his absence left my brother without anyone to care for him, so I'd been summoned home to babysit. I nodded as though hearing all this for the first time as we walked along.

I really liked Mrs Brown; all of us kids did. She was a petite, librarian-type woman with mousey-brown hair and the kindest aura you can imagine; she always had a smile on her face. Even now, as she escorted me, she was being kind: 'Will somebody be coming to collect you, Hayley?'

'Oh yeah, yeah, yeah,' I replied, trying to fob her off.

I'm not sure she fell for it. 'Well, will you promise me you'll call me once you're home safe?' she urged.

'Course I will, miss,' I said, and now it was my turn to smile at her reassuringly so that she'd let me go off alone.

I practically skipped down the steps that led to the public bus stop. While I waited, I took off my school tie and made sure that I properly did my coat up too, trying not to look like a schoolgirl on the skive. The adrenaline coursing through my veins took me onto the bus and lasted for most of the ten-minute journey to the meeting point agreed with Mr Willson, but it was seriously ebbing by the time I disembarked. Increasingly nervous, I hid in the archway of some covered steps while I waited for his car to pull in.

He was taking his time about it. I kept poking my head out, looking for him, but every time I did my pulse sped up. I was only about ten minutes from my house and any neighbour or family friend could drive by on the main road and see me. It was mid-morning on a school day; I had absolutely no good reason for being where I was. Skiving was so out of character for me that I felt genuinely alarmed by my actions. Even though I'd snuck out of lessons to see Mr Willson in his office before, I'd never, ever left the school grounds and I'd never fibbed in such a big way either.

The longer I waited for him, the more of a state I worked myself into. My heart was pounding and with each new beat a new question came: *Is he really going to meet me? Have I missed the car?* And then: *Isn't that my dad's mate?!*

It was: a friend of my father's from the fire station was driving past me in his car. He must have looked straight through me because he didn't slow down or stop, but the moment I saw him, I felt sick. I ducked back into the covered stairwell – proper ninja hiding – only hoping I'd moved quickly enough for him not to realise it was me. Yet the incident kept playing on my mind: maybe he'd put two and two together later and tell my dad he'd seen me skiving... It troubled me all day.

At long last, Mr Willson's car pulled in. The sight of him was so welcome, not least because I hadn't seen him since the last day of the previous term; school had felt empty without him in it. I spotted his big beaming smile through the windscreen and I just legged it, diving straight into the front seat, pulling the visor down and scooting right down into my chair, where I stayed for the next few miles, hiding, paranoid in case anyone else I knew saw me.

'Oh my God, one of my dad's mates has just gone past!' I wailed breathlessly.

I really was not in a good place; I felt nervous and scared. It was so not in my nature to break the school rules like this; I was petrified we were going to get caught. The whole occasion seemed frightening rather than fun.

As usual, however, Mr Willson shared none of my fears. Notwithstanding that, his attitude from the moment he picked me up seemed rather different from the way it had before. He'd always been self-assured, but this time he was like the cat who'd got the cream. It was like he was *free*, somehow; he didn't care as much. It didn't feel as cloak and dagger, even though it still was; still had to be because I was only fourteen.

'Did everything go OK at the school?' he asked me casually.

'Yeah, it was fine, sir,' I replied.

He cast a look down at where I was huddled in the front seat, and his next words perhaps revealed why things felt different now. 'You don't have to call me sir anymore, Hayley McGregor,' he said, with that sparkly smile I loved. 'I'm not your teacher now. Why don't you call me Andrew?'

I screwed up my nose in amusement. That would just be weird: he was *Mr Willson*. 'I *can't*, sir!' I retorted, giggling. But even though I couldn't call him Andrew, I think things had changed a little bit in his mind now that we weren't officially teacher/student anymore. I think it freed him up. He was less cautious, less constrained. All bets were now off.

I told him that Mrs Brown had asked me to ring when I got home, so we stopped off at a phone box and I made a quick call to the school to reassure the staff that I was safe. By that point we were quite far from Bacup, so when I got back in I felt confident enough to sit up properly in the seat. We held hands when he wasn't changing gear, or Mr Willson sometimes rested his hand on my knee. We listened to the radio and sang along. We were just like a normal couple, a proper boyfriend and girlfriend driving to a date. I started to relax, though in the back of my mind I was still panicking about my dad's mate – and about what was going to happen next.

Mr Willson eventually pulled up on a cobbled street before a row of Victorian-era, Yorkshire-brick terraced cottages. I felt a bit nervous getting out of the car and stepping onto the street, even though I didn't know anyone in the village, but Mr Willson bounded out of the vehicle with his usual verve. *He* wasn't nervous at all; he was on top of the world. He knew at once where the door key was, hidden under a pot or the front mat, and confidently slipped the Yale key into the lock and ushered me inside.

I remember feeling distinctly disappointed as I looked around: *Oh*. Even though it was a bright crisp day outside, it was dark and dull inside the house and it smelled fusty and damp, as if it hadn't had an air in a few days. I'd been picturing a romantic retreat like you see in the movies, but this place definitely wasn't cinema-ready. The front door opened straight into the living room, which was furnished with an old-fashioned rocking chair and tiny, uncomfortable-looking wooden sofas. The décor had no stylish female touches, yet it didn't feel like a proper boys' pad either – there was something almost grannyish about it, with the rocking chair and the antiquated patterned carpet on the floor. I imagine the owner wouldn't have been quite so willing to lend it to his friend if he'd known Mr Willson was bringing a schoolgirl back to it.

As in Mr Willson's house in Rochdale, the brown wooden stairs came straight up from the living room. I knew they must lead up to the bedroom, and my stomach suddenly twisted with nerves at seeing them. Part of me didn't want to do this anymore – I was worried about disappointing him, about not being good enough – but I'd gone too far now to turn back.

Mr Willson wasted no time dilly-dallying downstairs. As soon as we were inside the house he took me by the hand and led me straight up those wooden steps. I felt sick: excited sick and nauseous sick. There were suddenly two voices competing in my head: no, no, no/yes, yes, yes/wrong, wrong, wrong/but I love him/but his *wife*... Guilt was definitely part of my inner turmoil, along with all the rest.

Mr Willson took me directly into the bedroom, which was very plain, with magnolia walls and no artwork; almost as if his friend wasn't permitted to decorate. Big windows allowed the sun to stream in so it had a much lighter atmosphere than the dark and dank downstairs, which I found very welcome. But that was about the only good thing. Stacked beside the bed were piles of books and magazines, and on the bed itself the clean white sheets I'd been imagining were noticeably absent: instead, the bedclothes were grey and not very nice at all; the bed wasn't even properly made.

I don't remember much talking. Mr Willson started undressing me straight away – yet he took his own sweet time with it, savouring every single moment. First, my coat came off, and was abandoned on the floor. Then he started unbuttoning my school shirt, one slow, solitary button at a time, his movements deliberately considered and purposeful. Eventually, after what seemed like a very long time, he pulled the shirt from me and stood staring for ages at my breasts in their smart black bra. There were lots of noises coming from him, lots of grunting, and then touching; and after a while he slickly undid my bra so that he was gazing at my naked breasts for the first time.

'They're perfect,' he breathed.

It was chilly in the room – there was no central heating in the house and it was an icy January day – so he really liked it when my exposed boobs reacted to the temperature, my pink nipples hardening. 'They're small, but they're perfect,' he whispered again, his voice catching slightly in his excitement. He bent his head and kissed each one, sucking at my nipples as though anointing them.

He kissed every bit of me as he revealed it. It felt rather as though he was unwrapping presents and giving grateful thanks for each separate, precious gift he'd been given. He kissed my neck, my breasts – and then went on down to my flat, fourteen-year-old tummy, which he waxed lyrical about because it was so smooth and firm; my long-hated puppy fat was finally starting to drop off thanks to my dancing classes, though I still considered myself chubby. Mr Willson seemed so happy at seeing each new bit of me; he kept murmuring how very perfect the different parts of my young body were – better than in his wildest dreams.

Though there was a lot of positive language coming from him, it didn't relax me as it usually did. In fact, I'm sure he actually started telling me *to* relax. Because I wasn't saying anything back and I didn't know what to *do* back, either, so I was very, very quiet. Inside, I felt horribly inadequate. *Oh my God, I'm so rubbish, I don't know what I'm doing AT ALL*, I kept thinking forlornly, as he grunted and touched me and I simply stood there awkwardly before his eager gaze. This situation felt totally beyond me: I was in way over my head.

When Mr Willson had finished relishing my nude top half, he undid the button and zip at the back of my school skirt and shimmied it smoothly down my legs. I felt terribly unsexy standing there in my thick black tights, but he got them off pretty quick; my pants as well, tucking his thumbs into the waistbands and disrobing me in one swift movement that removed both my tights and knickers at once. Suddenly, I was standing there fully naked while he remained fully clothed.

I fidgeted before him, feeling really uncomfortable as he drank in the sight of my naked teenage body. No one had ever seen me nude since I'd passed puberty, and I especially didn't feel good having my bottom bits on display. Understandably, given I was only fourteen, I didn't look after myself down below as you do when you're older, so I was very '*au naturel*' – but he didn't seem to mind. He was just *very* excited; more excited than I'd ever seen him before. In contrast to my reticence, he seemed very, very happy, as though he'd been waiting for this moment for a very long time. He didn't rush any of it, he genuinely savoured it, and in truth I did feel a little like a goddess, because of the special way he was looking at me, as if he couldn't believe his luck. Yet my overwhelming feeling was one of weirdness: after all, when you have bad dreams you often picture yourself naked, with everyone else clothed and staring at you, and this situation was that nightmare brought to life.

Only once I was fully naked did Mr Willson start to undress too. He took off his suit jacket and shirt so that he was topless as well, and then he finally pulled me in for a much-needed hug, pressing his naked chest against my bare boobs. I really liked that, and the skin-to-skin sensation calmed me, even as I tried not to giggle at the ticklish feeling of his chest hair on my breasts. I felt safer in his arms than I did when I was stood on my own being stared at; I inhaled the familiar Eternity for Men scent of him and as I breathed out I tried to let go of my insecurities, and of the nagging feeling inside me that there would be consequences if I followed this through.

If I get away with this, I thought to myself, *I am one lucky girl*.

But I *was* a lucky girl, I knew that already. Even that afternoon, Mr Willson reminded me of it: 'I chose you, Hayley McGregor. Aren't you lucky that I chose you?'

Mr Willson and I started kissing passionately as we stood, skin-to-skin, pressed against each other. He led me to the bed and laid me down, so that my back and bum were lying on the grey bedsheets, but my legs were hanging off the edge. Then he started kissing me again, but not on my mouth. He worked his way down, down, down, kissing all down my body and all down my legs, relishing every part of me, and then eventually he started kissing me on my private parts, and he gave me the oral sex that I'd been giving him for the past few months.

It felt nice, at first, as he kissed and licked and sucked at me. Then I think he got a bit carried away as bits started to hurt; I didn't come. Instead, I sat up and with his encouragement and direction I started to take his belt off. It was almost as if he had it all worked out, how it was going to go, and now he'd gone down on me, it was my turn to do the same to him.

So I undid his belt and then managed to pull his trousers off. I struggled a bit with that awkward moment of him standing there in his pants and socks, so he took his socks off for me, which helped me out. Once he was naked, he stood before me and I gave him a blow job – here, thankfully, on familiar ground – while his hands tangled in my long blonde hair, pulling my hair all around me as I held him in my mouth.

He stopped me abruptly; I think he was about to come. In his plan for the day, it was clearly too soon for that. Afterwards, he lay down close beside me on the bed: one naked body pressed against another. There were hugs, and long kissy moments, but that wasn't really why we were there. For I don't know how long, we stayed in that bedroom caught up in a melee of different body parts as we touched and kissed each other all over, body parts rubbing against body parts as Mr Willson placed me in different positions, and we went down, went up, touching with hands and mouths and genitals, doing everything but full sex.

We were simulating it, though, just as we used to do on his desk at school – but this time we were fully naked and it was harder to control. At one point I remember being on top of him and he very nearly entered me.

'*No!*' he cried out, pulling away as though my bare skin had scalded him.

'Why not?' I asked in a whiny voice, like a child denied a Christmas treat. I felt rejected and hurt.

'I can't, I *can't*…' was all he said, and then he pulled me into another nude embrace.

By now I had relaxed a little, though I still had a nagging feeling in the back of my mind that we were going to get caught. Then my life would end because we wouldn't be allowed to be together. It was one of the very good reasons we had to wait till I was eighteen before we told anyone about our love affair, because *then* people would understand. We were risking everything by being together now, and it made me nervous.

After a while, some combination of the fingering and wanking and oral sex and dry-humping we'd been doing pushed Mr Willson over the edge and he came. I felt some sense of satisfaction in that: he might not love me enough to *make* love to me, but I took it as a sign of his affection that I could at least make him come, and so my self-worth notched up just that little bit higher as a result.

He does love me, he does. Here is the incontrovertible proof.

Afterwards, while we were both still naked, Mr Willson picked me up in his arms and carried me downstairs. We sat on the rocking chair in the living room, with me almost like a baby in his lap, my legs hanging over the arms of the chair, and we simply rocked there for a little while. I felt so safe and so loved. It was heavenly, actually, to be naked with him in that context, skin-on-skin, with him being all romantic and snuggly. He told me solemnly that he loved me and he wished he could be with me always.

I simply adored that moment with him; it made all the other stuff worth it. He even started to do butterfly kisses on my cheek as we were sat there rocking in the chair, fluttering his soft eyelashes against my flushed pink skin. I remember it making me giggle. I'd never heard of a butterfly kiss before and I thought it was so sweet.

Mr Willson had something else sweet in mind, as it turned out.

'Do you like Nutella, McGregor?' he asked me throatily.

'Yeah!' I replied enthusiastically.

When he disappeared into the kitchen, I genuinely thought he was going to make us something to eat. That sounded like a plan to me: it was about the time I usually had my after-school snack and I was dead hungry; I thought some Nutella on toast would go down a right treat.

But that wasn't what Mr Willson meant at all. He came back in with a big new jar of Nutella in his hands – but, to my disappointment, no toast. We snuggled up together on the rocking chair again and he unscrewed the lid while I watched in confusion. Then he dipped his finger into the chocolate spread and smeared it on my nipples. Watching me intently, he bent his head to my breasts and licked it off.

I watched him somewhat po-faced: I just didn't get it and it was doing nowt for me. He tried again, as it was clearly exciting him, spreading it on my boobs and on my tummy as well, and then licking it off. I observed all this with an odd sort of detachment – and more than a little amusement. Finally, as his tongue twirled in a ticklish manner on the chocolate spread that he'd laced around my belly button, I couldn't help it: a cheeky giggle erupted from my lips and burst forth loudly, as though he'd been cracking a joke and not attempting to seduce me.

I think that was the moment he realised it wasn't at all sexy for me – I was way too giggly about it. Unfazed, he followed my lead and jokingly dabbed a bit of Nutella on my nose instead, as though the plan all along had been to make me laugh. And we did laugh together after that; we giggled together. Yet it wasn't as free and easy as it might once have been between us – because we were both watching the old-fashioned clock that hung on the living-room wall, and we knew time was ticking on. *Our* time was ticking on.

I'm going to lose him after this, I thought dejectedly. How could it be any other way? He had already left the school; in the next week or so he and his wife would be moving to Northamptonshire, over 150 miles away. I was three years off getting my driver's licence and I had no independence from my parents; it would be impossible for me to contrive some way for us to be together. Consequently, I just wanted to get dressed and then stay there, in that dark, dank house; to stay snuggled with him forever; for him not to go back to his wife. I even said it out loud as we sat naked together on the rocking chair and the clock's hands edged unstoppably closer to half past three.

'I don't want to leave, sir,' I said miserably. 'I don't want to leave.'

Mr Willson stroked my hair in a comforting way. 'Neither do I, McGregor,' he replied, 'but we've got to.' He made me look at him then, staring deep into my eyes in that way he had; the way that could always make my heart skip a beat. 'You know this isn't the end, right? This isn't the end. We *will* be able to do this more in the future.'

Ultimately, his promises were the only thing that kept me going; that gave me the strength to get dressed, to walk out of the house, to get into his car. I knew I had to get home too – after all, if we hadn't been discovered already, we certainly would be if I didn't make it home at a reasonable hour – and that also spurred me on.

For I had more reason than ever now not to arouse my parents' suspicion, because in my mind my relationship with Mr Willson had moved on to another level: I was more in love with him than ever before. Therefore, I *had* to keep the secret, because if people found out now it would be too soon and it would blow the whole thing. I knew we were going to be together forever, because we were soulmates. I just needed to stay silent for a few more years.

Mr Willson didn't drop me home; instead, he dropped me near a bus stop close to the school so that I could get the bus home. We were too late for the school bus, which never waited for those kids who were running behind, but there was a normal bus that ran shortly afterwards, for those people who'd had detention or an after-school club – or an illicit afternoon with their former drama teacher, for that matter – and needed a later service.

There was a kiss goodbye between us in the car. Mr Willson gave me a special present that day too: the perfume Beautiful, which represented so much of what he always said about me: that I had beautiful eyes, beautiful hair, a beautiful smile, beautiful breasts... I felt almost speechless as he handed it over. No one had *ever* given me perfume before – I wore body sprays from Boots, like Charlie Red or Exclamation – and it felt terribly romantic and mature.

'I love you,' he told me, his face that of an impassioned hero bidding farewell to his dearest sweetheart on the eve of war. 'I'll see you soon, McGregor.'

His words, too, were a gift: a promise to keep me aloft, as though on the magic carpet from *Aladdin*. It carried me home, where I went straight into my usual after-school routine: wash up, dry up, vac up, take Tetley for a walk. No knock came on the door from my dad's colleague. All was well.

That night, I went round to Nicola's house and in a hushed undertone beneath her music, I told her everything that had happened. I think her reaction was tinged with shock, but in my blissful bubble I didn't notice. For I may not have lost my virginity that afternoon, but I did feel *different* nonetheless. A line of some sort had clearly been crossed and I was aware of that, at least. At the time I saw it only as a good thing: a precious stamp in my passport as I journeyed towards womanhood.

I told Nicola all about it with my eyes shining, the blue of them shimmering with a teenager's innocent pride in growing older.

'I'm a proper grown-up now, aren't I?' I sighed contentedly, even though I was just fourteen.

Chapter 13

Under His Spell

The power of Mr Willson's words was such that that magic carpet kept me afloat for quite a while after he left. Slowly but surely, however, I came back down to earth with a bump.

At first, it was my grief that he had gone that tore at my heart. Everywhere in school held a memory: the time he'd touched me on my arm, or snatched a kiss, or we'd simulated sex on the desk, my school skirt rucked up around my waist. There was nowhere I could turn where his ghost wasn't present, but remembering only emphasised his absence all the more. My disinterest in school increased; I wasn't even passionate about drama anymore. Mr Willson's replacement, Miss McGinn, was like a pale version of Olive Oyl from the *Popeye* cartoons; she spoke in a broad Scottish accent and was very old-fashioned in her teaching style. She never singled me out for praise and I didn't enjoy her lessons, not like I had Mr Willson's. I grew increasingly glum as January came to an end; and glummer still as February started and I realised it had been a whole *month* since Mr Willson had kissed me goodbye – and I hadn't heard from him once. Not once.

I made excuses for him, of course. He had to have been busy with the move; he had a lot on. When I subtly asked my parents about him, I learned that Dad hadn't heard from him either, so I reassured myself that it was OK, Mr Willson would call when he was able to; he *would* come back into my life, as he'd promised. Sometimes, just thinking about his voice and the sweet nothings he had whispered was enough to make me continue to believe in him, such was the hold he had over me. His charming voice was hypnotic, even when I was only imagining it.

The days went by, each as agonisingly empty as the last, and still no call came. A month is a very, *very* long time in a teenage girl's life, and I started to fear the worst. To begin with, I'd been crying myself to sleep because I missed him, but now I started crying because I feared everything he'd said to me was a lie and I wasn't special to him at all. Without his constant praise, my self-esteem dropped below zero. My heart would protest at these treacherous thoughts, but the evidence was hard to refute. After everything that had happened at his friend's house, I'd thought we were stronger than ever, but since he'd bade me farewell there had been nothing but silence.

After the afternoon we'd shared together, I'd kept the perfume he'd given me on the vanity table in my bedroom; I'd lied to my parents that Nicola had given it to me. At first, the sight of it had been reassuring and exciting, a token of Mr Willson's true love, but now it seemed to taunt me, as though it was some kind of peace offering to buy my silence or a price he'd had to pay for the intimacy of that afternoon.

Even though my head was getting more and more messed up by the day, I couldn't show it. I felt I became two different people: I was the good girl Hayley when I was out and about, being the person I wanted my parents and teachers to see, and then at night I became a heartbroken girl in my bedroom, sobbing desperately into my teddy bear's arms. I was utterly miserable.

I don't know what I'd have done without Nicola. She was an amazing support, but I think even she got sick of seeing me that way. One night in February, when we were both babysitting for my brother and I was moaning about how Mr Willson still hadn't been in touch, we egged each other on to take matters into our own hands. After all, we were independent girls in the modern era, why didn't I just phone him myself?

My mum kept all her numbers in an address book by the phone in the hallway, including the new Northamptonshire number of our family friends, the Willsons. I'd actually made sure I memorised it so that I didn't ever have to look it up, as doing so might have seemed suspicious to my folks: why would I need the number of my former drama teacher? But my parents were out at that moment: this was my chance.

Before I could lose my nerve I dialled the number and waited patiently as the long-distance line connected.

'Hello?'

Heaven. Mr Willson's voice was just heaven.

'Hi,' I said shyly, romantically. 'It's me.'

'Oh!'

He sounded shocked; it wasn't a nice reaction. He was very off with me; I guess, now, that I must have phoned at a bad time so he couldn't talk in the free way he always could when he chose to ring me himself. But I didn't rationalise it that way then. All I knew was that I'd been desperate to hear from him, I'd been worried sick he didn't care for me the way he'd promised, and now we finally had a chance to speak he was rude and cold and seemed only to be emphasising his distinct lack of interest in me.

I was hurt – but most of all I was angry. I made sure he knew it, too. I wanted to get back at him.

In my immature way, I racked my brains for a solution. What would really hurt him? I remembered how fierce he had been when he'd told me I couldn't kiss Kenickie as Rizzo; how he'd stopped me from sitting on Adam's knee. Like me, he was a jealous soul and I thought I'd stumbled on a brilliant idea to make him realise how much he wanted me; a way to bring him back: I would get myself a boyfriend and hope he would find out through my dad. It was still all about him, of course – for even though I was angry and sore, I still loved Mr Willson with every beat of my heart. We were soulmates, after all, and even a month of silence couldn't break that kind of bond.

School grapevines are wonderful for gossip of the 'my mate fancies you' variety. Having heard from Nicola, who'd heard it from Paul Brown's good friend Sedge, that Paul Brown fancied me, I soon started dating him. He was the receptionist's son, in the year above me. Tall with blond hair and blue eyes, he was a sporty lad with a footballer's physique. We got on all right; he was quite quiet, really. I waxed lyrical about him to my dad, though, hoping he would get the message back to Mr Willson that I'd got myself my first boyfriend.

Yet I couldn't stop thinking about Mr Willson, and I was constantly comparing Paul to him – and finding him lacking. It was very unfair of me, I know. Mr Willson understandably kissed in a very mature way: he knew where to put his hands and they were always in my hair and it was all lovely. Paul didn't have that same experience, of course – nor the same ability to make me swoon. He was a lovely, *lovely* boy, but in contrast to Mr Willson he seemed boring to me. We only lasted about two weeks before I thought, *This is unfair on him*, and I finished it. Whether or not my original plan had worked, only time would tell.

By now, it was March 1996 and my parents had started thinking about how to celebrate my upcoming fifteenth birthday. Dad couldn't stop the grin as he excitedly told me, mad Leeds United fan that I was, that he'd got tickets for all the family to go and watch them play in the League Cup final at Wembley. The game was scheduled for Sunday, 24 March, the day after my birthday, and the timing seemed perfect: Dad thought it was a brilliant idea to marry it all together. I was well happy about it: 'Wicked!' I exclaimed. 'What an ace day out!'

'Oh,' my dad then added, almost as an afterthought, 'and Andrew Willson's offered his house in Northamptonshire to us to break up the journey, so we'll be stopping overnight with them on the way home, all right?'

I wanted to scream and shout: 'YAY, I'M GOING TO SEE HIM!'

In reality, I nodded my head nonchalantly, well trained as ever, and simply said, 'All right.'

The instant my dad told me the news, all was forgiven and I was no longer angry with Mr Willson, not one iota. *He must have had a good reason for not getting in touch*, I told myself firmly. *And look – this is* better *than him being in touch, because he's actually arranged for us to see each other. I'm going to see Mr Willson face-to-face!* I knew the moment we looked into each other's eyes that our soulmate connection would still be there.

It would be strange, of course, being in his new family house with his wife and his son, but it wasn't as though I hadn't been put in that situation before by him. So even though I knew nothing was going to happen between us – after all, this wasn't a dinner party with a group of fourteen-year-olds who could be easily fooled while we snogged upstairs; my parents and my brother were going to be there too, for goodness' sake – I allowed myself to get excited about seeing him. It was the best news, and this was going to be the best birthday *ever*.

It turns out Leeds didn't get the memo: we lost 3–0 against Aston Villa, a real damp squib of a game. But even that couldn't dent my enthusiasm. Even as we made our way back to the car, all four of us McGregors kitted out in our Leeds United gear – shirts and scarves and hats, the lot; proper football family geeks – unbridled excitement was still simmering inside me. I was fifteen years and one day old, and that meant I was one step closer to being sixteen, when Mr Willson had promised he would make love to me at last; I thought I'd feel ready, by then, by the time I was sweet sixteen. Having turned fifteen, I was also one step closer to leaving school: I hated it, now, without Mr Willson there, and I couldn't wait to be old enough to leave it all behind. And in just three years' time, I'd be the magical eighteen and he and I would be able to go public and start our lives together. As if all that wasn't exciting enough, in just a few *hours'* time I would be seeing my soulmate himself. I felt like I was going to explode with anticipation.

As my dad drove through the Willsons' new village at the end of the journey from London, I could tell my boyfriend had done well for himself. It was a gorgeous setting, with all the old postboxes and lamp-posts still in place, and you could tell it was a 'beat the Joneses' sort of settlement because all the gardens we passed were immaculate, not a blade of grass askew and every bloom picture-perfect.

My dad pulled into the driveway of a massive detached house and I remember thinking, *Oh wow, this is nice!* It had a huge garden and was a truly stunning property. Mr Willson had said his wife's new job was well paid – well, this was clearly what money could buy.

Dad took charge as he always did and led the way to the front door, pressing firmly on the doorbell as I loitered towards the back of my family, suddenly apprehensive about seeing my teacher again. As he swung open the front door he looked *amazing*, charming and charismatic as always. He caught my eye even as he greeted my parents and there was that tell-tale twinkle that made my heart melt. He shook my dad's hand and they slapped each other on the back in the way that men do when they really respect and like one another. My mum got a kiss and a lingering hug and my brother an impish ruffle of his blond hair: my five-year-old brother simply adored Mr Willson.

And then it was my turn. He kissed me on the lips, knowing my parents wouldn't say a word; he was like that with everyone, after all, so he got away with it. As Mum and Dad and my brother passed into the house, calling out a greeting to Mrs Willson, I got my own special hug. It felt so incredible being back in his arms, like it was the right place for me to be. He gave me a long, lingering hug as his hand slowly but determinedly trailed down to that possessive place on the base of my back. I squeezed him so tight, wondering if he could hear my heart pounding; if he could feel how much I loved him through my embrace. It was wonderful simply to be around him, to be smelling his scent again; it truly was intoxicating. I felt like a creature in a cartoon, in *Tom and Jerry* or something like that, when they smell a tasty pie and they're suddenly alive. Mr Willson's aftershave and his personal, special smell tantalised me and – just like that – I was under his spell all over again.

I almost had to shake myself out of my daze as we eventually separated and he ushered me through the front door with a knowing little smile. Inside, the house was even more incredible: it was lovely and clean and bright, and Mrs Willson clearly had an eye for design as she had created a beautiful home. The front door opened onto a hallway and the stairs, and off that was a big playroom for their son and then a second, more adult-friendly living room. They had the biggest kitchen I think I've ever seen, with a large walk-in pantry attached to it, and upstairs was a huge bathroom with a beautiful free-standing bath right in the middle. The house had ancient wooden beams in the ceiling and old wooden barn doors with those metal handles; attractive period details that set it apart. I actually felt a little in awe of it: it was totally gorgeous.

After all our greetings had been exchanged, Leeds United and their poor performance that day was an immediate talking point. The conversation flowed so smoothly, as it always did with Mr Willson at the helm. He and his wife knew it was my birthday that weekend so I received a card and a present from them; with some guilt, I could tell that his wife had picked it out for me. There were even some jokes from Mr Willson to my dad about my age: 'Oh, she's fifteen now, Neil! I remember what it's like to be fifteen. Slippery slope now... She's all grown up!'

As the evening drew on, the Willsons' son and my brother were put to bed, but I was allowed to stay up late with the adults because it was my birthday. It was a lovely night: Mr Willson and my dad were having these big guffaws of laughter as they joked around and there was a really convivial atmosphere. Mr Willson kept telling me to call him Andrew, but I still couldn't; I found it really bizarre. As I've said before I found it difficult to call him anything but Mr Willson.

There came a point in the evening when my can of soda ran dry so I went out to the pantry to fetch another. It was a huge room, really, and just as you might imagine the typical pantry of a beautifully posh country house to be. Really bright, with nice chrome light fittings, it was full to the brim with packets of food and other household paraphernalia.

To my surprise, Mr Willson followed me in there. He came up behind me and I felt his warm hands on my waist, just as I'd first done in that long-ago drama lesson when he'd moved me to one side. Before I'd even had a chance to catch my breath, he lifted me up and onto the counter and started dry-humping me, as the crisp packets and biscuits around us shifted noisily on their shelves.

In between heated kisses and thrusts and fumbles over my clothes he was whispering to me, 'Oh my God, I've missed you so much, it's been so hard for me, McGregor.'

Then we heard a noise from just outside the pantry and our embrace was suddenly over, just like that, within a matter of seconds. I got my drink and some crisps and I was out of there, a fake smile plastered on my face, while inside I was dancing. It was a whirlwind, a fabulous whirlwind, and I treasured it as the only moment we could possibly have together on this trip. It was just too risky to do anything more; as it was, we had embraced for only a few seconds, but I cherished each one as evidence of his burning love for me.

He had missed me. He had said it, so it must be true.

Soon it was time for lights out. The Willsons explained the sleeping arrangements: Mum and Dad were in the guest bedroom upstairs with my brother, while I would be on a pull-out sofa bed in the playroom downstairs. I got ready for bed wearily; my dad always got us up at stupid o'clock on family days out and today had been no different. There'd been the drive to London, the buzz of my first time at Wembley, the match itself, and then seeing Mr Willson... I was exhausted from all the excitement, stifling yawns as I pulled on the traditional Leeds United pyjamas that Mum had packed for me; they were as geeky and as uncool and unsexy as they sound. I didn't care, though; it wasn't as if anyone was going to be seeing them.

I was out like a light the moment my head touched the pillow. It was a really comfy double sofa bed and a really comfy duvet: crisp, cool bedding which had been beautifully pressed. I was so tired that I wouldn't have stirred at all the following morning if it hadn't been for those lovely metal handles on the old barn doors. But as Mrs Willson left for work at 5 or 6 a.m. – when it was still pitch-black outside and everyone else was sound asleep – the metal clasp rattled a tiny bit behind her as she shut the door and I was rattled too, stirring out of my sleep just slightly.

I could tell it was too early to be awake, because the babies weren't even up yet and it was dark, so I lay there half-dreaming for a few moments, waiting and wanting to fall back to sleep. I heard her go, but I didn't think anything of it. Yet only five or ten minutes later, I heard another sound: the door to the playroom opening. I kept my eyes shut because I didn't know who it was.

But perhaps I should have done.

It was *him*.

Chapter 14

First Time

I lay unmoving, my eyes still shut. The sprawling layout of the large house meant that one route to the kitchen was through the playroom, so I thought perhaps he was simply on his way to make a brew and wasn't going to say a word to me. But, like a prince in a fairy tale waking a sleeping maiden from her long slumber, he stopped beside the sofa bed and crouched down to whisper in my ear.

'Hello, McGregor.'

Without another word, he got into bed with me. I stiffened: in embarrassment at my geeky Leeds United pyjamas; in shock because my parents were only upstairs and I couldn't believe even Mr Willson would be so brazen.

He started kissing and touching me at once, whispering sweet words in my ear with a striking urgency: 'I've missed you, McGregor. It's so amazing to see you and feel you. I can't stop thinking about you.'

I was listening, but I also had half an ear on high alert for my parents: was that a creaking floorboard I could hear, or a door opening upstairs? Every sense was on a knife edge: the tantalising spell I'd been under the day before simply wasn't there, for the bubble had been pricked and pierced by my acute fear of discovery. I wasn't comfortable doing this in his house, and was most definitely *not* in the moment: I was far too aware of everything else, of everything that could go wrong. My parents could walk in at *any* moment.

Yet it seemed Mr Willson was aware of that too. There was an urgency and a speed to his touch that I wasn't used to. His caressing of my breasts as he slipped his hands up inside my pyjama top wasn't soft and loving: it felt more like he was going through the motions. It felt *perfunctory*, and he didn't even bother to take my top off. He himself was bare-chested; trackie bottoms on below. After a very quick fumble of my boobs, he slipped his hand inside my pyjama bottoms and fingered me briefly, as though merely checking I was wet. Then he pulled off one leg of my pyjamas and pulled down his own trousers too. He'd been in bed with me for less than a minute.

My mind was racing, yet I still felt half-asleep, as though this could all be a dream. Yet as Mr Willson positioned himself above me and I felt the weight of him, I knew I was wide awake. And I knew too, instinctively, that this time we were going to go all the way.

Why is he doing it now? I remember thinking. *I'm only fifteen. This isn't my sixteenth birthday, it's my fifteenth. He's banged on about it so much. Why has he kept me at arm's length all these months if he's just going to do it now?* I felt bewildered and shocked. It wasn't how I'd expected it: there were no candles, no bath; I couldn't even say what *I* wanted, as I might have been able to do at his friend's house in January, because I was so scared my parents would hear. It was horrible: I couldn't enjoy the moment at all because I was petrified my parents would discover us. My head was buzzing, yet the one crystal-clear thought I had, over and over, was: *Why? Why now? I'm only fifteen…*

Almost as though Mr Willson could hear my thoughts, he started whispering in my ear: 'I can't wait. I can't wait any longer, McGregor. I know I said I would, but I crave you, I *need* you.'

The covers were over us, and I had the crazy idea that it was as if he had created a den for us to play in. But the game he had in mind was one I'd never played before...

I stared up at him. He was heavy and sweaty, lying on top of me and pressing me down. He must have used some protection, but I don't remember any delay before he positioned himself above me and I felt his penis nudging and pressing at me firmly. I tensed up: *This is it, this is the moment...* I was hoping it wouldn't hurt too much and that, if it did, it would be over quickly.

He went straight in, as much as he could; he had to push hard. I took a sharp intake of breath. *Don't make a scene*, I told myself, *do what he wants.*

Mr Willson was moaning and whispering in my ear: 'It feels *amazing*, McGregor. You're *so* tight...'

Then he simply went into his panting, breathing heavily in my ear, clearly enjoying himself. As for me, I remember it feeling friction-y. I was not relaxed at all – on tenterhooks both because of my parents being upstairs and the situation itself – so I took no pleasure from it; instead, there was a wincey pain.

Although there was no pleasure, there was a bit of pride too: that I was doing it; that he wanted me; that he'd missed me so much he couldn't resist. I liked the fact that I was pleasing him – I *always* wanted to please him. This had been the one thing I'd been unable to give him, but now he was claiming it for his own.

It was all over after only a few thrusts. For me, there was a strange sense of anti-climax: I'd thought losing my virginity would take place in a proper bed, to start with, and that we'd both be naked and take our time with it, making it special. Instead, I had only one leg out of my Leeds United pyjamas and Mr Willson's trousers were around his ankles – and we were lying on a sofa bed in his front room. It wasn't quite how I'd pictured it. I'd always thought making love with Mr Willson would be like what I thought our true love was: pure and passionate – not just having sex. But it had felt mechanical, in a way; there wasn't a sensuous, loving, cinema-ready angle to it, as I'd come to expect from my teacher. It all felt very out of character for the man I was in love with. It was a side of him I hadn't seen before. Perhaps it was the pressure of my parents being upstairs, but there was none of the 'savouring' that had gone on before: it was abrupt, and urgent, and almost like he wanted it to be over with.

After he'd shuddered to a climax in my arms, he grinned down at me.

'I love you, McGregor.'

'I love you too.'

Then I felt it: this feeling of happiness and elation because he wanted me like that and we'd finally done it. I thought it had cemented us for the future; I could give him everything he needed now.

Still moving quickly, Mr Willson raised himself up and got out of bed, faffing about; I guess, now, sorting out the condom. Still a bit dazed, I pulled my pyjama bottoms on fully – and was so embarrassed to see that where we'd made love there was a small smudge of blood on the sheets.

Oh, that's horrible, I thought. I felt worried and a little bit upset.

I was looking at it and Mr Willson saw it, too. He laughed and seemed almost proud, the very opposite to my reaction.

'It doesn't matter,' he said in an upbeat way. 'It happens, you're a virgin.' He grinned at me again.

No-nonsense, he pulled the sheets off the bed and put them in the wash straight away. While he did that, I started folding the remaining bedding, my helpful, good-girl instincts coming to the fore. I felt stunned as I mechanically smoothed down the duvet in my arms. *Did that happen?* I wondered, now the evidence had gone. How *did that happen?*

Mr Willson came back in and finally he embraced me, as we both stood awkwardly beside the sofa bed.

'Cool pyjamas,' he noted.

It made me laugh. I didn't feel embarrassed – there wasn't a lot I could do about my outfit now, and at any rate, it hadn't put him off! Standing there in his arms, as always I started to relax, as though he was a drug and I was getting high. I started to feel good about myself and quite grown up.

Not only is it my fifteenth birthday weekend, I thought, *I am now a proper woman*.

As we stood hugging, the household started to stir. It had gone from dark to light in the time Mr Willson had been with me. I heard his son and my brother cry out as they woke and the house creaked and settled around us as the heating came on. Before too long, my mum and dad pottered down the stairs – but by the time they did, there was nothing untoward to see.

'Good morning!' Mr Willson called out cheerily as he greeted them. 'How did you sleep?'

I followed his lead as the casual conversation flowed over breakfast as fluidly as milk. Mr Willson was always there so I had no chance to speak to my parents alone – though, of course, my lips had been sworn to secrecy long before. His presence made certain of my silence.

I tried to hang on to the positive feelings I'd had in his arms about what we'd done. As we breakfasted and then started to gather our stuff together for the long journey north, I tried not to worry about the fact that I was leaving and I didn't know when I'd see or hear from him again. *He had sex with you because he loves you*, I told myself. *This cements it. This proves it. He wouldn't have done it if he didn't care.*

There were hugs and kisses all round as we said our goodbyes. Mr Willson squeezed me in that oh so special way – as he did my mother, too – and that was it. I climbed into the back seat of the car, behind my parents, and as the vehicle turned the corner he was lost from sight.

In my head, though, Mr Willson and what we'd done were all too visible. I plugged myself into my CD Walkman and listened to Alanis Morissette's *Jagged Little Pill* album all the way home. My parents commented on how quiet I was, but I simply said I was tired and that I didn't sleep well. That was always a good excuse to make them back off.

Though I might have seemed quiet on the outside, inside me an argument was raging. It was as if I had an angel and a devil on my shoulder and they were fighting all the way home. I had such mixed feelings. *Sex has made us stronger*, the angel said. But the demon spoke louder:

Sex was all he wanted. Don't be surprised if you never hear from him again.

After all, now we'd done it, there was no reason for him to wait for me. All the milestones we'd planned – sex at sixteen, going public at eighteen – lay discarded in the dust, trampled by his eagerness to claim my virginity now, when I was only fifteen years of age.

He loves me, the angel said. But the demon cried: *He loves me not.*

Chapter 15
Reality Check

I'd thought, now that I was a woman, things would be different. From what I'd seen, when men lost their virginity they started to walk around like they were kings of all they surveyed. I'd believed losing my virginity would magically make me the happiest, most confident woman in the world... but the magic I'd believed in wasn't working anymore. The bubble had burst: the princess, fairy-tale bubble that had been my world for the past few years had well and truly popped. Cold hard reality set in instead.

My heart aching and fearful, my head confused, I told Nicola what had happened in Northamptonshire. She wasn't impressed; I think that was the moment when she took a big step back and started to reassess her former glowing opinion of Mr Willson.

'Why has he done that?' she said, sharp and critical. 'Why didn't he wait?'

Suddenly, 'He said he couldn't' didn't seem a very powerful argument. Nor could I tell her that he'd done it because he truly loved me – because *if* he loved me, wouldn't he have been in touch?

The weeks passed; March turned into April, and still no call came. Mr Willson had had sex with me, and then he hadn't called: it was that simple. As I had done so many times before, I turned to the teenage magazines for advice, poring over the problem pages for a solution. Yet they all said that boys who behaved as Mr Willson had were only using you. I had no contact with him at all and slowly, over the next few months, as his silence held and the spell stayed broken, I spiralled down, down, down…

School became a joke. Everything that had once been easy for me now wasn't. My mind elsewhere, fixated on Mr Willson and his betrayal, I started to forget books for class or even to take my PE kit in on the day we had Phys. Ed. I even lost interest in my beloved dance classes after school; I had no energy for them anymore. I was fighting this triple-headed monster – grief at being without him, pain at his dismissal, shock at the way my bubble had burst – and everything else seemed impossible. I lost my sunshine. My grades went sharply downhill and the deadlines I'd started missing at the beginning of the school year, when I'd neglected my GCSE coursework because I'd only wanted to spend time with Mr Willson, finally started catching up with me.

We had a parents' evening and it was my first bad parents' evening *ever*. Not knowing the reason behind the change in my behaviour, my dad was absolutely fuming. As usual, we went round all the different subject teachers and pretty much all of them had the same thing to say: 'Hayley's not her usual self; she doesn't seem as focused; she's missing critical deadlines for her exams.'

The teachers asked me what was up.

'I'm tired,' I said weakly, the lingering magic of Mr Willson's spell still powerful enough to bind my lips.

And that excuse, at least, was true – because I was crying myself to sleep every night. I would sob into Bedtime Bear and all my other teddies, but not one bear in my extensive collection could offer me comfort now. I started to rock myself as I lay sobbing on my bed, and unbeknown to me the sound of the headboard bashing against the wall travelled down to my parents in the living room below. Mum came up to investigate the noise and found me really distressed, crying and rocking on my bed.

'Hey,' she said. She held me and stroked me, smoothing back my long damp hair: in my anguish I was sweating heavily, working myself into a right state. I was aware of her coming in, but despite her presence I didn't stop crying; I *couldn't* stop crying. After a while, too, I even started to sleepwalk that summer, something I'd never done before.

Though my parents were worried and made a few comments about the change in my behaviour, I was never sat down and spoken to as an adult about what was wrong. I think they probably thought, given my age, that, whatever was troubling me, it couldn't be *that* serious – maybe it was exam stress, or my break-up with Paul Brown, or simply hormones playing havoc with my peace of mind. My mum would put her arm around my shoulder and jolly me along. I didn't want to tell them the truth; I felt like a fool. And, despite everything, I still loved Mr Willson and I didn't want to get him into any trouble.

Of course, it wasn't only him who would be in the firing line if the truth came out: I'd broken school rules, I'd lied to my parents, I'd knowingly had an affair with a married man. I was ashamed of my behaviour and the last thing I wanted was for Mum and Dad to look at me with disgust or disappointment, which seemed to me the only possible outcome if they knew what had gone on.

Nevertheless, in my own, immature way, I did once try to tell them. I wrote a note telling them everything; emphasising how much I was in love with Mr Willson as though that might mitigate my culpability. And I was all set to give it to them – when they asked the 'right' questions. To help prompt them, I left Madonna's 'Papa Don't Preach' playing on my stereo on repeat. I thought the lyrics were uncannily apt and was hoping my parents would 'read between the lines' and ask me outright about my situation.

Unsurprisingly, of course, they didn't think anything of it – when I loved a song or was trying to learn it for drama, I would play it on repeat until the whole street was sick of it, so the message was completely misunderstood and the 'right' question never came. I never had the guts to go through with it unprompted. I really don't blame my parents for not asking me – after all, they never had the slightest suspicion about their friend Andrew Willson because he had charmed them just as much as he had charmed me.

As the only person who knew my secret, Nicola was an incredible source of support. I was very, very lucky to have her. Because, to us, my relationship with Mr Willson was that of boyfriend and girlfriend, she did what any other sixteen-year-old would do to help her bezzie mate get over a boy who had hurt her. We had a girlie night in, and she tried to cheer me up as we ate sweets and read magazines and were simply silly and young; a kind of 'wash that man right outta my hair' evening. She carefully copied out a poem from *Just Seventeen* onto her best 'Forever Friends' notepaper and gave it to me, hoping its lyrical wisdom would help me – it was all about forgetting his name because he had chosen to be with the other woman.

Because all the time Mr Willson was silent, of course, I knew where he was: *with his wife*. Was everything he'd said about her a lie, too? But I told myself it couldn't be; he had been so convincing. I didn't know why he was ignoring me now, but I knew at least that while we were together our relationship had been pure and true. That house of cards he had built of his affection was on shaky ground, but it still held up.

I listened to Alanis Morissette over and over: 'You Oughta Know' was the soundtrack to my sadness. Her songs could have been written about my life, I felt. April turned into May, turned into June, and there came a morning when I woke from yet another night of crying to find my eyes sealed shut.

'*Mum*!' I called out in panic. I actually thought I'd gone blind overnight.

My parents took one look at me and marched me off to the doctor, equally concerned about my swollen red eyes; I couldn't see anything. The GP examined me, making notes about my tiredness and lack of energy too.

'We don't really know exactly what it is,' he concluded, 'but we think it might be caused by stress.'

I was so ill, I had to miss two weeks of school, so I missed all my mock exams. My mum was an absolute sweetheart, caring for me; I was very well looked after. It felt so nice, after all the grown-up dramas of that year, to simply be a child again, with Mum mopping my brow. Aware of how far behind I had fallen with my studies –

the good girl in me was aghast that I was missing the chance to practise my GCSEs – I tried to study while I was signed off sick, but Mum insisted on taking my schoolbooks away from me.

'I'm not having it,' she said protectively. 'You're stressing yourself out too much. There'll be time for all that when you're better.'

The time off school marked a turning point for me. Under my mum's care, and perhaps with the passage of time, too, I did start to get better. For a while, I even felt angry with Mr Willson and that emotion gave me some much-needed strength. The Spice Girls' 'Wannabe' came out that summer of 1996 and I fully embraced their 'Girl Power' message: I was an independent woman! When Mr Willson phoned to speak to my dad – for their friendship was still as strong as ever – I'd pass him straight over without engaging in chatter.

In time, my anger faded and I started to look at what had happened in Northamptonshire more positively: *at least I lost my virginity to him, to the man I loved.* I felt used, it was true, but somehow it didn't bother me anymore. After all, I didn't know any different; I'd never had any other relationship. *Maybe*, I thought, *this is just how everyone feels.* I owned the betrayal, and over time I made so many excuses for him that it didn't seem like a betrayal at all. He hadn't been in touch, true, nor planned a way for us to be together, but he *couldn't* really be in touch properly: it was too risky. *It wasn't his fault.* I could still hear his voice in my head telling me all those things he once had – that we had to wait to be together; that when his son was in a special school and I was eighteen, *then* would be our time – and so I now took what I thought was a very mature approach to things. Mr Willson did love me and he was still going to be my future husband, it just wasn't the right time *now*. He would be my future boyfriend, when the time was right; but for the present, I just had to get on and live my life.

As Year 11 began in September 1996, I was back on an even keel. I'd caught up with my schoolwork and began knuckling down for my GCSEs. Still embracing my 'I'm going to live my life' motto, I even started dating Oliver, the little lad in my year who looked like Penfold and was rumoured to have fancied me since Year 7. He was not so little anymore, though; he was nearly six foot now! A petrolhead, he was properly into cars.

Dad, naturally, was worried about my having a boyfriend, particularly in this all-important exam year, but Oliver and I were both quite studious so it was fine. My over-protective father didn't need to have any worries on any other fronts, either, for Oliver and I only really saw each other at school; he never came round to my house to hang out in my bedroom. We mostly necked on in the schoolyard (till the teachers told us off) or held hands on our way to lessons. It all seemed so simple after the rollercoaster ride of being with Mr Willson and I liked it: we went out together all year.

One Saturday afternoon in the winter of Year 11, Dad came back from the footie and started chatting to me in the living room. I got all my news of Mr Willson through him now. I still missed my ex-boyfriend like crazy, so I was always interested to hear any titbit my dad could drop – I'd perfected my 'I'm not that bothered' face even as I listened eagerly for just hearing Mr Willson's name could make me smile. Though I wasn't in touch with him myself, I was glad to know he was OK. All in all, I was really pleased that Dad was still in contact – I thought it would make things so much easier when the time eventually came for me and Mr Willson to be together.

I was sat on the sofa and my dad was standing up, having just come in.

'Good news!' he exclaimed.

'Ooh, what's that?' I said, eager to hear the gossip.

'Mrs Willson's pregnant!' he announced.

And the house of cards came tumbling down.

Chapter 16

A Stolen Kiss

I kept a fake smile plastered to my face. 'Oh, that's nice!' I said numbly.

Even though the revelation was new, there was a horrible familiarity about the situation: once again, Mr Willson – the man who supposedly loved me, according to his passionate declarations – had put me in the position of hearing what to me was devastating news from my father. To reveal my true emotions would give the game away; I had to keep everything inside and adapt my behaviour with Dad in order to keep the secret.

When I was finally able to express my emotions, I found I didn't cry: I was *angry*. Absolutely seething. The dream castle I'd been living in came crashing down around my ears. Mr Willson had always promised me it was over between him and his wife; he had vowed once his son was old enough, we would be together. But now they were having another child. It meant they were still intimate. It meant, just as his son was growing older, that they were starting afresh with a new baby. It was less than a year since he had taken my virginity in his son's playroom, two days after my fifteenth birthday, and the swift reversal of his promises left me reeling. *Everything had been a lie.*

Yet even though it was painful, there was nonetheless something that felt inevitable about the pain – like I deserved it, like I'd had this coming. I'd got into this situation with my eyes open, after all: I'd known he was married from the start. Consequently, I felt my distress wasn't his fault, but *mine*: I shouldn't have got in so deep.

Even now, even after everything, I was making excuses for him so that I didn't have to knock him off the pedestal I'd raised him up on. That was the hold he had on my heart. And from the ache in my heart at the news of the pregnancy, I realised that, even though I'd *told* myself I was moving on, I'd still been pining for him, all this time. With it having been mere months since Mr Willson had made love to me, I'd still had hope that – *eventually* – we would be together. But once I heard the news about the Willsons' new baby, that hope was gone.

I thought I was done with Mr Willson. Instead, I focused on my exams, on my plans to go to college in September to study A levels in English, dance and drama. In March 1997, I turned sixteen, but it wasn't the momentous birthday I'd thought it would be, once upon a time. In fact the only momentous thing about it was that Nicola bought me some make-up and my dad finally allowed me to wear it – only on special occasions, of course, and only through gritted teeth, but it was a milestone nonetheless.

Oliver and I broke up in the summer: at the end of the day our relationship was just a teen romance, and once we weren't seeing each other every day at school, we both sort of thought, *I can't be bothered with this* and happily went our separate ways. I don't remember that summer because of the freedom of being single and having left school at last, however. I remember it because of the wedding.

It was the marital union of some family friends. Except they *weren't* family friends; they were friends of Mr Willson. My mum and I both found it a little odd we'd been invited, to be honest – when I saw the invitation propped up in the glass cabinet in our dining room, I actually exclaimed in surprise, and Mum said, 'I *know*! Whole day as well!'

Us McGregors love a good wedding, so we were all looking forward to a knees-up – and I, of course, was stupidly excited because I knew Mr Willson would be there. I thought the wedding gave me the perfect opportunity to show him that I'd grown up. But I wasn't going to go running to him; if he had anything to say to me, after everything that had happened between us, *he* could come to me. Girl Power ruled OK in the summer of 1997.

I don't think I've ever taken such care over my appearance; I made a real effort. I even went to the hairdressers with my mum and they gave me a really posh-looking up-do. No longer was I hiding behind my curtain of long blonde hair; instead, this sixteen-year-old was going for mature sophistication. I wore a little black dress with a scoop neck and a purple fitted jacket – and my first-ever pair of high heels. Given it was a special occasion, Dad even allowed me to wear some of Nicola's birthday make-up. I finished off the look with my silver ballerina necklace, a present from my mum and dad when I'd first started secondary school.

Having gone to all that effort, I felt really confident as I strutted into Rochdale Town Hall on the day of the wedding. We saw Mr Willson at once, as he was helping to usher guests to their seats.

It was the first time I'd laid eyes on him since we'd slept together the previous year. Despite all my preparations and my determination that *this time would be different*, simply in seeing him I felt as though magic fairy dust was sprinkling onto my shoulders. He gave me a beaming smile and I could tell by his look that he'd clocked the effort I'd gone to with my outfit and appreciated it. I was trying to be the strong, independent woman I always heard the Spice Girls singing about, but I was amazed at how wobbly my resolve suddenly became. I'd forgotten the power of Mr Willson. There was something about him, in the flesh, that despite myself I was still infatuated with. I'd loved him since I was twelve years old. It was so hard to remember he wasn't the perfect prince I'd fallen for back then.

Luckily, there was no chance for us to be alone. As he disappeared, busy with wedding duties, I regained my equilibrium and recalled what I'd wanted to achieve that day: to show him I'd moved on and that I was no longer the puppy-dog schoolgirl. The wedding progressed as standard – ceremony, wedding breakfast, speeches – with the reception held upstairs in one of the town hall's large function rooms. Loads more people turned up for the evening and it became a very busy event. My mum and dad were having a good old drink and a dance and I almost forgot about Mr Willson being there as I joined them on the dance floor. Hour by hour passed, and the guests grew more and more inebriated. I, of course, was stone-cold sober, being underage.

Quite late on in the evening, I told my parents I was going to the loo and slipped out into the corridor that led to the toilets. He must have been watching me and followed me out. I heard running footsteps behind me and then I felt a hand on my arm as he stopped me and pulled me round to face him, just like in a movie.

'Our song' had warned 'Don't Stand So Close To Me', but Mr Willson didn't take its advice. He stood so close that I could smell that familiar Eternity for Men aftershave… and it felt like I was *home*. There was another smell, too, one that threatened to overpower it: alcohol. Mr Willson was drunk.

'I haven't had a chance to speak to you, McGregor!' he said. 'How are you doing? How were your GCSEs?'

I answered him politely, but I think I was a little bit off. He might be acting as though the past year hadn't happened, but the emotional rollercoaster ride *I'd* been on wasn't all that easy to forget.

'You look so beautiful,' he told me. 'Every time I see you, you grow more stunning.'

He'd noticed my hair was up, and told me that I looked grown up.

'You're growing into a woman now,' he slurred. 'You look *amazing*.'

To be honest, I thought *he* looked pretty amazing, too. He looked like the love of my life – just as he always had.

People were milling around us on their way to the loo. Nevertheless, despite the audience, Mr Willson pulled me into him for a snog. It wasn't long, but it was passionate. I let him kiss me; of course I let him. He'd said all the right things, done all the right things, and I was sixteen-year-old putty in his hands.

Afterwards, he gave me a cheeky slap on my arse. 'You go to the loo, McGregor,' he said, and so I did as I was told. Then I went back into the melee of the wedding and danced the night away, feeling like I could feel his eyes on me; feeling the secret of that stolen kiss as if he'd burned my lips with love when he'd kissed me. It felt like a gift, like a reward: *you are loved*.

With Mr Willson I'd always equated our physical intimacy with affection, so I treasured that kiss almost as much as the scholar in me did my GCSE results, which arrived just a few weeks later. They were good, despite my academic troubles in Year 10, but for me the most important thing about them was that they enabled me to go to college. A new chapter was beginning: Mr Willson and my secondary school were now just a part of the past.

Chapter 17

End of an Era

There's something really special about those first couple of years after you leave school. Even though I was still in formal education, studying my A levels, it was my *choice* to do so and that made a huge difference. I *chose* to go to college, I *chose* what to study, I *chose* to start going clubbing at the weekends and to begin experimenting with drinking and smoking. When you're a child, you don't have a choice, and I loved the fact that I was now more able to assert my independence. Even the fact that I didn't have to wear a school uniform anymore felt revolutionary at that age. I was a proper teenager at last and, unlike the past couple of years, there was nothing to complicate my enjoyment of that formative time.

On a night out clubbing in Rochdale during my first term at college I met a really nice young man and we started dating. It quickly became serious. As he was only a year older than me, I didn't feel nervous or inadequate when I was in bed with him. After all, I knew what I was doing – thanks to Mr Willson. I was no longer the student studying my craft.

My boyfriend and I felt so comfortable with one another that we were happy to experiment in bed; we even tried role play. It was me who suggested we recreate a teacher/student scene – but I wanted to play the teacher. I'm not sure why. Maybe I wanted to see what it might have felt like for Mr Willson; maybe *I* wanted to have the power for once. But my boyfriend wanted to do it the other way round, so once again I found myself playing schoolgirl to a seducing tutor.

It was odd, but I didn't like it. The scene wasn't anything like it really had been, of course – for a start, I played it much more cocky and promiscuous than I'd ever been when I was really thirteen or fourteen years old, when all I remembered of my emotions was feeling uncertain and ill-prepared – but nevertheless I just kept seeing Mr Willson, rather than my boyfriend. I might even have said his name at one point. I couldn't get him out of my head.

As for the real Mr Willson, though I no longer saw him, thanks to his friendship with my dad, he was still in my life, albeit at a distance. I'd get the odd update from my father – just that he was working supply now or simple chit-chat like that – and I was always excited to hear the news and to know he was OK. He even helped me get my first theatrical agent – though as he'd been promising to do that since I was in school, I didn't feel especially grateful, it was more like: *About time*. I'd actually given up on the idea, thinking it was just another broken promise, but my father is much more dog-with-bone than I am, and because Mr Willson had also mentioned to him about getting me an agent – 'Your daughter's going to be a star, Neil,' he used to say expansively – Dad had persevered until finally Mr Willson had set up a meeting for me with those agents of his in Manchester and they'd taken me on. I did a bit of work for them in my spare time, being an extra on shows like *Hollyoaks* and *Corrie*.

Due to the shared nature of our chosen profession, Mr Willson was very good at getting information out of my parents about me. 'I've got this lead for Hayley,' he might say, or 'I've heard about this audition' and then he'd add, 'Could I get her email address to let her know, please?' By now, the technology revolution had taken place and I had my own email address and my own mobile phone. But, as I soon discovered, it wasn't for professional reasons that Mr Willson wanted to stay in touch.

The first email arrived after my eighteenth birthday. I was still with my boyfriend, very seriously in love, and I wonder now if Mr Willson had got wind of that via my parents and if that's why he chose that particular moment to break his silence of so many years.

I didn't have my own laptop, so I was checking my emails on my boyfriend's desktop computer in his bedroom. When I saw I had a message from Mr Willson, my heart skipped a beat for, although I was very serious about my current relationship, you never forget your first love. I think a flame still burned within me for my former teacher, it had just been doused for a while by meeting someone else.

I clicked on the email and opened it, wondering what he had to say.

There were no pleasantries. It was a dirty email, straight away: straight into the sexual content, just as he'd gone straight into the sex when he'd taken my virginity.

I didn't like it, not least because I was with my boyfriend now and I didn't relish the guilty feeling that receiving such an intimate message provoked. Nonetheless, I didn't mention it to anyone. Maybe because part of me was also quite pleased to get it – it gave me a huge boost of confidence to know that Mr Willson still got turned on by me. He obviously couldn't get me out of his head, just as I couldn't get him out of mine. No matter how hard we tried, we were always coming back together. It was star-crossed lovers' time all over again.

There was another benefit to the email, too: I started to feel in control. I'd *never* felt like that before with Mr Willson. I replied, but not with anything filthy myself – that really was not me – though I definitely stroked his ego. After that the emails continued, but very irregularly. They were always about him being hard for me or he'd tell me he'd been thinking about me that day. He might have driven past somewhere and it had reminded him of me, or he'd been listening to our Police song and it had taken him right back. He said he thought about me when he masturbated.

I always replied, but I wouldn't say I encouraged him outright. Neither of us ever suggested we meet. Our lives were poles apart, but for this slim thread that kept us looped together.

I finished my A levels and moved out of my parents' house to take a three-year dance course at another college. Unfortunately, I absolutely hated it. You had to be weighed when you went into class and, even though I'd lost my puppy fat and was actually quite fit from all that dancing, I was in no way a slim ballerina. My self-esteem hit rock bottom. Most of the other girls felt the pressure too: they were all on laxatives and throwing up in the changing room, so it was really not a nice environment. I was eating a Nutri-Grain, a banana and a sausage roll for my daily food intake, topping up with fags, and on trips home to see them my parents noticed my becoming more and more emaciated. I was trying to be the girl I thought people wanted me to be, and it was making me utterly miserable.

It was my dad who forced a change. 'What's wrong?' he asked me, at the end of my first year. I burst into tears and admitted that I hated college.

'Right then, you leave,' he said bluntly. It was the obvious solution, but I'd been trying so hard to please everyone that I hadn't been able to see it. I loved my dad for being able to help me out in that way; to help me in a way I hadn't allowed him to do when I'd been so miserable about Mr Willson a few years before. 'But you don't sit on your backside,' he added in his no-nonsense Northern way, 'you make sure you get a job.'

So I did – and pretty darn quick. I got hold of a copy of *The Stage* newspaper and began taking myself off to auditions. I landed a job working at Longleat Safari Park in that summer of 2000, entertaining the queues and putting on a kids' show four times a day. It was a summer of fun, really, and after that I got a job at the Millennium Dome down in London as a costumed character host. My boyfriend and I tried really hard to keep our relationship going, but we were young and it was difficult now that we were living at opposite ends of the country. After a series of jealous rows we eventually finished between Christmas and New Year: the final nail in the coffin was that I found out he'd been unfaithful while I'd been working away. It hurt, but I also thought, *Karma*. It was the least I deserved given I'd been with a married man.

Now I was older, coming up to my twentieth birthday, I'd started to judge myself a lot for that betrayal. I felt like such a bad person – a bad *woman* – for having done that to another woman. It wasn't a nice thought to have, so I tried to make excuses for myself – I was young, I was in love, he'd told me their marriage was over – but the nasty aftertaste still lingered.

After my boyfriend and I split up, I found that I hankered after affection in whatever way I could get it. I think, after my heart had been broken not once but twice by men who had ended up with other women, I was desperately searching for a way of feeling in control because I felt rejected and unloved. One of the lessons Mr Willson had taught me was that sex equalled love; I knew it only in my subconscious, but whenever I was feeling low I'd go out and find a man to have sex with, as though that would make everything better. Being in love made me feel soft and weak – it seemed from my past history that I allowed men to walk all over me if I fell in love – so for a time I blithely used them for sex and enjoyed having no strings attached. The noughties was the time when ladette culture was becoming mainstream and I told myself over and over that I was an empowered woman because I was strong enough to be on my own. And if I wanted to have sex at the weekend, I would: simple as that.

It wasn't simple, though. Not least because there started to be a pattern to these flings. I would go out drinking – I was always drunk when these things happened – and I would get with a man… and he would turn out to be married. Sometimes I knew it from the outset, but more often than not I would find out after the event. It seemed typical male behaviour; I almost expected it in the end. Why it kept happening, I didn't have a clue. Better the devil you know? Was that just my type? I guess, after the rejection I'd felt after losing my virginity when Mr Willson had gone back to his wife, maybe I experienced a warped kind of euphoria at 'winning' *this* man, at least. I couldn't be with Mr Willson, but there was a victory and some kind of self-assurance to know that someone else wanted to be with me.

On the surface I said I didn't care about their marital status – they were the ones with the wives; it was their choice and it was nothing to do with me – but inside I was hurting. It was almost as though I was punishing myself because, when I was honest in my heart about what was happening, I did feel guilty and I did feel hurt and I did feel used. But it was as if I didn't think I was good enough to be with someone who could actually love me. Even if I was with a single man, I assumed he was going to cheat and I'd be jealous and suspicious until the fling soon fizzled out. Though most of the time I professed myself to be a confident modern woman, cut from this new ladette cloth, there were nights when I'd weep on my own, shut up in my room, confused as to why I always seemed to end up in these destructive relationships. I'd thought for a long time I was a bad person because I'd had an affair with a married man when I was younger; now I was repeating the behaviour, it seemed only to emphasise the point.

So I'd push the thoughts away. I'd drink through them; I'd paste on that sunny smile of mine that Mr Willson had always adored and I'd get out there again as though nothing was wrong.

In the summer of 2001 I joined a kids' cartoon roadshow event which toured all over the country. With my parents still in contact with the Willsons, they told them proudly that I'd be performing in the Northamptonshire area that August.

And so the Willsons invited me to stay.

It felt *so* strange walking into their big detached house again. We all gathered together in the playroom at first as it was the room closest to the front door, so everyone was stood right in the place where Mr Willson had taken my virginity five years before. *Weird.* So much had changed since then – but other things were just the same. When Mr Willson greeted me, he kissed me on the lips and wrapped me up in a special hug that lasted just a beat longer than was necessary.

I wasn't quite sure how I felt, seeing him again. Other than the sporadic emails and an even more occasional filthy phone call, we hadn't stayed in touch; we'd lived our own lives. On that day he seemed very much the family man. His daughter, who had been born shortly before the wedding where he'd kissed me, was now four years old and a gorgeous little thing; his son, now eight, remained severely disabled, of course, but he could engage with you and it was nice to see him again. As for Mrs Willson, she was as polite as she always was to me and she and Mr Willson seemed happy and relaxed together. *That's that done then*, I thought, of what Mr Willson and I had once shared. So I boxed it up: a schoolgirl crush, another fling that didn't stand the test of time. I had once loved him, but it was the stuff of dreams and it now seemed insubstantial.

We all spent the evening together, sitting out in their big garden, smoking and drinking wine. I was twenty years old, no longer on the cans of soda; it was just one more thing that was different. I stayed the night in the guest room that my parents had used when we'd visited as a family all those years ago and I was pleased not to be on the sofa bed – that would have brought back a memory too far.

In the morning, when Mrs Willson left for work, the metal clasp on the barn door probably jangled as it had done five years before. And something else echoed from that long-ago day, too: for the moment she left the house, Mr Willson changed.

We were stood together in the living room; the children were in the kitchen and we could hear them banging about. In one smooth, fluid motion, he pulled me to him and kissed me passionately.

Though taken aback, I went with it.

When he came up for air, he told me, 'I've missed you, Hayley McGregor.'

I replied instantly, falling into our call-and-respond pattern of old, 'I've missed you too.'

Just like that, we clicked back into our old intimacy. The truth was, even after everything that had happened, there was no one I felt more comfortable and confident around. It felt easy and familiar. That day, it was almost like Mr Willson made me his girlfriend. I helped him dress and feed his kids and we went together to drop them off at nursery. Then he and I went for a drive, just like old times. This time, however, he had a very different car: the messy automobile I remembered from my youth was gone and in its place was a mid-life crisis dream: a sporty little red Mazda MG. He put the top down, and we drove through the twisting country lanes on this gorgeous summer's day, with Mr Willson's hand on my knee and my long blonde hair flowing in the wind. It felt perfect; it was everything I'd ever wanted from him. In a heartbeat I'd gone from thinking the night before that he didn't want me anymore to him completely bowling me over. That day, it felt like we were a couple – just as he'd always promised me we would one day be.

We spent all day together, blissfully happy. After the drive, we returned to his house and had lunch. We got a bit passionate downstairs, so Mr Willson stood up and led me upstairs to the bedroom. At last, the crisp white sheets of my teenage imagination sprang into being. Yet there was something wrong with the fantasy now it was brought to life.

For they were lying on his marital bed.

I knew what was going to happen, of course. I had a really odd feeling about it – it wasn't eager anticipation, more like I felt it was an opportunity to explore my feelings about what had happened five years before. It seemed like a dream, sometimes, the way I'd lost my virginity, aged fifteen: Mr Willson sneaking in to see me in that dark before dawn and then everything between us suddenly stopping afterwards, just like that. Was it real? Did it happen? I remembered the way it had hurt, the way it hadn't lived up to my teenage expectations, the way something about it just hadn't felt right. I hadn't enjoyed it. I wondered, now, if it was going to be better this time; whether *we* were going to be better together. I was still waiting for that filmic love scene, I think. If anyone could make it happen, surely it was Mr Willson, because I'd blatantly never loved anyone the way that I loved him. I wanted to confirm whether we were soulmates, or whether my negative feelings about sleeping with him were in fact the right way to feel. My memories of our affair were of me loving the romantic elements of being with him, but not the sexual side. I had longed so often to be older, so that I could enjoy it more. Well, now was my chance.

We had sex together. I won't go into detail, but it wasn't good – for me, at least. Afterwards, he cuddled me briefly and reeled out his greatest hits of compliments: 'That was wonderful; your body's so amazing; you're so tight…'

But they didn't work on me the way they used to. Lying in his arms, I realised that I didn't feel the same way anymore. It was unsurprising when you thought about it: I was just fourteen when I was with Mr Willson; I was now twenty years old. Yet he'd had this hold on me for so long and I loved his personality so much that I'd thought we were meant to be.

I didn't say anything to him; I didn't want to hurt him and I had no idea how to let him down gently. I think I was scared, too, in case he agreed it was over – I'd often daydreamed that one day he might stop my future wedding with a passionate, public declaration of his love for me, and it seemed strange to think that, when I got up from that bed, I was also walking away from the romantic narrative that had sustained me for so long.

But I was a grown-up now. I was sad about my feelings, but I knew they were right. Sleeping with him had confirmed it: this was wrong, this wasn't how things were meant to be. Mr Willson wasn't my shining knight in armour after all – all that was just for fairy tales.

And that was the last time that I was ever intimate with Mr Willson.

In more ways than one, it was the end of an era.

Chapter 18

A Man Unmasked

A week after I stayed at the Willsons' house in Northamptonshire, I started a new job. For the next year, I was to be working with a leading theatre-in-education company, going into schools up and down the country to perform short plays and run workshops inspired by key issues for young people. We covered bullying, drug and alcohol abuse, teenage pregnancy, road safety and much more. I was touring with two lads in their twenties and the three of us did this whole programme of different plays and sessions with the kids, actively going into schools and working with the teenagers.

It was strange, being back in a school environment but being so much older than when I myself had gone to school. I felt like I was seeing it with new eyes. What I found especially striking was how I was acutely aware of the teacher/student relationships that I witnessed in these different institutions. I could instantly tell which teachers were, shall we say, *close* to their students. It was almost like I had a radar for it, and when I observed the elbow touching, or the light placing of hands on shoulders, or the discreet caress of an arm, I recognised what was going on at once. Obviously schools are hotbeds of raging hormones, and it was clear there were crushes going on all over the place from the young kids towards the good-looking teachers, but I would say, from my observations at least, it was apparent Mr Willson wasn't the only one who was perhaps too tactile with his students.

Yet that was something I'd discovered from my conversations with my peers, as well. My tongue loosened by my increasing maturity and the passing of the years, by now I'd happily told friends and boyfriends that I'd been in a relationship with my drama teacher at school. I still didn't want my parents to find out about it, but I didn't see any problem in discussing what I simply saw as a previous relationship. And that's how everyone else saw it too. It was amazing how many people said to me, 'Oh, me too' or 'I had a thing with my art teacher'. Or their maths teacher or their science teacher, or the man who taught them French. No one batted an eyelid; it seemed like it was rife.

But it's one thing to be in the moment, age fourteen, and then to think it was normal once you'd grown up with that secret stitched inside your soul. It was quite another to observe the youth of some of these girls that we were working with now. And they looked *so* young to me. I couldn't fathom how any adult could find them attractive. That was true even of the older kids in Year 11, who were officially past the age of sexual consent. Although you could identify those pupils who had all the physical attributes to go on to be a heartbreaker, their immaturity was such that it didn't matter how tall they were or how chiselled their newly stubbly jaws, they just weren't attractive to any well-adjusted grown-up. Through their behaviour and even merely their use of language, it was obvious they were still just kids inside. I actually thought, *You've got to have something wrong with you if you're going to go with that age group and not your own.*

But even though I could see how young *these* kids were, I didn't marry what I was seeing to what Mr Willson and I had shared. After all, *I* was different. I really *had* been mature – that was what he had always told me. I could remember his words even now, so proud had they made me feel: that I had an older, wiser head on my shoulders than anybody else in my year. I hadn't been like these girls when I was twelve, or thirteen, or fourteen: I was special. What we'd had was special; Mr Willson had truly loved me. I didn't see anything wrong with it.

The months passed and I continued to work closely with the kids in the schools we visited. Becoming a teacher of sorts to them, I began to develop my skills in building a rapport with the children. It was amazing how clear it was, to me as an adult, which kids needed a bit of a confidence boost or who was being overly confident in our workshops because they actually felt incredibly insecure inside. When we're teenagers, we think the secrets of our hearts are inscrutable, but in fact we're broadcasting them with every bit of body language we have.

I was good at my job. I worked with all sorts of kids, including some with special needs or major emotional problems: drama can be a fantastic key for unlocking some of their communication difficulties. I felt really proud when I was able to get a student to trust me. In such cases, you become their confidante. And through these relationships that I was building – as 2001 turned into 2002 and the early months of the new year passed by – I started to realise there was a mark, a line, that you should never, ever cross with a child. If they trusted and respected you, liked you – even if they had a crush on you – that was a gift that would enable you to help them grow into a mature and well-adjusted individual. With that special relationship in place, you were in a position to offer guidance and encouragement. You could help them grow, become confident, aspire to achieve their dreams. It was a privileged position; it wasn't a trust you should *ever* take advantage of.

On Saturday, 23 March 2002, I turned twenty-one. The night before I'd been out clubbing to celebrate and I was really hungover. Despite that, I had to get up at 9 or 10 o'clock in the morning as my dad was picking me up: he took me to the hairdressers because we were having a posh family meal that night and my parents had told me I'd want to look smart. I did my best, despite my aching head. The hairdresser gave me a Rachel-from-*Friends* do – a really sophisticated to-the-shoulders cut that was the shortest I'd ever had it – and she dyed it in that classic noughties zebra style with alternating streaks of blonde and brown. I wore black knee-high boots and what looked like a black dress (but was actually a skirt and top), which had a really funky emblem of a Chinese dragon in white on the front of it. The pencil skirt tapered sexily to my knees and I felt really confident in the outfit; I'd lost weight through touring and was a slim size 10.

The meal with my mum and dad and brother was quite early in the evening, and on the way home my parents said airily, 'Oh, we've just got to pop into Bacup Cricket Club to drop off your brother's subs.' My eleven-year-old brother was a really keen cricketer so I didn't think anything of it. After Dad had parked, though, he turned around and suggested casually, 'We may as well go in for a quick drink while we're here.'

As soon as I walked through the door, I heard, 'Surprise!' and the DJ started playing that cheesy 'Happy Birthday To You' record.

I froze at once in the doorway. But my immobility wasn't caused by the shock of the unexpected party. It was because *he* was there.

Mr Willson was standing by the stage area of the function room, wearing a dark suit and a smart shirt. And for the first time I saw an old man – a man who was so much older than me. He'd started to go grey and his hairline had receded, but as though battling the passing of the years he'd had an earring put in since I'd last seen him: a little gold hoop. It looked a bit desperate, to be honest. I'd always thought Mr Willson was cool and suave and sophisticated, but seeing him now he looked rather geeky to me. It was as if a mask had fallen and for the first time I was seeing someone different from the handsome prince.

A totally unexpected emotion rose up inside me when I saw him standing there, looking utterly at home among my closest family and friends on this special birthday that marked my official transition into adulthood.

I felt *hate*.

I was amazed by how strong it was – I think my experiences in the schools had changed me more than I had thought. Because, for the very first time, I thought: *You should have said no.*

You should have said no.

Yes, I'd had a crush on him. Yes, when I was twelve, I'd thought he was the most incredible person on the planet. But I'd had no control over my infatuation – *he* had been the adult, and *he* had had the power.

My eyes narrowed as he smiled smugly at me from across the room. *You should have said no.*

My mum, standing by my side, nudged me gently. She thought I was in shock because of the surprise party. 'Well, go and say hello to your guests then!' she prompted cheerily.

My parents had organised this amazing event just for me; it must have taken an awful lot of hard work. I knew I had to switch out of the moment I'd been in and focus on the task in hand. 'Sorry, Mum!' I said, pasting the smile back onto my face, changing into good-girl mode instantaneously, as I had learned to do so easily after all these years of subterfuge. 'I'm shocked!'

I started to make my way around the room, greeting friends, neighbours and family members. As I did so, I could feel his eyes on me. I knew the weight of that gaze so well, for he had been watching me closely for almost ten years now.

Despite my feelings, I couldn't ignore him all night: he was a guest, specially invited by my parents. I noted he hadn't brought his wife. Eventually, though I tried to put it off for as long as possible, our paths crossed and I found myself face-to-face with him. I actually gritted my teeth as he greeted me. It was his usual repertoire, of course: he went to kiss me on the lips, but I turned my head away. He embraced me passionately, but I wriggled out of his arms as quickly as I could – I could still feel that hatred burning inside me.

He looked hurt. No wonder, really: the last time I'd seen him, I'd jumped into bed with him the moment he'd said, 'I've missed you.' I think he'd thought I was his for life. He kept trying to catch up with me all evening, but I wasn't having any of it. I made sure I was always around people so that he couldn't say anything intimate to me and in so doing charm his way back into my good books. Instead, I spent all evening hanging out with my mates, including Nicola, who naturally was there to celebrate the big twenty-one.

She was even less impressed than I was at seeing Mr Willson there. I'd told her that we'd slept together the previous summer and she was completely switched off to him now. Both of us, in different ways, had arrived at the conclusion that he really wasn't a very nice person. It had taken us years to see it, but as it happened the boyfriend Nicola had brought with her to the party that evening saw through him at once.

He'd clocked Mr Willson watching and hugging me, you see. 'That's your *teacher*?' he exclaimed in surprise when Nicola told him who the old bloke with the earring was. 'He's a bit familiar, isn't he? What a perv!'

As the night drew on, it turned out that Mr Willson wasn't only a special guest at the do because he was my 'favourite teacher'. Unbeknown to me, my parents had asked him to put together some entertainment for the evening. A hush fell as I was ushered to a chair before the stage and then this half-hour skit began, with Mr Willson and a mate of his dramatising – in a really over-the-top way – my life story, from birth to present day. It was hilarious, actually: they played me, they played my parents... They were prancing about the stage with this amazing energy – and talent. Mr Willson always was talented.

I sat before them like a child at a birthday party, clapping my hands in delight. It was pretty special: not many people get that on their twenty-first birthday – a bespoke drama piece written just for them, all about their life. It was lovely. And so the rollercoaster ride of my relationship with Mr Willson took another turn. I had this hate, but I also had this conflicting feeling of gratitude and appreciation. When I hugged him after the skit had finished, our embrace was longer and warmer and I thanked him with genuine emotion. There was still a dislike there, but once again I started making excuses for him. He *wasn't* the perv that Nicola's boyfriend was making him out to be; what we'd shared was more special than that. And so, despite my newfound knowledge of lines that should never be crossed, I tried to make Mr Willson's crossed line right in my mind – because I really didn't want it to be wrong.

Maybe six months or so after my birthday, I met an amazing man. He had a girlfriend at the time – but when had that ever stopped me? I was still drawn to people who couldn't commit. Unusually, however, this time *I* stopped it. I felt there was something different about him.

'I can't do this anymore while you are with her,' I told him. 'I'm not making you make a choice, this is just *my* choice to walk away.'

Two weeks later, he came to me and told me he'd finished it, so we got together properly.

I fell hook, line and sinker for this man. It was a different love from anything I'd ever felt before. I knew clearly, when I met him, that what I'd felt for Mr Willson was just infatuation – girlie silliness.

I could tell, in my gut, this was the real thing.

Chapter 19

Charming Men

Robert was a very charming man – not unlike Mr Willson, in that way. He was Asian, and had beautiful brown eyes and the softest skin. Everyone thought we were the perfect couple. And, to begin with, we were.

It was my fault things changed; at least, that's what I thought at the time. I found it very, very difficult to trust my partner whenever I was in a relationship. I didn't know why, exactly; all I knew was that in my experience men lied and cheated – *all* men did. After all, most of the blokes I'd been with had always rolled that way.

I started to have a go at Robert. Niggle, niggle, niggle; nag, nag, nag. All my insecurities, my jealousy and my fear of rejection came out. Our relationship had begun with him cheating on his girlfriend: I told him over and over that he was going to do the same to me.

'But I chose you,' he would protest.

But another man had told me that, once upon a time, and he had been lying through his teeth too.

My conversations with Robert weren't reasonable, rational discussions because, when it came to trust, *I* wasn't reasonable and rational. I started to be a bit of a crazy girlfriend, banshee screaming at him. Then one night he snapped. He pushed me against the wall and grabbed me round the throat, hard, till I started choking and crying, and then he let me go.

He said sorry for it, afterwards – he was shocked, I think, that he'd even done it. He'd never hit a man before; he'd certainly never hurt a woman.

Robert was very good at talking me round, just like another charming man I'd once known. So I accepted his apology, without a moment's hesitation, because in my head I *deserved* it: it wasn't Robert's fault.

Maybe you can guess what happened next, though I didn't see it coming. But it's like any story of domestic violence you've ever heard: there is no twist in this particular tale. Once you forgive a moment of violence, it's going to happen again.

To begin with, it would only occur in the heat of one of our increasingly toxic arguments. Robert would reach a point where he couldn't cope with my vicious verbal attacks anymore and he'd lash out with a push or a grab, or a throttle. I forgave each one. Sometime after the second or third incident, we were rowing in the car one day as I drove us to the airport when our argument suddenly escalated and he punched me in the face.

Luckily, I managed to retain control of the car. Everything went deadly silent, both of us shocked. He wanted to leave and I begged him to stay. By then we were on a slippery slope, and though he never hit me in the face again, the violence grew steadily worse until every argument we had would end up in a physical fight. Each time, I felt I deserved it so I stayed. On the surface our relationship was strong as steel; over time we even moved in together.

In the beginning, I used to fight back, but I slowly learned that I could never, ever win. That lesson was both physical and mental because, once Robert realised that he could physically dominate me, he used his charm and his articulate manner to put me down, too. He told me I was stupid, talentless, ugly, fat, and I began to believe him until I had no confidence. Once he could see his words were working, I think he started to relish the power that he had over me; to enjoy the fact that this formerly strong, vivacious girl was now under his control. His actions became even more manipulative: he'd stand in a doorway and not let me out; he'd steal my bank card or hide my car keys or break my mobile phone; he'd leave the house and lock me in it; he'd throw my handbag from a moving car. All of that intensified until he really savoured taking my things, smashing them and then throwing them down on the ground and making me get them: it was almost, 'Fetch, dog'. And once I was down there on my knees, he'd spit on me or kick me. One time he kicked me in the leg so hard that I started bleeding through my jeans; I still have the scar.

I didn't tell a soul what he was doing. Part of that was embarrassment, I guess – I was ashamed of what I was forgiving. Another part was because I still loved him: though he hurt me badly, we were also bezzie mates. It was two sides of the same coin, and it didn't feel unfamiliar; it was almost like I expected this double-sided aspect to my relationships: abuse and affection went hand in hand. The final part was fear – fear of not being believed. After all, the stereotypical image of a battered woman is mousey Little Mo from *EastEnders*. I certainly wasn't such a meek and mild girl. Robert convinced me that no one would believe me, and categorically that they wouldn't believe me over him. As far as the wider

neighbours had phoned for me, hearing
the walls, but Robert believed I'd never
to call his bluff.

ong. And when the police arrived, despite
to be Mr Wonderful in front of them,
said eventually wound him up so much that
his true self and he went for me. The police
instantly and bundled him off in their van.
brilliant, actually. Two weeks later he came
llect his stuff, and that was the end of that. I
ert wanted it to be over too, really – I don't
liked the man he had become.

as around this time that my brother had an
nt trial for a cricket club. The whole family went
port him, travelling down to Northampton. And
hould we meet in the pub afterwards, given we
in the area? None other than Andrew Willson, of
se. Now aged twenty-five, I finally felt able to start
g his first name.

I was in a bad place at the time. I'd broken up with
obert, but I was vulnerable and very, very thin. I was
noking, not eating; my friend said she had to look away
when she saw me changing costume at work because she
could see my ribs and the bones along my back. I wonder
now what Andrew Willson thought when he saw me; it
had been years since we'd last had contact and the trauma
of the intervening near half-decade must have shown on
my body, let alone my face.

The moment I saw him, I couldn't help it: my
heart fluttered. The hate I'd felt for him at my twenty-
first birthday party simply wasn't there: all my hate was
directed at Robert. What I'd been through with him was

world was concerned, he was Mr Wonderful. Ironically,
although I concealed my injuries as best I could – and I
lived in polo necks to cover up the bruises – on occasion
he hurt me so badly there was no way I could hide it, so
I'd have to lie and say I'd got in a fight because of my
gobby mouth or I'd even been in a car accident (I looked
so awful, people actually believed me); and then Robert
would get all the praise for caring for me on my sickbed!
Once again, I'd got myself in a situation with a charmer
who could charm the world.

I started to go into myself. Once upon a time, I'd have
been the one entering a room with charisma and vitality –
'Hiya, everyone!' – but now I always let him go in first and
I'd follow meekly in his wake. I lost touch with many of my
friends; even Nicola didn't see me for years. Despite myself
and my natural personality, I became that quiet, don't-
say-boo-to-a-goose girlfriend. I was afraid of Robert, and
afraid to speak. Because although we'd begun this journey
with his violence sparking only in the heat of an argument,
over time his fuse got shorter and shorter and shorter –
until there simply wasn't one. All it took was one look at
me to make him want to smack me or spit on me, or pull
out a clump of my hair. It got to the point where he hurt
me every single day. It got to the point where he only had
to raise his hand and I'd flinch in abject fear.

I could tell you so many stories, reading my script
from the scars upon my body. The mark by my temple
where he shoved me down the stairs. The spot on my
shoulder where I tried to jump out of a moving car to
get away from him and the resistance of the opened
door pushed me back in and nearly broke my arm. The
dint on my eyebrow from a PlayStation controller that

was lobbed at me; it was my fault I got hurt, apparently, because I didn't get out of the way in time.

It was *always* my fault I got hurt, though. I had such a low opinion of myself that I thought I deserved it. One of my mum's favourite sayings is 'Everything happens for a reason'. I took that, and – just as I'd felt when my teenage boyfriend had cheated on me – I thought: *This is Karma*. I was such a bad person, and I'd done so many bad things in my life, I'd had this coming for a long, long time. This was my lot – I just had to take it. I didn't even fight it anymore, I let it happen. I didn't scream and I didn't shout – that way it was over quicker. God forbid I should try to stop a man controlling me.

There was barely a pretence of a relationship anymore. Robert used to do the cooking, but if he didn't cook, I didn't eat. I lost so much weight that I was almost a size 4 on my top half. We barely went out; we were living separate lives in separate rooms, simply circling each other in this house that I'd bought with some financial help from my dad, and things were really, really nasty and really, really bad. I couldn't see any way out… except one.

One night, everything came to a head for me. After drinking heavily, I went round the house taking this concoction of tablets – anything I could find. I wanted to go to sleep, never wake up, and just fade away.

Yet even that desperate cry for help didn't work: I threw everything up and woke in a cold, stinking pile of my own vomit.

Wow, I thought, *you turned into that girl*. It was hardly the future I'd dreamed of for myself, lying next to Bedtime Bear in the pink, poster-covered bedroom of my childhood.

That lov
I thought. W
when I told h
having a fucking

So I went on
and said, 'What's
supposed to be the
get-together watching
us, including Mr Wond

'I think we're done,
from the tremble in my v
sat me down and put the
him everything – except for
way Robert had manipulated a
enough just to tell him that.

My dad was fuming about
without him,' he said.

That night I stayed over at my
when I went back in the morning I'd
strength to stand up to my abuser.

'Where the fuck have you been?' he
walked in.

'I stayed at Mum and Dad's,' I said. Th
deep breath before adding, 'We really need to
cannot go on, you cannot treat me like this.' I
whole speech, which ended, 'And you need to leave

He just laughed at me, of course, in that beli
way he had, and he didn't believe me when I said I'd
the police if he didn't get out right now. Why would h
I had cried wolf about that so many times before, hoping
the threat of bringing in the Old Bill would stop him
hurting me, but I'd never actually had the courage to

call. In the past
my cries throug
be brave enoug
He was wr
his attempt
something I
he showed
were on hir
They were
back to c
think Ro
think he
It w
import
to sup
who
were
cou
usi

definitely wrong; he had *definitely* crossed a line; he had *definitely* hurt me. In contrast, Andrew Willson seemed perfect; in a way, even more perfect than he ever had before. After all, I had *tried* to move on from him – and look where it got me. I think most people have that one former relationship that is 'the one that got away'; the one crush they return to after every break-up; the ready excuse that says, 'Well, that didn't work out because I'm meant to be with *this* guy'. I was drawn back to him like a migrating bird, wanting to come home. Now I was twenty-five, in a parallel world it was more than feasible that Mr Willson and I could be together now, if we wanted to be. It wasn't beyond the realms of possibility anymore. After all, I was now the age he was when we'd first met: I was a *proper* grown-up at last. As he kissed me on the lips and swept me up in that gorgeous Eternity-for-Men-scented hug that I knew so well, my heart leapt in a hopeful way that it hadn't done in a very long time.

Perhaps he sensed the much warmer reception from me. At any rate, he was straight back to his old ways as we sat beside each other in a family country pub, resting his leg against mine and tensing and twitching his thigh muscle as he had once done in class. Then he got more brazen: he put his hand on my leg under the table.

Though pleased to see him, I hadn't expected that. We were with my parents, sat at the same table as them – my dad was immediately across from him and my mum was to his side. What was he thinking? I moved away.

But he kept on touching me. I moved again; I felt really uncomfortable. Yet he didn't get the hint: once again his hand slithered onto my thigh as we sat with my family. It really wasn't the time for making his advances yet, no matter what I did, he kept his hand on my thigh, almost possessively, and – as he had always been able to do – he kept up the chatter with my parents as he groped me under the table, as though nothing untoward was going on.

I didn't like it anymore, but I couldn't say anything. As had always been the way, no words came to my lips to tell him: 'No'. I had almost resigned myself to an afternoon of his unwanted touch when something unexpected happened.

'Mr Willson!' we heard from behind us.

He snatched his hand from my leg, as fast as he had once dropped my arms in the technology corridor on the day after we'd first kissed, when that teacher had disturbed us. There was something guilty in the movement; he didn't want to be discovered. Turning around, I'm not sure what I was expecting to find: from the way he'd whipped his hand from my knee you'd have thought it was his wife, but I knew it wasn't Mrs Willson. The voice had been too young and flirtatious for that.

There were four kids standing there, two boys and two girls; they were college age, I guessed. I could tell which girl had spoken from the way she was coquettishly tossing her long hair over her shoulder, and I felt this weird, jealous, worlds-colliding sensation as I stared at her.

She looked exactly like me.

Not the me who was sitting beside Mr Willson in the pub, age twenty-five, you understand: the me who'd attracted his attention as a schoolgirl. She had a comforting curtain of thick blonde hair, sparkly blue eyes and a lovely smile. Her hair was nicer than mine, I will add. Mine has a curl to it; hers was classically

Timotei-advert beautiful. But the similarities were close enough that I couldn't fail to see them; it felt horrible.

'Hello,' Andrew Willson said to the pretty little blonde, in a cheeky, twinkly voice that I knew so well. She almost visibly twinkled back.

It was as if a door slammed hard in my brain: *I am done. I am done with him.*

Because he has done it with her.

It was only my opinion, I must add. But, in my opinion, I saw this dynamic spark between the two of them. To me, with my radar and my intimate knowledge of my former teacher, it seemed as clear as day. Science students could have studied the chemistry between them. And why else would he have snatched back his hand in such a guilty way?

All this time, I'd thought I was special. I'd thought I was different. We were soulmates, that was what he'd always said. He'd never felt this way before. I was the one, the only...

But I didn't think that now.

We were only there for the afternoon; we wrapped things up and us McGregors all piled into my parents' car for the long journey home. All the way back, I couldn't stop thinking about what I'd seen. I felt embarrassed at myself: for ever believing in him, for wasting so much of my time and my headspace in love with this man. I felt disappointed in him, too. I felt let down.

Perhaps strangely, I wasn't worried for the girl. She seemed happy as Larry – as I'd once been, of course. But the thing was, I didn't see anything wrong per se in what I thought Mr Willson had done with us both. Instead, I felt hurt and betrayed and jealous that I wasn't so special, after all. I even wondered if he'd had a blonde in every school he'd ever taught in, but that was too much to deal with, so I put it back in Pandora's box.

Whenever I felt rejected, as I did now, I could think of only one way to feel loved. Once again, I fell into a pattern of sleeping with older, married men. It was destructive behaviour and I didn't know why I kept doing it, but I couldn't seem to stop. I'd have a drink, and then another, and it would suddenly seem like a good idea. One time, when I was working away in a hotel, a lone businessman started giving me the eye and later slipped a note under my door inviting me to join him for 'a bottle of wine' in his room. And I did. The wine was rank, the sex was rank and the whole situation was wrong: he was blatantly married.

There is another incident I particularly remember. It was a one-night stand and I'd invited the bloke back to mine. We were in bed, getting it on, and he turned out to be a man who really liked to be in control. Now, I'd learned over the years that I really didn't like it when men told me what to do in bed: for some unknown reason, I had an aversion to dirty talk, when men would tell me to go harder, faster, lick it underneath... For me it was a turn-off. This bloke did some move – and I can't tell you now what it was; it was just some way that he moved me to put me in the position that *he* wanted and I didn't have a say – and I completely flipped out.

'Get the fuck out of my bed!' I screamed.

The poor bloke didn't know what had happened. 'Woah, woah, woah,' he said, his arms raised high in peaceful demonstration. 'It's OK, it's *OK*!'

But I'd gone. I can't remember what I said, all I remember is this naked bloke looking absolutely petrified.

I wouldn't even call him a cab and he didn't have a clue where he was, bless him. I just told him to get out, get out, *get out*!

I didn't know what had come over me. *I am mental*, I thought, *I am actually going mental*. Clearly I had some sort of problem – something in that scene had traumatised me and set me off – but I had no inkling what it could be.

Needing a change of scene, in October 2007 I took a nine-month contract working on a cruise ship. I would be acting in afternoon plays, compering the quizzes and bingo and running the entertainment lounge. I loved it, actually, especially the compering, because I wasn't playing a part: I was *me*, and to present *as me* I found empowering.

I was still lying to myself that I found sex empowering too, however, and I began sleeping around on the ship. I'd never have done it without the drink, but with my white wine or my vodka Red Bull in hand I felt invincible, beautiful and confident, in a way I never did sober. Unfortunately, that feeling of invincibility led me to do silly things.

The thing about being on a ship is that you can't get away from anything. Everything you do, people find out about – especially when you're clearly doing the Walk of Shame back to your cabin the morning after, still dressed in your evening gown from the night before. I started to sense lots of nastiness being spoken about me, but the thing was, the gossips couldn't be any nastier to me than I already was to myself in my head.

There were a lot of young, gorgeous girls in the dancing crew on the ship, and now I was nearly twenty-seven I looked at them and found myself lacking. So I'd have another drink to make myself feel better, as though I could drink to forget. I'd get absolutely wasted – and then have to eat massive fry-ups and burgers and whole tubes of Pringles to get over my hangover, in order to have the energy to do my job. The weight piled on till I was almost a size 16. That made me feel even worse, yet the only way I knew of to boost my self-esteem was to hear a man say he wanted me, so I'd go out on the prowl again and the cycle would start all over.

In the January of 2008, I met a man on the ship, and after I talked about how I wanted to learn to dive he offered to give me some free lessons – one-on-one, as he considered himself something of an expert. Then, in the evenings, I noticed my teacher kept appearing by my side in the bar: he'd buy me drinks and tell me I looked utterly beautiful. He'd reminisce romantically about the first time he ever saw me. He was a popular, charming man with surferish good looks and a muscly physique. He was ten years my senior, and there was something about his smooth voice, his persona, his power, his likeability – and, yes, the fact he was my teacher – that reminded me of Andrew Willson.

I wondered if this was me meeting my soulmate at the *right* time. I wanted so desperately to find my happy ending. It was a different man, in a different guise – could he be The One?

Chapter 20

The End

I wanted it to work out between us so badly that I ignored any warning signs that this man could be trouble. I wanted that happy ending, but I was searching for it in all the wrong ways. Instead of warning signs, I concentrated instead on his compliments and on the generous gifts he bought me: rings, necklaces, earrings, chocolates… perfume. I'd never been with a man with money before and it was lovely to be showered with presents like a princess. He resided in a passenger cabin, which was much, much nicer than the windowless hovel I lived in as a lowly member of staff. I was still drinking heavily as we started dating; the difference was, he was now paying for it.

Within the first month he had our lives planned out: I was to be a kept woman and he was going to sort everything out for me so I didn't have to worry my pretty little head about it. Wherever I went on the ship, he was always there. Just as Andrew Willson had once done when we were at school together, my boyfriend had looked up my timetable to find out where I was. At first I thought it was just coincidence, but the truth was it was controlling. In bed, we could never just sleep sweetly together, we always had to have sex. It became a bit much for me, but

I'd never not consented to something a partner wanted, and I didn't change the habit of a lifetime now.

It was a relief when, just before my twenty-seventh birthday, his holiday on the ship came to an end. I'd felt smothered, and not having him in my face all the time I finally felt able to breathe again. But on 1 April 2008, I received a phone call that took all the breath from me: my beloved grandma had died suddenly.

It was a major blow, and I was devastated. I was very close to my mum's mum: we used to sit and watch old movies together – Ginger Rogers, Fred Astaire – or I'd dress up in her really cool clothes from the 1960s and we'd lark about. I thought she was brilliant, and the moment I heard she'd died, it was the end of everything as far as I was concerned. I wanted to finish with my boyfriend, I wanted to get the hell off the ship... I just wanted to be with my nan.

Even though my boyfriend wasn't onboard anymore he tried to keep tabs on me. He was not the type of bloke who could countenance me having my own life – at least, that's the way I saw it. He was constantly phoning the ship because in my grief I was ignoring his calls and my crew director kept saying to me, 'Hayley, he's trying to get hold of you, can you please tell him what's going on?'

But I wasn't ready to speak to him; I just wanted to go home.

When I stepped off the plane in Manchester, unexpectedly my boyfriend was there, waiting for me with a big bunch of flowers. It was a proper *Love Actually* moment – but it was the worst surprise ever. I didn't want him there. He didn't know my family, he didn't deserve to be at my grandma's funeral; he'd never even met her. Most importantly, *I hadn't invited him.* All week he hung around like a bad smell, accompanying me to my parents' home, where he expected them to put him up. He didn't seem to cotton on to the fact that I didn't want him there – that *none* of us wanted him there. This was a private family occasion and we'd only been having a fling for a couple of months; in my opinion, it was inappropriate.

'I've got a surprise for you,' he announced after the funeral, as I prepared to return to the ship to see out my contract. There was nothing I wanted to do less, but they offered a generous bonus if you completed your contracted months and I needed that money to live on during the summer.

'Oh, brilliant...' I said sarcastically, though he didn't pick up on the derision in my voice.

'I'm coming on the ship for another week's holiday!' he declared ecstatically.

On the second day of his vacation, I finished with him. I don't know why I wasn't bolder earlier, really. By then, I thought he was full-blown stalker crazy. He went absolutely ballistic when I broke it off; by my own admission, I was quite blunt with him when I did it. We were then stuck with each other on the ship all week; he was heckling me from the back of the entertainment lounge and eventually had to be removed.

Still grieving for my nan, and wounded by the failure of yet another relationship, my spirits spiralled down and down. Why did I keep attracting these men who wanted to control me? Why was I drawn to these charming blokes who were always something else behind their oh-so-convincing masks? The problem must surely be me.

After he left, those final few months of my contract are a blur; I really don't remember them. By then I was drinking from morning to night, back to my old ways with men, and I did not care. Out of control, I was breaking every rule on the ship; some mornings I wouldn't even get up for work and the boss would be banging on my cabin door as I buried my head in my pillow, not yet ready to face the world and what I'd done the night before. I wanted to be fired, I think, but they were so short-staffed they couldn't replace me.

Finally, July came round and I was able to return home. I left the ship to cheers from the safety team, who'd had the thankless task of getting me up in the mornings – and I was pretty happy about it too. I got settled back in at home – it's amazing how you lose your land legs after months at sea – and on my second day back I nipped to the supermarket to get some groceries.

I was in the pharmacy aisle when a thought suddenly struck me. *When did I last have a period?* I couldn't remember so I bought a £3.50 pregnancy test and did it in my bathroom at home. It was a warm summer's day so while the test did its thing I went out in the garden and sat on a bench in the sunshine with it facing down, all the while thinking, *Please no, please no, please no...* But the test was positive. And I had no idea whose baby it was.

Despite the unexpectedness of my pregnancy, there was no question that I wasn't keeping the baby. I'd *always* wanted to be a mum – it was one of the dreams I'd often talked about with Andrew Willson, when I was a giddy fourteen-year-old planning our fantasy future family – and no matter what my age or circumstances when I fell pregnant, I would always keep my child. As soon as I found out the news, I started taking health supplements specifically designed for pregnant women and booked an appointment with a doctor: they told me I was already more than three months gone. Now I was *really* excited about it. I thought the timing was beautiful, too, with my grandma having so recently passed away: one life gone, but a new one beginning. It seemed to fit.

The whole thing seemed like a lifeline, in a way. I'd been on this run of self-destructive behaviour for so long, but now I'd been given this gift to turn my life around. I knew I would sort myself out for my child, because there was no question in my head that a child comes first. For the first time in a long while I felt hope for the future and a newfound sense of purpose in my life.

Happily, a really good friend of mine called Kirsty was also pregnant at that time. A couple of weeks later she came over for a girlie night. She was further on than me, about six months pregnant, and she looked *amazing*, all big and 'snuggly mummy'. I love the way pregnant women look anyway, but Kirsty really was blooming. It was incredible to think that, in a few months' time, that would be me. We sat in my lounge drinking fruity water and giggling away at each other, chatting about our plans for motherhood, and eventually we went to bed; she was staying the night as we had an awful lot to catch up on.

It still hurts, what happened next. I woke in the middle of the night with horrific tummy pains. For some strange reason, and I still don't know why I did this, I phoned my parents. They didn't know I was pregnant yet; from my description of the horrendous stomach pain, Mum thought it must be appendicitis. 'Get to the hospital,' she urged me.

I'd been on all fours on the phone to my parents, my head pressed down into the bed, so it was only when I got up to tell my friend about the terrible pain that I saw the dark-red blood that had stained the white sheets. I burst into tears and went into Kirsty's room, crying my eyes out. She was brilliant; she went straight into sort-it-out mode and called an ambulance for me. I was rushed to hospital with the sirens blaring.

It was a busy Saturday night; the emergency department was rammed. I was left lying on a trolley in the corridor with loads of people walking past me, in a lot of pain. I could just feel the blood oozing out; the new life inside me ebbing away. They gave me gas and air, but nothing was enough to anaesthetise the hurt inside. I knew what was happening: I was losing my baby. Even though the pregnancy had been a mistake, I had wanted to keep my child. I felt such a failure... *again. I must be really shit*, I thought. *Even God doesn't want me to have a baby.* I thought I was being punished.

My parents came to collect me and took me home from the hospital. Kirsty, bless her, had washed and changed all the soiled bedding before she left for work. She was an angel. And so many other people were nice about it: I told the lads I was on tour with and they looked after me all week. I tucked the hurt inside my heart and carried on with my life.

What else could I do?

The life of an actor is always transitive: you move from one short contract to the next. Over the next few years I did more theatre-in-education work and some corporate training gigs, and in 2009 I started the first of several different Saturday jobs for various theatre schools, teaching kids aged four to eighteen dance, drama and singing. Though my pregnancy hadn't resulted in a baby, it had encouraged me to turn my life around and I was in a pretty good place: I was together, I was holding down a job and I wasn't behaving self-destructively anymore.

With a clearer head, those Saturday-morning sessions became very interesting to me. Just as I'd had to do previously with my theatre-in-education work, part of the job was bonding with the children. Those kids became like my family as I led them through their training and started working towards end-of-term shows; rehearsals could be intense. I divided them into age groups for the sessions: five to eights, nine to twelves, thirteen to eighteens. No matter what age they were, I really got to know them, inside and out. I learned about their home lives; I hugged them when they were down. And they responded: the five-year-olds were always all over me, as though I was a second mum; the teenagers developed a crush. It was always evident when the young boys had an infatuation; it generally makes them do whatever you say – and no teenager is that obedient unless there is some other power in play. I had a couple of them try to befriend me on Facebook and I said no, immediately. It wasn't appropriate.

I adored the kids I taught and wanted the best for them. Once again, I was made aware of the line I knew that I would never cross. Once again, I started to think, *How could Mr Willson have done it? Why would he have done it?* I began to have questions that circled round and round in my head: *Was what happened to me wrong? I feel like I need to tell my parents, should I tell them?* But I'd always talk myself out of it or make excuses. I pushed the questions away and shut them up in a box; I thought I would deal with them later, much later, when I was an old, old woman and everyone caught up in this tangled web – my parents, even Mr Willson himself – was dead and buried.

As time passed and I continued to mull over what had happened, I actually thought maybe I'd write a book about the experience one day – *The Diary of a Schoolgirl Crush* or something like that. I was feeling such a confused mishmash of emotions about my affair with Mr Willson that I thought writing them down might help me to make sense of them. But I didn't want to do it now; it would cause too much trouble if I asked too many questions now.

They continued to play on my mind though. I asked Bill, a sandy-haired welsh guy who was a close friend of mine, about what I was feeling, but like all the other friends I'd talked to before, he didn't see anything wrong with my having had a relationship with my teacher; in contrast, people found it amusing or exciting.

'I'm confused,' I'd say to him. 'Was it right? Was it wrong?'

He'd listen sympathetically. 'I don't know,' he'd reply. 'I mean, it depends. Is it affecting you now?'

I thought the answer was no.

At this time I hadn't seen Mr Willson since the summer of 2006, when he'd put his hand on my leg underneath the pub table. I was quite happy to keep it that way, especially with all the thoughts I was now having about our affair. I wasn't hating him – I just didn't want to see him. I thought he'd been wrong to do what he'd done, yet I believed that I was equally culpable. It was a schoolgirl–teacher affair and we'd both played our parts, for I had wanted it just as much as he had. He was wrong, but so was I, and I decided I didn't want it coming out either. I wouldn't tell my parents; I'd keep the secret. Long ago I'd learned the lesson that we'd *both* be in trouble if I told.

At the start of 2010, I received a phone call from my mother. My dad's fiftieth birthday was coming up in February and she wanted to organise a surprise party.

'And I've had a great idea,' she gushed, her enthusiasm audible. 'Maybe we could get Andrew Willson to do a little skit for your dad, like he did for you at your twenty-first?'

My stomach clenched. I didn't want to see him. It had been fifteen years since I'd been taught by him at school, why was he still in my life and attending these special family events? It suddenly felt like an infiltration, and nothing like a friendship.

I cleared my throat. 'Do you think Dad would really want that?' I said lightly. 'Do you not think we'd be better off with some sort of Rat Pack tribute band or a Michael Bublé impersonator?'

I tried everything I could think of to put Mum off the idea of Andrew Willson, but she wasn't having any of it. She knew him only as a charming, generous, talented man, and she remembered how delighted I'd been with his skit at my birthday eight years before. She thought Dad would like it. She thought it would be a treat for the whole family.

She wouldn't take no for an answer.

Mum asked me to organise it – because she lived with Dad it was harder for her to coordinate such a surprise behind his back. So it was me who rang Andrew Willson to ask him about the party, dialling those digits that I'd memorised so many years ago, when I'd felt so very differently about him. I phoned at a time when I hoped everybody would be in, and I was glad when Mrs Willson answered. I had a quick chat with her and made sure to invite the whole family to the surprise party: it was a *family* occasion, after all.

'Hayley McGregor!' Andrew Willson exclaimed when his wife passed over the receiver. He sounded as charming and as suave as ever, but I didn't engage with him: I kept the call as businesslike and short as I could. He happily agreed to provide some entertainment for my father's party and I got off the phone as quickly as possible. He insisted that I take his mobile number – in case anything relating to the party should come up.

The do was held on Saturday, 20 February 2010 at a place called Coco's in Burnley. I went full-out with my look: blonde hair extensions, spray tan, a strapless pale-pink bodycon dress teamed with a little white jacket and killer gold sparkly heels. Now twenty-eight years old, single and happily so, I felt great about myself. Although I wished I wasn't going to see Andrew Willson, at least this time I knew in advance he would be there – and I knew that I could cope; he was just an ex, after all. As it happened, Nicola was also invited to the family do so I knew she would have my back as well. I was actually more worried that everything would go smoothly for my dad. Luckily, it did. But as the birthday boy walked into the room and everyone yelled, 'Surprise!', who should be at the front of the queue to greet us McGregors but Andrew Willson himself?

The moment he saw me, he shoved a drink in my hand and zoomed in for a kiss on the lips. I turned my head away. It felt like he was taking liberties; he had no right to kiss me.

Strikingly, I felt no butterflies and no magic fairy dust settling on my shoulders when I laid eyes on him – I think for the first time *ever*, for even at my twenty-first I'd warmed to him by the end of the evening. Instead, this time I wanted to recoil. He looked old: receding hairline, greying hair, mutton dressed as lamb. He was dressed in skinny jeans, a black shirt and a waistcoat, as though attempting to emulate Russell Brand's sartorial style. Frankly, I thought he might have started to grow old a little bit gracefully by now, but I guess that wasn't his way.

He used his body to block me into the doorway; I'd barely got over the threshold. I could see my parents and brother working the room – 'Hello, how are you?' they said as they mingled with our guests – and I wanted to be with them. After the way Robert had used to block my path by standing in doorways, too, I really could not *stand* what Andrew Willson was doing.

'I've got to go,' I told him abruptly. 'You're not the only person in the room.'

I was rude to him, and unapologetically so. As I strode off into the party I hoped that would be the last I'd have to see of him.

If only. Despite my invitation to the whole Willson family to attend the event, once again it was only Andrew Willson who'd come along. He didn't bring anyone with him, yet he didn't really know anybody else there – not to spend the whole evening with them, at least.

Consequently, he was following me around like a lost puppy dog. Nicola even came over to me at one point and whispered, 'He ain't making this half obvious!'

'You look beautiful, Hayley McGregor,' he told me, words that once would have swept me off my feet. 'How is everything? How have you been?'

I was short with him – I even told him directly to leave me alone on numerous occasions – but he kept chatting away as though I hadn't cut him dead.

'I'm staying in a hotel on my own, you know...' he said, his eyebrow raised suggestively.

I stared back at him blankly. 'Very good. Good for you.'

'What are *you* doing?'

'I'm going home, with my parents and my brother,' I told him bluntly, 'because it's *my dad's fiftieth birthday*.' I couldn't believe his gall.

As though *he* couldn't believe that the magic no longer worked, he trailed his hand down my arm and placed it possessively on the base of my back, because once upon a time that would have sent me silly. I pulled away; walked off; moved on to someone else. Nevertheless, he kept layering up his suggestive comments all evening – in the same way he had once built a house of cards of his affection. Now, I could see how weak and pathetic his attempts to seduce me really were. To begin with, he said, 'I've got my own room,' with a suggestive twinkle of his sparkly eyes. Then it was: 'Why don't you make an excuse and come back with me tonight?' And finally he brought out the big guns, the intense, passionate lines, delivered with his best Heathcliff-style smouldering eyes: 'I just want to hold you again. I want to feel you again.

I *really* miss you. Please, it's the only chance we'll get. Can you not make an excuse, Hayley McGregor?'

'No, I don't *want* to make an excuse.'

Hearing his chat-up lines, I wanted to squirm. *I can't believe I used to fall for this.* My rose-tinted glasses had been whipped off and I was seeing and hearing him clearly. It was weird. I could remember how I used to feel – as if hearing an echo, I could still feel that infatuated want and adoration – but this time it made my skin crawl. For the first time I could hear him speak and I was able to tell that it was a lie, that it was all fake. I felt disgusted with myself for ever falling for it, completely foolish and stupid.

I had to remind myself that I was only a little girl, the first time he'd tried his tricks on me.

He gave up, eventually, and that evening he struck up a friendship with a mate of my mum. The next day, I felt so strong waking up in my parents' house, knowing I had told him no. I had *never* said no to Mr Willson before. It was a nice feeling. It was an empowering feeling. But it didn't last long. Maybe a couple of weeks later, I saw I had two missed calls from my mother's pal, whom he'd befriended at the party. She never usually called me, why was she suddenly phoning now?

Panic shot through me, right into my heart: *What if he's said something to her about us?* I started to think it through. *What if he twists this around? What if he comes out about it first, but not about the affair at school, just what we've done since I've been an adult? What if he says I seduced him?* I could just imagine my parents' shock and disapproval. *If I counter at that point,* I thought, *if I say that actually the seduction started at school, it might make me look like a liar. No one will believe me.*

Nervous as hell, I phoned my mum's friend back. I think I need hypnotherapy to actually recall the conversation, because it's a big black panic-ridden hole. All I know is that I did have to do some sort of damage limitation: he hadn't told her I was a schoolgirl, of course, but she did know something had gone on.

Afterwards I was in an absolute state. All those questions that had been circling round my head, all the doubtful feelings I'd shoved into a box to think about *later*, were suddenly set free and my brain and body couldn't cope. I was hyperventilating, my heart was pounding; I couldn't catch my breath. I phoned my friend Bill and he couldn't understand a word I was saying so he drove over in alarm.

'He's said something, he's said something!' I cried when he arrived. I couldn't believe how worked up I felt about it. This had been our secret and, although I'd mentioned it to a few pals over the years, I'd never wanted to tell my parents – that was a step too far. His telling my mum's friend was dangerous; it brought it into my backyard. It threatened to ruin everything: to ruin me, to ruin him. He was playing a dangerous game and I didn't want to be his playmate anymore.

I think part of it, too, was the way he had taken control. He had told the secret, but he had told it in *his* way. I wasn't twelve or thirteen or fourteen in this tale; I wasn't on the sofa bed in my Leeds United pyjamas. The storyteller has the power to shape the world the way he wants it to be – I felt like he was rewriting history and I had no voice to be able to tell it like it *really* was.

Even through my panic, things were crystallising for me. I had no voice now – and I had had no voice then. I felt manipulated now – I'd felt manipulated then. I hadn't been able to see it at the time, but I began to appreciate how very much I'd been controlled all those years. He'd controlled my conversations with my parents. He'd kept me quiet by always being there after he'd done something, so I couldn't speak up even if I'd wanted to. He'd had this power always to make me fall in line with what he wanted – and some part of me now realised that it was always what *he* wanted. I saw how often I'd done stuff for him and not for me; how he'd coaxed me along and pulled my strings and I'd danced and performed for him as though on a wire. He had always been able to charm me. Every time I'd had a doubt, even as an adult, he had always been able to turn it around. Robbed of my rose-tinted spectacles, I could see it, now, in a way I never had before. And I was done with feeling manipulated.

It was time for me to take control.

Still shaking, I dialled his mobile number, Bill by my side. I can't remember any words that Andrew Willson said that day; I'm not sure I even gave him the chance to speak. It was *my* chance now. And I went absolutely ballistic.

'I don't know what you drunkenly said, what you drunkenly meant or what you're playing at!' I shouted. 'But *you* listen to me now, you listen to *me*!' I took a big, deep, shuddering breath, sucking up air as though it could give me strength. 'I do not want you *anywhere* near me from now on. If I'm at a Leeds game, you make sure you stay away. If my parents try to organise any other surprise for me, you say no. They are going to want to invite you to my wedding: when you get the invitation you rip it up and you say no, you are not coming. You are not coming anywhere near me ever again. You do not see me ever again. Otherwise, *I will tell.*'

I put the phone down and burst out crying. Then I got angry. Then I burst out crying again. It was very surreal: the whole thing felt like an out-of-body experience. I couldn't believe I'd just done that: spoken up, spoken out, *threatened* him. I was shocked at that specifically: it came from a place of pure, unadulterated anger, and I think it came from my increasing knowledge that *he* knew what he'd done was wrong. I still thought what *I'd* done was wrong, too, but I sensed my threat had some special power for him that it didn't have for me.

For hours afterwards I was still trembling at my audacity in speaking up to him: Andrew Willson was a teacher, someone I respected, someone who had controlled me all these years, but I'd found the strength to say, 'No! *Enough*. Enough now.'

And that phone call was me taking the control back. I drew a line under it then: *we are done*. After that I never asked my parents about him anymore; if his name was brought up, it was not by me. And if this *had* been a fairy tale, this would have been the moment when, in big looping script, the words 'The End' would be stamped across the page.

And they all lived happily ever after…

I was still so innocent in so many ways, you see. I thought I was done. I thought it was that easy to walk away from what had happened.

But, once again, I was wrong.

Chapter 21

Falling Apart

Whenever we move on in our lives, we pack up our baggage into sturdy cardboard boxes, sealing the contents in with tape. That's what I now did with my affair with Mr Willson. I packed it all away and, over time, as with all former relationships, I got what I thought was a bit of perspective on it. I didn't like the man much anymore, and our fling seemed flawed on both sides, but it wasn't *all* bad. Inside that cardboard box, along with the troubling memories I also kept a few treasured ornaments from our time together, protected by bubble wrap to keep them safe and sound: his praise for my talent; his love of my looks; the confidence he had given me as a teenager, which ran like a ribbon through to today. Mr Willson might have been controlling, but he *had* loved me. And when you've felt love like that, it's like a trampoline, allowing you to fly high. I still treasured such mementoes, just as Cinderella might her sole glass slipper on the night she returned from the ball. She and Prince Charming weren't together, but she had still loved the way they had once danced cheek to cheek.

As I passed my thirtieth birthday in March 2011, I had never felt as free or as focused. I loved my life. By now I had worked as a professional actress for over a decade; that was something to be proud of. My personal life was finally shaping up too: a month or so after my birthday, my close friendship with Bill blossomed into romance and I had high hopes for our future together – especially because he was nothing like my former partners. I'd told myself: *If you do what you've always done, then you'll get what you've always got.* So Bill was different. I'd deliberately chosen someone who was quiet, reserved; even grumpy at times. He wasn't a charming man, in the way Mr Willson was. I hoped that might mean we'd live a charmed life – but fate had something else in store.

In June 2011, to my horror, I woke up in bed covered in these red, raised patches all over my body, from my chest down to my toes; it was particularly bad on my legs. These itchy, flaky marks had appeared overnight and I had no idea what they were. Yet when I consulted a doctor, he was unable to diagnose them: he simply gave me some oily cream for dry skin and I battled on with this weird skin condition for the next six months, keeping myself covered up as the red marks were terribly unsightly. It wasn't until early 2012, when I went back to my GP and demanded to see a skin specialist, that a diagnosis was finally given.

'It's psoriasis,' the expert doctor said. I'd never heard of it before. It's an auto-immune skin condition where your body starts attacking healthy skin cells in error, leaving sufferers with the ugly, crusty red patches that were disfiguring my body.

Now I had a name for what it was, I hoped the doctor would instantly prescribe me with the cure – but it turned out there was none. 'You can treat it, but it will never go,' the kindly doctor explained. 'You will find, whenever you're stressed, that the condition will flare up and come back.'

'Stressed?' I echoed. 'But I'm not stressed now.'

The doctor gave me a sympathetic smile. 'Yes, you are. Have a look at your life. What's your lifestyle like?'

As it happened, I adored my job so much that I pretty much worked seven days a week, so I told him that.

'Slow down, then,' he said. 'You're obviously doing too much.'

I didn't want to take his advice, but in the end my body forced me to. In January 2012, I was hit by a debilitating viral infection that left me bedridden for a month; I couldn't even make it upstairs. Wiped out by vicious migraines, I couldn't sleep, couldn't breathe, couldn't swallow, couldn't keep anything down – not even water. Eventually I came out the other side of it, but with an asthma diagnosis as a parting gift. Not long after that, I developed Irritable Bowel Syndrome (IBS) too.

I was absolutely baffled by the decline in my health. I'd never been like this before: all my life, even as a kid, I'd never been sickly. It was odd and I was really quite worried. I put it down to my age: *I'm getting old now, over thirty: it's all catching up with me, my misspent youth is coming back to haunt me...* So I quit alcohol, went gluten-free, aimed to drink two litres of water every day. The doctors kept lecturing me to slow down so I was trying to eliminate stress from my life, but the funny thing was I didn't *feel* stressed at all. To my knowledge, there was nothing in my life now causing me concern. If anything, I had never been happier.

That year, I started a new Saturday job, teaching drama to young kids in Huddersfield. Once again I found myself bonding with the children – and there was one girl in particular who caught my eye. Aged about twelve, she had long blonde hair and was polite and helpful: a genuinely nice, good girl. She was a triple threat – equally good at dancing, singing and drama – but despite her major talent she was nowhere near as streetwise as she thought she was. Something about her innocence really reminded me of myself at that age.

At thirty-one, I found I could finally be real to myself in a way that I hadn't been when I was twenty. Then, I'd looked at the young girls I was teaching and told myself: *I was more mature than them at that age.* Now, I knew that to be absolute rubbish. I may have *thought* I was mature, because we all think we're more grown up than we are when we're teenagers, but I was as young and innocent as they were. I was just as unstreetwise as that pretty blonde girl.

Watching her, it took my thoughts back there, back into the past. Like a scratchy old record, it started to play on my mind: seeing how young she was; realising how young *I* had been. I'd give the kids two minutes to rehearse something and while they did I'd find myself looking around at the class, at that sweet blonde girl, thinking about me and my experiences at the same age. Without my noticing, those two minutes became five, became ten... My reverie would be broken only when one of the more confident children tapped me on my arm: 'Do you want us to show you our work yet, miss?'

As it happened, around that time a friend of mine on Facebook began uploading old school pictures to the social-media site. It was quite amusing, to begin with, seeing the photos and remembering my school days, but one snapshot in particular caused me to do a double take.

It was taken on the night of the wrap party for *Smike*, when I was in Year 8. There I was in my oversized stripy shirt, hiding behind my curtain of long blonde hair. It was shocking, in a way, to see it – for if anything I thought I looked even younger than the girls I taught in my drama class every Saturday. I wasn't wearing make-up, I hadn't done anything with my hair, and I hadn't stuffed socks down my bra to make my boobs look bigger. Though I'd now grasped that I *was* young at twelve and thirteen, until confronted with the photographic evidence I really hadn't appreciated quite how baby-faced I was.

But I wasn't the only one in the picture. Someone had captioned it: 'Spot the knobhead!' That surprised me. I'd thought everyone was a little bit in love with Mr Willson. I hadn't realised till then that, to some, he was unpopular: an unlikeable man.

He was standing with his arm around me; you couldn't see where his hand ended up behind my back. I scrutinised the image, having never seen us pictured together at this age before. It was taken before it all happened: before the scene in the classroom where he got lost in my eyes and I had swooned at his words, falling head over heels; before he had kissed me in his car on the way back from rehearsal; before he had snuck so stealthily into my bed. Though I vaguely remembered the party, I didn't recall this moment; didn't remember the camera shutter closing with a sudden flash of light.

As I've said before, I love the camera. I beam instantly when one is near; it's second nature to me. And my memory of my love affair with Mr Willson was that I was infatuated, swept away, happy and content.

Why, then, did I look so uncomfortable in this picture?

It freaked me out. The girls I taught were like family to me and I knew, if ever I saw a photograph of them with that expression on their face, I would be concerned – and concerned enough to ask, 'Are you all right?' I didn't look happy; I didn't look in love. Instead, I looked awkward, maybe even frightened, as though something wasn't right and I found it very, very troubling. I tucked these disquieting thoughts away, stuffed into my cardboard box filled with memories of our love affair, and I shut the lid tight.

Yet it seemed as if forces were at play not to keep it that way. In September 2012, the newspapers were filled with the story that Jeremy Forrest, a maths teacher, had run away to France with his fifteen-year-old pupil: the two had been secretly having an affair at school. There was a manhunt and Forrest was eventually found and brought back to England, facing criminal prosecution for his actions. The coverage was widespread and I found I was drawn to it; as I was to coverage the following month of Operation Yewtree, a police inquiry set up to look into historical allegations of child sexual abuse by the disgraced celebrity Jimmy Savile and others. I found myself reading everything I could about it; if I heard a story on the radio or TV, I'd turn up the volume and listen intently. I felt so much empathy for the victims; I believed every word they said.

Oddly, that same autumn, as I read more and more about these cases I found it harder and harder to get up in the morning. At first I thought I was just being lazy, but as I made excuse after excuse not to go to work, not to get out of bed at all, it seemed maybe it was something more. I couldn't understand it: normally I bounded out of bed, eager to get on with my day, to go to work in a job I adored. But now I found myself crying for no reason and snapping at people; poor Bill bore the brunt of it. At times I'd get so worked up and emotional that I found my chest tightening and my breath hard to catch; I thought it was just a bad asthma attack.

By now, Bill and I had been dating for over a year and we were relaxed and confident with each other physically: it was a warm, safe and loving relationship. Yet that year I recall my feelings changing about that. One day, we were being intimate with one another. Feeling his hands in my hair, something revolted inside me: I went crazy at him, screaming and shouting. It was just like the time a few years before when I'd freaked out on the one-night stand – and I was equally clueless as to the cause of my distress. Confused, ashamed, embarrassed, hurt, I ran away from Bill, curled up in a ball and tried to rock myself to sleep, crying hard because I didn't recognise who I was or what was happening. What the hell was going on with me? My psoriasis was inflamed and really bad at that time; I even lost out on a Halloween job that year because I was unable to wear the costume.

The only bright spot that autumn was that I made a very special new friend. I'd always wanted a dog of my own and I heard that a friend of a friend had some German Shepherd/Akita-cross puppies who were looking for new homes. When I went to look at the litter, this little darling of a dog came over to me and carefully untied the laces on my Doc Marten boots with his teeth.

'Er, excuse *me*, mister!' I said, before picking him up. He was so small, he fitted in the palm of my hand. When I cuddled him he nuzzled straight into my neck and stayed there happily. I looked up at the owner with an equally happy grin: 'I'm having this one!'

I called my new dog Biffy, after the Scottish rock band Biffy Clyro, who are favourites of mine. After Biffy's arrival, I at least had something to get up for every morning. For the next couple of months my puppy lifted my spirits, but in the depths of winter I started to feel those dark, negative emotions that had kept me in my bed earlier in the year resurface. I felt emotional all the time, unable to cope. We went round to see my parents at Christmas and they asked me to keep Biffy outside, which seemed unreasonable to me. But whereas normally I'd have been able to deal with that situation, now I couldn't: I broke down, sobbing, overly sensitive to my mum telling me I was soft. 'How can you be so mean?' I wailed at her.

Bill was totally at a loss as to how to cope with the new me. The sunny girl he had started dating simply wasn't there anymore. I was anxious all the time and those 'asthma attacks' I'd been having soon became full-scale panic attacks where I'd be hot and flushed, coughing and crying until I was unable to breathe, red in the face with a tight chest that felt as if it was going to squeeze me to death. The smallest thing could trigger them: being in a crowd; having an argument; hearing an unexpected knock at the door. They happened every couple of months, and I found them terrifying. Struggling, as every day got harder and harder to live through, I gave up my bid to be teetotal and started drinking again, looking for answers in the bottom of a bottle. Bill didn't drink at all, but by the end of the night I'd be throwing two empty white-wine bottles into the recycling bin. It wasn't like we were enjoying a drink together, I was drinking in a dangerous way.

I pushed Bill away. It got so that I couldn't bear him touching me: I'd wriggle out of his embrace or pick up Biffy and sit him on the sofa between us so that Bill's thigh wouldn't press against my own. I didn't want sex at all, which perplexed me; I'd always been a sexual person but now it was all locked off. I didn't want Bill ever to touch me in that manner; as the months drew on, he wasn't even allowed in my bed.

He may not have wanted to be there anyway. I was horrible to be around, and we seemed to have row after row. Some of them were caused by Bill's clumsy attempts to address what was going on: 'What's happened to you?' he would say angrily. 'I don't know you anymore. Why can't you snap out of it?' He'd call me a bitch – and he was right, I *was* being a bitch but somehow I couldn't *help* being a bitch – and his aggression and hatred would make me hate myself even more. Before, when I'd been sunny, Bill and I had been each other's yin and yang: he was a grumpy man but his grumpiness used to make me laugh and I'd always been able to bring him up if he was down. Now that *I* was down, his natural personality was such that it wasn't enough to shine for us both. We sniped at each other constantly. Only Biffy gave me any comfort: when things became dark and cloudy in my head, he would put a paw on my leg or rest his head in my lap, and I would know that he was there for me.

In June 2013, Jeremy Forrest was jailed for abducting his schoolgirl lover. Headline news, it prompted discussions at work about student/teacher affairs. As ever, I wasn't the only one with a story to tell. Around that time I was working with an actor named Leroy, a warm, funny Londoner who made a mean cup of tea and gave sterling hugs; he was ten years older than me. Unusually, as he listened to the stories being shared around him, he didn't react as others often did to that conversation about teachers sleeping with their pupils. Instead, he shook his head. It was rare to see someone disapproving. He'd tut: 'Bang out of order, that is.'

I didn't know about that. What *was* bang out of order was the way *I* was behaving; it just wasn't normal. My emotions were on a knife edge and I was miserable and short-tempered all the time.

I hated it; I hated myself. But I didn't know how to change, or what it was that was making me feel this way. For months I buried my head in the sand, but that summer the time finally came when I couldn't ignore the horrendous feelings anymore. And Bill hadn't been able to ignore them either. It turned out that, amid the accusatory arguments and the sniping, he'd been doing some research to try to help me out. And so, one night in that summer of 2013, he showed me a YouTube video he'd found, which was made by the World Health Organization.

It was called: *I had a black dog, his name was depression.*

Chapter 22

The Big Black Dog

The D word. It sounded so serious. And 'depression' was almost a dirty word in my family; we didn't discuss mental health. With some trepidation, I pressed 'play' on the video.

It's only a short film; four or five minutes long. It shows a cartoon dog – representing depression – really small, so you can pop it in your hand and control it; and it shows the dog really big: so big you can't get out of bed because he's lain so heavily on your chest. By the end of the movie, the narrator has got to a point where he can walk the dog on a lead, in charge of the big black dog at last.

I watched it and I burst into tears. It described exactly how I'd been feeling for the past ten months. This horrible beast *did* have a name, after all.

There was a video for carers too and I encouraged Bill to watch it, though I'm not sure he did. Through it, and my further research around the subject, I learned that many of his comments to me were textbook 'what *not* to say to a depressed person' – but it wasn't his fault. He didn't understand, and I was very hard to live with. And at the end of the day, Bill couldn't get me out of this situation. Only I could do that.

It was a scary thought, that I might have depression. To label this morass of feelings with such a loaded term felt serious. Was I really *that* ill? But being open to the idea of maybe having depression, learning about it, admitting to it, at least gave me some control over it. I hadn't felt in control of my feelings for a very long time now. Like a drowning woman, I grabbed at the rope.

In August 2013, I bravely made an appointment with my GP. She was absolutely wonderful. I told her how I was feeling and she said gently, 'It sounds like depression.' It was so strange hearing a professional say the word, and my instinctive reaction was to deny it – us McGregors didn't get depression, there was no such thing; and anyway, I was a bright, sunny actress, always upbeat and smiley, how could depression affect a girl like me?

The GP calmed me down as I spluttered and protested at her diagnosis. 'Anybody can get it,' she told me sympathetically. She printed out information for me and I started doing my own research too. It was obvious when you looked it up: from my symptoms, I clearly had anxiety and depression. Why the conditions had developed in me, though, I didn't know. I thought perhaps it was to do with the domestic violence I'd suffered in my twenties. I'd never really dealt with that and I wondered if the terror I was now feeling could be traced back to that trauma.

For several months, I battled against the diagnosis and didn't seek further help. But things got worse and worse and eventually I returned to the doctor and was prescribed anti-depressants; I also joined a waiting list to see a counsellor, but it was many months long.

Going on the tablets was tough: the side effects were brutal, including headaches, dizziness, insomnia, increased anxiety, throbbing legs and nausea. They often made me throw up; Biffy became alert to the sound of retching and would rush in to offer comfort when he heard me being unwell. But the pills *did* help. Before, I thought I was worthless and often idly contemplated suicide, running through the options of ways to end my life as if choosing which fruit to buy at the supermarket – but those suicidal thoughts subsided once I went on the drugs. It was still hard, though. I felt exhausted, yet I couldn't sleep. My limbs were like lead. I'd walk into a room and be convinced that everyone hated me – and no surprise, because I hated myself. I thanked God that my job at least gave me a chance to get out of my own head: it was actually a relief to go to work and spend hours playing another character. It was harder by far to make it through the night as *me*.

In February 2014, Bill and I sat down to watch a Channel 4 documentary called *Sexting Teacher*. Inspired by the Jeremy Forrest case, they'd produced a special on student/teacher relationships, interviewing people who'd experienced them. As with the news coverage of the Forrest case and Operation Yewtree, I specifically wanted to watch it: I wanted to know what it felt like for other people who'd conducted an affair in school.

It was very weird to watch. I remember one woman in particular who was interviewed. She and her teacher had had an affair when she was fifteen and he was thirty: they'd been discovered and he had gone down for what he'd done. This had happened back in the 1980s, I think, but to this day she didn't blame him: she blamed herself. She said she had been promiscuous and that she had done all the chasing; it was all her fault. She defended him and made excuses. Bill and I exchanged a look: we thought she sounded warped. *You're a fool*, I thought, *it's not you*.

Yet there was another part of me that postured: *Maybe she's not such a fool...* My brain was oddly split – my angel and demon of old residing once again on either shoulder – with one part of me thinking, *She sounds deluded* – yet a tiny part of me also recognising: *She sounds like me*. Because I still thought it was at least partly my fault that Mr Willson and I had begun our affair; we were equally to blame for following our hearts. I still thought I was different to these girls, who had been victims, because Mr Willson had *loved* me. Even though I could see that what had happened to these women was wrong, when it came to *my* teacher–lover I always talked myself into a grey area, where black and white and right and wrong swirled together in a murky paint palette that coloured my world with confusion.

I jammed these unsettling feelings back into the box. It was becoming harder and harder to do that these days because everything that was happening – Operation Yewtree, looking into historical sexual abuse; seeing that photo on Facebook; observing the innocent blonde in my class – was layering up and up, building a picture I didn't want to see, and the box was threatening to burst open. So I squished everything down and ignored it, like a child with her fingers in her ears singing loudly to herself, trying to drown out the sound of the approaching storm.

That same February, I had to go away on tour. Bill, who was struggling to support my battle with depression and probably didn't fancy being up all night on the phone with me while I sobbed my heart out from some provincial town, suggested that I tell one of my colleagues about my illness 'so that you can talk to somebody' while I was away.

I took his advice. I chose to tell Leroy – we'd worked together off and on for quite a while by then and we were good mates. He was unbelievably brilliant when I confessed my dark secret; I think he had experience of dealing with mental illness and he knew all the right things to say and how to listen without judging me. I valued his friendship so much. With him being ten years older than me too, he had a bit more wisdom to him and the mature and helpful way he supported me through my struggles was invaluable. I honestly don't know what I'd have done without him.

Over the next few months, Leroy and I grew closer and closer. At the same time, Bill and I were growing further and further apart. We didn't bother to talk to one another while I was away on tour, and when I came to the end of the job I found I really didn't want to come home. At the end of June 2014, Bill and I sat down together on the bench in the garden to have the conversation that we knew had been coming for a good long while.

'I hate to say it,' I said, 'but I don't think I'm in love with you anymore.'

Bill looked at me solemnly. 'I don't think I'm in love with you anymore either,' he admitted. We both had a cry, and that August he moved out.

Meanwhile, Leroy continued to be an amazing friend to me. We had an incredible emotional connection and understanding. We did everything together, from morning to night; our colleagues teased us that we were like an old married couple. There wasn't a start date, exactly, for when our friendship spilled over into love, but that made it all the more precious: we built our romantic relationship on this bedrock of friendship and it felt all the stronger for it.

While Leroy shared many characteristics of men I'd been with before – older, charming, talented – in other ways he was worlds apart. He was a big friendly teddy bear of a man. Crucially, he understood depression. My big black dog still made me act unreasonably at times, and I still had serious issues when it came to trust and jealousy – issues, when I thought about it, that had plagued *all* my relationships over the years... Leroy understood that it wasn't *me* who was lashing out, it was my fear and insecurity making me act that way. So while he might have been hurt that I didn't trust him, or that I pulled away sometimes when he wanted a cuddle, he didn't pick a fight with me about it. In my past relationships those things would have caused a huge row, but Leroy knew to take himself away and take a deep breath, and he never took the bait. Instead, we would talk through my complicated emotions, sitting on what jokingly became known as 'the counselling bench' in the kitchen.

All this time, Leroy was my *only* counsellor – but in October 2014 I finally received an appointment with a professional: at last my name had risen to the top of the waiting list. By then I was desperate for assistance, for, although Leroy was amazing and did his very best, even picking up tips from the book *Counselling Skills for Dummies*, the big black dog was an unruly beast. I could feel its weight growing heavier and heavier, affecting more and more of my life, and shortly before the counselling session my GP signed me off sick from work with anxiety and depression. I was no longer able to manage to do what had previously been an escape. It simply took too much effort to plaster the smile onto my face; to wear a mask of happiness when inside I was screaming with pain and distress; to be around other people, when I was convinced they were all whispering about me and hating me.

I was devastated not to be able to work, though. I'd worked since I was fifteen years old, when I'd taken on a waitressing job, and it was another way of many that made my life not feel my own: this wasn't me, this *couldn't* be me. But I knew that it was.

How had this come to be?

I hoped deeply that the counselling might give me some answers. Even getting there was like climbing a mountain, though. My anxiety was so bad that I couldn't manage to make it to the appointment on my own. Earlier in my life, I'd toured in Italy for a while, breezily driving on the other side of the road in foreign towns where I'd got totally lost and never once batted an eyelid, but now I was so distressed at the thought of finding a parking spot five minutes down the road that it sparked a panic attack that gripped me with such intensity that I couldn't catch my breath.

In the end, Leroy and I went together. Going in I felt absolutely petrified – I wasn't used to talking about myself. Whenever I got into deep and meaningful conversations with friends, I was always the one solving my mates' problems, it was never me doing the chatting. It felt very scary to think that the focus was to be on me alone. Plus, the counsellor was a stranger *and* he was a man, so both these things added pressure.

In my head, I'd imagined that the counsellor's office would be a cosy, comfy place, with sprawling sofas and positive quotations framed upon the walls. Yet it was nothing like that: it was a GP's surgery that was cold and clinical, furnished by upright chairs with stiff backs and sturdy legs. I sat down gingerly, feeling incredibly apprehensive.

From the beginning, the counsellor tried his best to put me at my ease. A very skinny man – one of those wispy chaps whose legs look like they're disappearing into their trousers – he was rather old-fashioned, with a long, thin face. It was warm in the room so he wore only a shirt, no jacket. The first thing we had to do was paperwork, which again surprised me – I think I've watched too many American TV programmes and I was expecting tea and sympathy straight away. Eventually, though, the paperwork was done and we finally began to talk.

Leroy was allowed to stay for the first part of the session. The counsellor asked me how I was feeling and about the background to the build-up of my depression.

'Well, I'm not very happy with myself...' I began.

Understatement of the century.

Nervously, I grinned, then immediately worried that I looked too chirpy and not 'depressed enough'. 'I'm drinking too much,' I admitted. 'I've not got the same verve for life that I used to have...' I told him that I thought my depression might have been caused by the physical abuse in my twenties, or maybe losing my baby when I'd miscarried; I still grieved for my lost child and considered the loss a kind of punishment for the mother's sins, because I didn't deserve to have that kind of love. I talked through my cripplingly low self-esteem; my trust issues; the way I had forgiven Robert for everything, thinking I must be to blame.

I didn't mention Mr Willson once. *That doesn't have anything to do with this*, I thought. Though I had disquieting questions and disturbing thoughts that poked and prodded away at my psyche – it was wrong, you were a schoolgirl – the demon on my shoulder spoke louder: 'Remember all the fun times singing in the car and all the times he held you and hugged you, and said you were soulmates. He loved you. It was a positive relationship. It hasn't caused you any harm…'

After about twenty-five minutes, the counsellor asked Leroy to step out of the room so we could speak alone. I felt nervous watching him leave, but he gave me a supportive smile and I tried to draw strength from it as I turned to face the counsellor for our one-to-one chat. He began to question me, starting, perhaps obviously, with the topic of family.

'What's your relationship with your father like?' he probed.

It was Psychology 101; I'd almost been expecting that question. 'Oh, it's fine!' I said cheerily. 'He's a bit strict, but it's fine.'

'And what was school like?'

'Fine again!' I could feel the good girl inside me yearning to please him, wanting to give all the right answers. 'I did great; I didn't have any problems.'

The counsellor sat silently, giving me space to speak, but I didn't know what else to say. 'I got picked on a bit, but I wasn't badly bullied,' I added.

Still the counsellor sat silently. I wanted to fill that silence so I said: 'I was in a relationship with my drama teacher…'

The counsellor sat forward in his upright chair. 'Let's revisit that.'

I sat up a bit straighter too. My heart was pounding for no reason I could tell.

'How old were you when you were in a relationship with your drama teacher?' my counsellor asked.

'Twelve, thirteen,' I replied. 'It went on till I was fifteen. I saw him again when I was twenty.'

As I spoke, I had the most peculiar feeling. It was as if that cardboard box inside me was quivering, as though all the secrets inside it wanted to come out. The angel and the demon were arguing at full volume in my head but for once I ignored them both. I took a deep breath. Finally, I let some of those questions and thoughts that had been building up over the past few years rise to the surface of my mind. They'd been there all along, drip-drip-dripping a realisation to me that I now, finally, confessed to very, very weakly: 'I feel like that relationship might have affected me in some way...'

The counsellor locked eyes with me. 'Hayley,' he said gently, 'it's affected you in *every* way.'

Chapter 23

Shattered

The world went from being light to dark. I experienced this nauseous sensation of impending doom – a dread that what I'd feared *was* the truth, and that the counsellor was about to reveal it to me, as though exposing the Wizard of Oz to be a fraud and a fake. I didn't want to see behind the curtain anymore, but it was too late to shut my eyes.

Through the shadows, the counsellor kept speaking.

'Everything you've just told me is related to it,' he went on. 'Your low self-esteem; your relationship with men; how they control you. It's a pattern, Hayley. You're repeating a pattern. And the pattern began with him.

'He would have complimented you to start off with,' the counsellor said, settling into a patter. He was clearly on familiar ground, but I felt the ground beneath me was crumbling, the foundations on which I'd built my life falling away into nothingness. 'That would have made you feel good. That would have boosted your confidence and encouraged you to enjoy his classes. It's no coincidence that he was a drama teacher and you are now an actress.'

I spoke up numbly. 'He always used to tell me how wonderful I was. He used to ask me to demonstrate things to the class. He told me talent was a big turn-on for him.'

The counsellor nodded sagely. 'He would have complimented your looks – nice eyes, nice smile. You'd feel relaxed around him, happy. You'd feel loved.'

How does he know? I wondered. I hadn't told him anything that Mr Willson had said or done, but he seemed to know what had happened before I'd even said a word. It was almost as if the counsellor *had* read my mind, for he answered: 'It's terrible, but this happens all the time, Hayley. People have all got their own individual stories, but this is what *all* perpetrators do. It's typical grooming.'

As I heard him say the word, I felt like I'd been punched. *Grooming.* It was so loaded. The demon on my shoulder was shouting: '*No!* You weren't groomed, you were *wooed*!' Mr Willson had been my Prince Charming – all those wonderful words he'd said had been romantic, it had been a courtship. But now this expert was telling me something different.

I can't explain properly how it felt. Words simply cannot do it justice. My world turned upside-down, the rug came out from under me… but really, simply, what I felt was shattered. My world was shattered, just like Cinderella's glass slipper: smashed to smithereens and broken beyond repair. For if I was groomed, then I wasn't loved. And all the things I'd thought were lovely and romantic were now nasty and manipulative. Happy memories turned to ashes, grey and filthy dust. I felt sick and dirty; I felt *used*. I felt so very, very stupid for falling for it. And for the first time – the first time *ever* – I felt like a victim. An abuse victim. A victim of an historical sexual crime.

No, no, no, no, no! It didn't feel right. That wasn't the story I'd grown up with. I had lived for twenty years thinking this was all right; I'd had a few questions as I'd grown older, a few moments of doubt, but it had been my fault too. I was just as culpable. And my failed relationships were my fault as well; they had to be.

'I cannot stress enough, Hayley,' my counsellor said, 'how *wrong* what your teacher did was.'

No one had ever said those words to me before. No one had ever said that what Mr Willson had done to me was wrong. And it wasn't just anybody who was saying it: this was a professional, he knew what he was talking about. He had just listened to me talk for fifty minutes and this was his verdict.

As I felt my world lurch again, spinning me 180 degrees, I went from feeling empowered about my relationship with Mr Willson to feeling horribly abused. I'd always thought it was my decision and my choice to get involved with him – even that *I* had had the power, making him succumb to my feminine wiles – but the counsellor's explanation said no, I was a victim of something that someone else had done to me.

'I cannot tell you that enough,' he added.

I couldn't excuse it anymore; I couldn't stick up for Mr Willson anymore. The curtain had been pulled away and in the place of the wonderful wizard was just a sad little man. But what did that make *me*? If he had groomed me, he had lied. *But I had built my life and my career upon his words.* I had had the confidence to become an actress *because* of Mr Willson. He was the one who had told me I was talented. Now, I questioned whether I *had* been good enough for the parts of Mrs Johnstone and Rizzo – roles that had acted as a launchpad for me, propelling me confidently into my future. I questioned everything. Maybe I was only given them to allow him to continue what he was doing. Perhaps he offered them to me as if they were sweets and like an idiot I'd swallowed them unthinkingly. Mrs Johnstone's opening song in *Blood Brothers* suddenly haunted me: 'Tell Me It's Not True'. Oh, how I *wished* with all my heart that it wasn't.

The counsellor cleared his throat. 'Is he still teaching?' he asked. He said it lightly, but the impact of his words was such that it was as though he had hurled a grenade.

'I think so, yeah,' I replied. I felt sick, for the implication of his words was obvious. For the first time in years, I had a sudden vision of the coquettish young woman I'd once seen in a pub in Northampton: another one of Mr Willson's former students who had, in my opinion, perhaps been a little *too* pleased to see him.

My counsellor sat forward in his chair to stress the importance of his speech. 'If this was a year or so ago when Operation Yewtree was at its height,' he said plainly, 'and you'd disclosed this information to me then, I would have had to go to the police.' Panic whirled in me at his alarming words – I'd barely got my head around being a victim; it was still alien to me that my beloved love affair was in fact a horrible *crime* – but he continued quickly, 'We don't do that anymore. So I can't do it and I won't do it, because I don't think that's fair to you.' He held my gaze. 'There is no pressure *at all* about what you choose to do now, Hayley. Go home and think about it. And whether you go to the police, or whether you don't, or whether you just keep coming to see me and we use these sessions to help you become stronger, it is *your* choice.'

I nodded, grateful for the agency he was giving me – but he hadn't finished speaking. He cleared his throat again and said: 'All I would say is, have a real think about whether he could still be doing this...'

Well, theoretically, I thought to myself, as I sat frozen on my upright chair, alarm bells ringing in my head, *yes, he could be...*

The angel and the demon were scrapping on my shoulder, the demon screaming that he couldn't *possibly* be doing it to anyone else because he had *loved* me.

But he didn't love me, I thought sadly, *I was groomed. And was I really the only one?* I felt the dead weight of responsibility hanging around my neck. As I thought back over the past two decades my stomach clenched with guilt. *What if he's been doing this for twenty-odd years?*

My counsellor had planted a seed, and even as I stood up at the end of our session and thanked him for his time, even as Leroy and I made our way home in the dark October evening, even as I closed the door on the world and was left alone with my thoughts, that seed was sprouting.

And so Leroy and I talked through everything the counsellor had said. Leroy – who had said from the moment I'd told him about Mr Willson and me, 'That's bang out of order' – agreed with everything. I think he'd been trying for a long time to help me see that maybe there was a connection between that relationship and my battle with depression, but I hadn't been ready to listen. Even now, as we sat on the counselling bench at home and talked about what I should do, I found that old demon on my shoulder speaking through my mouth.

'But what if I was different?' I wondered aloud. 'I've read all the stories about grooming, I've read how girls can be manipulated – but what if he really *did* love me?

Because the man I knew back then, he would never hurt me, Leroy. It *was* love.' Even as I spoke, the angel corrected me. 'It *felt* like love, at least.'

Leroy listened patiently, not devaluing my feelings, simply trying to help me come to my own conclusions.

'What if he did love me and I'm about to ruin his life?' I asked him desperately. 'Is it *always* wrong for a teacher to fall in love with a student?'

As much as I didn't want to, with the counsellor having opened Pandora's box with his talk of grooming and historical sexual abuse, I even questioned paedophilia. Was Mr Willson a paedophile? What makes someone a paedophile, anyway? Desiring a two-year-old is different from desiring a twelve-year-old, surely – or isn't it? Are both equally as bad? These horrifying thoughts swirled in my head and I wanted to vomit at the very idea. Yet these visions – memories – of Mr Willson unwrapping me like a gift at his mate's house flooded unwillingly into my head. He had treated me like a goddess and I had felt so very grown up under his gaze. But was his delight at my body in fact because I *wasn't* grown up at all?

I couldn't cope with that idea. Instead, I batted it away: *no, no, no, no, no*! I moved on to another argument: *he must have genuinely liked my family, otherwise why did he stay around us for all these years*? For the counsellor had said I wasn't the only one who was groomed, that Mr Willson had manipulated my parents, too. Those days out at the footie with my dad had made my father trust my teacher implicitly. Without their friendship, I would never have found myself on a sofa bed in Mr Willson's house two days after my fifteenth birthday, and he never would have had such an easy opportunity to seduce me.

He wouldn't even have found himself alone in a car with me, able to make that first move when he had first and forever after crossed that line.

I questioned whether Mr Willson thought it was wrong at the time. He had seemed so confident about it, maybe he thought it was OK. He was only young himself, in his mid-twenties, with his head in the clouds. He had always said our souls were the same age – maybe *he* had been the immature one and didn't know it was wrong?

Leroy and I went round and round in circles.

'At the end of the day,' my boyfriend told me, 'it doesn't matter. The bottom line is: it was wrong. And I think he knew it was wrong because of his age and his position. When you're a teacher, you don't abuse the power you have. You know that, Hayley. After all, you're a teacher yourself.'

It was true, I was – and I think my knowledge of all the young girls I'd worked with over the years gave me some strength to see this for what it was, and the clarity of vision to know what I *had* to do next. For I would never want any of my girls to be hurt in this way – and if I didn't go to the police, other girls just like them could still be in danger.

There was no other option, to my mind: I had to report this to protect other people. That was my overriding thought. If what the counsellor was saying was true – that Mr Willson's actions had caused the horrific depression and anxiety I was currently suffering – then I had to act now before anyone else endured the same fate. I wouldn't wish depression on my worst enemy; I didn't want him to have the opportunity to do this to anyone else.

In all honesty, I didn't think beyond that. I wasn't imagining a trial or even desiring justice for myself. The very idea of my having been the victim of a crime was still so new that my decision wasn't about that. It was more that, ever since the counsellor had shown me this was wrong, a suffocating darkness had eclipsed my world. I didn't know how to make that darkness lift, other than to tell.

But if I was going to go to the police, then first I had to tell my parents.

My parents… The idea of revealing this to them made me want to cry. It was something I had promised myself I would never, ever tell them. *If* they believed me – and I actually thought there was a strong chance they wouldn't, because my depression taunted: *who would believe a girl like you?* – then I thought they'd say it was my fault. I'd always fancied Mr Willson, and they knew that well; I could still remember Mum's teasing words about my 'schoolgirl crush'. I thought they'd be disappointed in me – for having an affair with a married man, if nothing else – and I never wanted to let them down. Even after all these years I still strived to be the good girl for them, bringing home an impeccable school report. To admit to this seemed like admitting to failure. I'd have to tell them that I'd lied – lied for over twenty years, and to their faces. I'd no longer be the shining good girl. Instead, I'd be a dirty girl, an abused girl, and I couldn't bear to see that proud, innocent light fading from my father's eyes.

I was consumed by the need to tell my parents but also felt a conflicting desire to protect them from this terrible revelation. My insomnia, always bad, worsened until I was going for days without any sleep. It made me a little bit crazy, I think. At times Leroy would say to me in concern, 'Do you realise you're not making any sense?' My words would slur even without the aid of alcohol. I tried to make sense of things by writing poems, lots and lots of them, in the wee small hours, pouring my heart out onto paper. It helped me to be creative, to transform the horrible reality into something artistic: it was like going into another world, and it gave me a different perspective.

Through these poems, a vision sprang into my mind's eye of a little blonde Pinocchio doll. She danced, and simpered, and followed her master wherever he went, doing whatever he commanded. It was weird, but I knew that's how I really felt about what had happened to me as a girl. Whatever I had tried to tell myself, I had *never* been in control of what went on between me and Mr Willson: he was always the one pulling my strings, he was my puppeteer. And just like that marionette in my mind's eye, I had been powerless to disobey.

A lot of the time, when I was up late at night wrestling with the thought of telling my parents and the knowledge that I *had* to because I had a duty to tell the police, my demon kept on whispering to me, telling me over and over that the counsellor was wrong. It ridiculed his conclusion that all my troubles in life – all my failed relationships and my low self-esteem, my depression and anxiety – could stem from this one love affair when I was young. The demon made the whole idea seem far-fetched.

So the angel made me research it. I found websites that contained expert psychiatric reports on the impact of enduring sexual abuse in childhood and adolescence. Twitter was a massive help too: it hosted groups for sufferers of depression and for CSA (childhood sexual abuse) survivors and I felt like I was understood on these forums. People often tweeted helpful links. I'd click on them and read this report or watch that video. I did a lot of reading. And I came to learn that what my counsellor had said was backed up by reams and reams of research.

'Sexual abuse can be taken on by the child's brain as a form of attachment and relating, which gets wired into the child's brain, and then repeated in adulthood.'

That was why I always went for older, charming, attached men – men just like Mr Willson – and why I allowed men to control me. Because Mr Willson had controlled me sexually, it had seemed normal to me when Robert had controlled me physically and mentally, and when my diving instructor had 'stalked' me on the ship. Unconsciously, I'd been attracted to partners who would abuse and manipulate me – and I never questioned it because it felt familiar and 'right'. I learned that, when adults haven't resolved abuse they've suffered as a child, they frequently tolerate such abusive relationships because their self-esteem is so terribly low.

'The child rises above the shame and starts to create a false self based in the sexual identity as the core identity of the person, where self-worth is linked to sexual favours.'

Sex equals love, wasn't that the lesson Mr Willson had really taught? Throughout my twenties, I'd felt so lost and unloved that I'd tried desperately to find my happy ending by sleeping with men. It had never worked, which made me feel even worse about myself, which in turn drove me to try to make another sexual conquest in the hope that the next frog I kissed would turn into my prince. I'd developed what's called a 'compulsive repetitive response': I was locked in the pattern, always trying to 'get it right this time', but left feeling more and more like a failure, as each time my attempts ended destructively.

With Mr Willson having lied to me – about his intimacy with his wife; about us being together *one day* – I found it hard to trust that partners were telling me the truth. With his having rejected me in favour of returning to his wife, I often felt jealous and expected rejection in the future. This was at the root of all the many, many arguments I'd had with my partners over the years. I'd never known why I'd been so jealous and untrusting: now, I had an answer.

I even learned that there was evidence that many CSA survivors develop psychosomatic health conditions: physical problems caused by mental illness, stress and worry generated by the abuse. My psoriasis, IBS, asthma, even my viral infection – they had all been caused by this toxic secret that had been rotting inside me all this time. I'd packaged up that cardboard box of memories, but the poison had seeped out, infecting my body and my brain until my life had totally fallen apart.

Even though my research gave me answers, in some ways what I learned was devastating, too – because it was yet more expert opinion that the 'romance' I'd believed in was in fact damaging abuse. I'd thought Mr Willson's compliments had given me a rich seam of confidence, running like a ribbon through my life, but now I realised that silken ribbon was in fact a chain, keeping me locked into the cycle of hurt. I could follow that chain all the way back to my childhood. And at the end of it was that charming man, smiling and twinkling and pulling my strings.

I spent days crying; I had panic attack after panic attack as another memory came to me and was tarnished like all the others. Then, for a short time, I started to blame my parents: why didn't they see it? Why didn't they stop it? Why did they let him into our lives?

Since I'd been diagnosed with depression, my parents had found it a difficult condition to understand – but they definitely didn't understand the animosity that I now started firing in their direction. My parents are reactive people, and tensions between us intensified till our relationship was at breaking point.

'They don't understand what's going on, Hayley,' Leroy would remind me as I railed against them. 'I know how close you are to your parents, you can't let this break you.'

But my worry was that telling them *would* break us – break the whole family. I felt as if telling this secret would change us forever. Once it was out, we would no longer be able to be the family we once were. *I'm about to ruin everyone's lives*, I thought, *and for what? For me. Isn't that selfish?*

I went back to see my counsellor and talked it over with him.

'Tell them in your own way, and do it when you're ready,' he advised me. 'It's on nobody else's terms but yours.'

So I continued to mull it over, wanting to protect my family, yet also wanting to protect other women. I knew I had to go to the police, but I also knew I couldn't report this until I'd told my parents: it would not have been fair to them to do it any other way. Each day was such a struggle: crying, panicking, not sleeping. Each time I got a text from my parents, I felt more hatred and even more dark. 'I'm done,' I'd hiss to Leroy. 'Get them out of my life. Tell them I don't want to see them again.'

But Leroy knew it was the depression talking, and not me. Yet he could see that something had to be done: we couldn't go on this way. With my blessing, he drove round to visit my mum and dad.

'Neil, Andrea,' he said, once they were all seated in my parents' living room, 'your daughter loves you to pieces. Truly. All this is not about hating you, it's about your daughter struggling with something terrible that's happened in her life. I have no right to tell you what that is. It has to come from your daughter.

'Please, come and see Hayley tomorrow.'

My date with destiny was set.

Chapter 24

Telling

It is a day I will never forget: Sunday, 23 November 2014. I felt so nauseous at the idea of telling my parents – of sharing this toxic secret that I knew couldn't help but infect them too – that I was physically sick before they came round. My body looked as though it was covered in angry hives, my psoriasis reacting – as the doctors had told me it always would – to this latest stressful situation. Yet I had *never* faced a situation like this before. It was beyond my comprehension. I was about to shatter my family, and I felt guilt and fear and doubt – but nonetheless I was driven by the knowledge that the truth had to come out.

My family was going to call round in the evening. I spent all day working myself into a state about it, sweating and panicking. There were massive bags under my eyes from my insomnia and my hair was lank and greasy; I'd long ago stopped going to the hairdressers because the idea of having to chat to a stranger for an hour gave me anxious palpitations. I looked a wreck, but that was nothing compared to how I felt inside.

As I rattled around the house that day, I picked up my phone to message an old friend. It had been a while since Nicola and I had been in touch, but the friendship we'd forged in our teenage years was so strong that it never mattered whether it had been a week or a year since we'd last had a chat, we were always able to pick up where we'd left off.

I'm coming round to the idea that what Mr Willson did to me was wrong, I texted her. *And I mean* really *wrong. I'm really poorly, Nicola, and I'm having to tell my folks. I didn't think it would ever come to this.*

But I didn't mention the real reason I was now sharing the secret: that I was eventually planning to go to the police. That would be a shock too far for my bezzie mate, I thought. I wanted to ease her in gently to what was happening.

Oh my God, she texted back in surprise. *I hope you're OK. I hope they're going to be OK.*

I'm telling them tonight, I texted. Even typing the words made me start to hyperventilate.

Her reply came swiftly: *Good luck, my angel. I'm here if you need me.*

What I needed was for this nightmare to be over – but it was only just beginning.

At about 6.45 p.m. there was a knock at the door and my family filed into the front room: Dad, Mum, my brother. I had invited my brother to this family meeting too – I wanted to show him respect in telling him myself, at the same time as my parents, so that he didn't learn about it second-hand, communicated after the event. He had a right to know too – I felt he deserved that – and at twenty-four he was old enough; he didn't need to be treated with kid gloves.

Even before I said a word, I was shaking. We exchanged pleasantries to begin with, which was almost surreal; Leroy made everyone a cup of tea. And then the moment came when I couldn't put it off any longer. We all sat down in the front room and my family turned to me expectantly.

'Thank you all for coming,' I said, a bit formally. Even just saying those innocent words made my voice catch in my throat. It was wobbling all over the place, the emotion coming through; I was completely unable to control it. 'I'm sorry things have been so difficult between us lately. As I know Leroy said to you, I have something to tell you…' I had to pause then, hovering on the threshold of *before* and *after*. I took a deep breath. 'I've been to see a counsellor,' I went on, 'and he's told me to do this in my own way. And my own way is that I'm going to read you a poem I've written to explain a little bit about how I'm feeling and what's been going on.'

My parents and brother settled back in their seats, their faces neutral and ready, wanting to hear the poem. I'd written it at 3 a.m. the day before and I'd decided that it was the best way for me to express what I had to say.

I cast my eyes down to the poem; I was shaking so much I could barely read the words. Leroy was rubbing my back, trying to calm me down – he could feel me trembling even before I'd uttered a single line. My living room had never been so silent; you could have heard a pin drop. But my family weren't there to listen to dropping pins – they were there to hear me break the secret of so many long, unhappy years.

I took another deep breath and read aloud:

My true darkness has descended
I'm drowning, feeling worthless.
All these years I have pretended.
Letting thoughts bring me to obsess.

Feeling so alone is painful and scary.
No one truly sees, do they care?
No one will believe me, I feel wary.
My secret isn't one I can share.

I'm trapped until I have a voice.
Until I feel I will be believed.
A prisoner that has no choice.
Will you see, if it's me you grieve?

There's no happiness nor hope.
I feel neither. There's no joy.
Only pain, only fear, can I cope,
Hiding the secret of a nasty boy?

This 'boy' is MY big black dog.
The reason for my darkest days.
The reason my brain is a fog.
Why my mind is just a haze.

Will I ever be rid of these thoughts?
Can I hide the pain forever?
Can these battles really be fought?
Does it have to be now or never?

I'm drained, I'm tired, I'm lost.
I hate myself every single day.
What will my historic truth cost?
Do I even know the words to say?

I will bring lives crashing down.
My own, my family's and his own.

People may question, may frown:
'To lies – she may be prone.'

He's my wound that once held tight,
Now the stitches have disappeared,
It's oozing, getting harder to fight.
All that I've held inside and feared.

I'm falling under this weight
Of a secret buried deep.
Have I left it all too late?
Should I put myself to sleep?

This feeling of being alone
Only makes things worse.
My wound never truly sewn
Will I take it to my hearse?

I don't want this illness to win.
I want to fight to the death.
I want to right my sin
Tell all with all my breath.

But I can't. I can't even speak.
This heavy heart is broken
No energy yet, no sleep
My truth still unspoken.

I'm that little girl who's scared
Feeling that I shall ruin it all
If only I felt that people cared
And listened to my call.

I don't know who I am anymore
I'm frightened and I'm broken.
Of my future I can't be sure
Should my truth be spoken?

I can't move on until I tell.
Then I'll only remain here
Under his manipulative spell,
Under the control of a puppeteer.

I still don't know how I got to the end of it. In fact I barely managed it; I was gulping for breath and my voice was seesawing. I felt this weird unstoppable sensation: *no going back now*. Part of me was feeling relief that finally they would know, but the other half felt trepidation that I might not be believed. When I think back to that moment now, it's a blur. I didn't look up as I was reading, I kept my head down, trying to focus on the words through the tears in my eyes. I simply couldn't look at my family. But eventually the words ran out.

I knew they weren't enough. The poem said a lot, but it didn't spell it out and my family *had* to get it; I was only doing this once.

With the poem's final word ringing like a clear bell in my front room, I said: 'That puppeteer, and the man that I'm talking about, the reason for all of this, is Andrew Willson.' One more deep breath – and then I threw the grenade: 'When I was at school, he sexually abused me.'

There is one thing I will say for my parents: at once, they *believed* me. For that I thank them from the bottom of my heart. Unfortunately, in the heat of the moment their reaction was not to absorb and support, but to question.

'Why didn't you tell us?' my dad said, almost instantly.

In my heightened state, I took the question as an attack.

'You should have told us, you should have told us, Hayley!' he continued.

I heard Dad's words as an accusation, the 'should have' of his sentence inflamed me.

I'm not you, so don't tell me what I 'should have' done!

'Things were different back then,' I told him, stress making me snipe at him. 'You had a four-year-old and you were looking after him and it didn't seem to me you were part of my world!'

If I was honest, I'd always felt the burn of sibling rivalry. From my perspective, the baby of the family had always been treated better and more fairly than me – I'm sure other older siblings might share the same view. My emotions running high, I didn't have the words to even try to explain to my dad that it wasn't until recently that I'd even seen what Andrew Willson had done to me was *wrong*. In many ways, there had been nothing *to* tell when I was a teenager because I'd thought I was in love. Unable to articulate that, and feeling attacked, I went on the counterattack in telling him it was *his* fault I hadn't told.

As for the boy at the centre of my speech, my brother was simply sitting in deathly silence in his armchair. I think he was very hurt at that moment; he had really liked Andrew Willson. He didn't say anything but just sat there, brewing.

My mum, too, was still and silent. She looked very flushed. Everybody looked really angry, in fact, and at the time I took that anger to be focused at me, though in hindsight I think we were all just really emotional and it simply came out in raised voices and angry words and accusatory stares.

'We love you the same!' my dad shouted angrily. 'We would never have not listened to you!'

'I didn't think you'd believe me!' I shouted back. I had never expected, nor could I cope with, this barrage. Dad leaned forward in his chair and I took it as an aggressive gesture, that he was coming at me, and so I leapt to my feet. I was crying and screaming; I couldn't think straight.

'You can fuck off and get out if you're going to be like this!' I bellowed, reeling from everything that was happening. I had never, *ever* spoken to my family like that before but the emotions inside me were out of control. I flung open the door to the stairs and hurled myself up them, slamming the living-room door behind me with a deafening crash. Up in my bedroom, I threw myself onto the bed, sobbing and rocking, just as I'd once done after Mr Willson had first betrayed me. And as at that time, it was my mum who came to my rescue.

Quietly, she came up the stairs and into the bedroom, not bothering to knock. She came in and lay down next to me on the bed, her familiar figure pressed alongside mine. Then she hugged me and she stroked my hair. It was so lovely, I think I cried even more at that moment because of her unconditional love. It was exactly what I needed from my mum at that time. I knew it was superficial salvation – that she was hoping this hug could be like the plasters she used to press to my knees when I scraped them in the playground, and that it would all be OK if only she could hold me tight enough. I knew that her arms couldn't always keep me safe. But in that moment, it was all I needed and I let her love me as only she knew how.

After a while, my dad came into the bedroom too. He stood at the edge of the bed and in his gruff, Yorkshire way he muttered an apology.

'I'm sorry too, Dad,' I said, my words still catching in my throat. 'I didn't mean to swear at you.'

And then my father scooped me up in a bear hug and I had a big, long cry in his arms. We were there for a while, my mother, my father and me, simply holding each other, trying to stand strong against this tidal wave that had sucked up all the sand we'd stood on all our lives and then battered us with walls of water that tried to drag us under.

Eventually, we returned to the living room, where my brother was still sitting in the armchair. He was very quiet. My dad went into fix-it mode – I suspect because he was so enraged by his friend's betrayal that he had to do something to stop himself from hunting Andrew Willson down.

'What do you want to do about this, Hayley?' my dad asked me bluntly. 'Are you going to the police?'

At this I nodded my head; the decision had been made for me after that first session with the counsellor. I couldn't let this secret stay hidden, not if it meant someone else might get hurt.

My dad nodded too. 'Good! That's what I wanted to hear. When?'

I hadn't been expecting that question: all my focus had been on telling my family and I hadn't thought beyond that before-and-after moment. 'Um, I don't know,' I stuttered. 'Tomorrow?'

'Well, why not now?' Dad said quickly. 'While we're here?'

It was that much of a whirlwind. I'd only told the secret about an hour before, but within seconds I had a phone in my hand and I was dialling 101, the non-emergency police number.

As the call was picked up I felt petrified. *What am I doing?* My family were all sat around me in the living room; it was totally bizarre. I'd never pictured it this way. I didn't know what I was going to say but, as the female operative answered, I had to come up with something quick.

My default position was apologetic. 'I'm so sorry,' I said, trying to find the words, 'I don't know if I've got the right number, or if I'm doing this correctly, but I'd like to report a case of historical sexual abuse. It happened to me when I was at school and I don't, um, I don't really know what to do…'

I tripped over my words, but the woman could not have been kinder. I was believed straight away, which had been one of my greatest fears about speaking out: that people would think I was lying. I think the police are specially trained to deal with this sort of case now and there was no question of my not being taken seriously. 'OK,' she said. 'Let me stop you there and I'll take a few details. When did it happen?'

We talked through it briefly. Instantly, this was not an interrogation of me, it was about how the police could help and move it forward and get closure for me. The woman was gorgeously kind and sympathetic – I couldn't have asked for anyone better to be the first 'official' person I told.

'I'm so sorry that you've been through that,' she said sweetly after she'd made some notes. Then she became more businesslike: 'We've got an officer in your area, I'll get someone round to you right away.'

She was true to her word. Less than half an hour later, there was a knock at the door and a uniformed officer was there, ready to take my statement. The family were all still sitting in the front room, drinking brews, as this tall, thin lady came into the room and joined us on my leather sofas.

Though she was thin, she had a presence about her. The moment she introduced herself, I could tell that she cared. It almost felt as if she had *chosen* to take my case; as though when it came over the radio she had responded swiftly with, 'I'll take that one.' I couldn't believe how quickly an officer had come round.

As Leroy got her settled with a cup of tea and she got out her notepad, she cast her eyes over my parents and brother, sitting on the couches. The emotion was still evident on their faces, though they were almost supernaturally calm.

'Are you sure you want your parents to stay for this?' she asked.

In truth, I would have preferred them to go, but I didn't feel that I could ask that of them. I looked at my mum and dad in turn and their gestures seemed to say, 'We're cool being here.' So I let them stay. It was only going to be a preliminary interview to get the bare facts, or so I thought, so I wasn't too concerned.

The officer smiled at me warmly. Though efficient, there was nothing about her manner that made you feel she was simply doing her job: her care and empathy came through in everything she did.

'OK, Hayley,' she began, 'I've heard you've made a complaint of historical sexual abuse. We don't have to get a *lot* of detail right now, but anything you can remember can really help your case in the future. OK?'

I nodded.

'Take your time, then. I am in no rush. If you cry, you cry – that's absolutely fine.'

I nodded again. But oddly, given I'd spent much of the past month – if not the past few years – crying my eyes out, I didn't actually feel like crying at that time. Instead, I felt incredibly surreal. I'd imagined talking to the police a lot over the past few weeks: now I was doing it, I kept expecting to wake up. It was like an out-of-body experience where I could hear myself saying words but I wasn't sure that it was me who was saying them. My mother was sitting next to me and I was about to report my historical sexual abuse. Days didn't get much more unexpected than that.

'OK, let's start at the beginning,' said the officer.

So I told her about the first lesson: how I'd been waiting in the queue outside the arts theatre when I'd laid eyes on Mr Willson for the very first time. I told her I was twelve years old when we met. I told her about his praise, about his special looks, about the way I'd felt he was sometimes looking only at me. I told her about his hands on my waist, about the *Blood Brothers* rehearsals and his offer to drive me home.

As I talked, she made notes in her pad. 'Mm hmm,' she would murmur. 'Hold on a sec while I get that down. So was this in Year 9 then? And what happened next?' Her questions were excellent, leading on from where I'd got to and inviting me to tell her more. When did it start? How did it start? How long did it go on? What sort of things did you do…?

It was peculiar, talking it through – I hadn't thought in detail about our 'relationship' for many years. The major things I could remember well, but the day-to-day details were harder to recall. In my head, it had been a loving relationship where we went from kissing to fondling to sex. I remembered the 'highlights', but not exactly which date it was when *Blood Brothers* was performed or exactly when he put his hand on my knee for the first time.

The story spooled out of me, like film reel on a cutting-room floor. I had always thought that Mr Willson had romanced me like a movie star, but telling a policewoman what he had done was hardly the cinematic fantasy of youth. Matter-of-fact as I told my story, I concentrated on the bare facts.

With my parents listening, I talked her through the first kiss, and how things had grown more serious on the night of the *Blood Brothers* wrap party. I found it extremely uncomfortable talking about it all, especially because my mum and dad were there. And it seems they were finding it pretty tough too.

'I was in his office one day,' I continued, remembering a long-ago and very unexpected lesson that Mr Willson had given me, 'and he made me give him a blow job.'

At that, my father stood up. He announced abruptly, 'I'm going to take Biffy for a walk.'

I fussed over that dog like a baby. 'OK, do you know where you're going? Do you know where the lead is…?'

'Yep,' said Dad brusquely, cutting me off. He went out into the kitchen to fetch Biffy and he swiftly left the house. He didn't want to hear anymore, and who can blame him? I was very worried about him, but I knew that a walk would be the best thing for him: my dad has always gone for walks to clear his head.

My mum was still sat there though. She sat beside me, occasionally rubbing my back or my leg reassuringly as I spoke on, describing what had happened to me. I never felt her eyes on me so I think she was staring at the floor. She listened as the policewoman matter-of-factly asked me about Mr Willson's penis. Did he have a mole on it? Was he circumcised? She wanted to know if there were any striking physical characteristics that would make him stand out.

I wasn't expecting those questions. To be honest, I hadn't expected that we'd be discussing *any* of the intimate details of what had gone on, but as the policewoman asked her questions and scribbled down my answers in her notepad, she built up a full picture of everything that had happened. It was very awkward at times; it was much easier to speak once my dad was no longer there. As I talked about the drives in Mr Willson's car, and about our visit to his mate's house when he'd smeared Nutella on my naked body, I felt my mum growing angrier and angrier by my side. And then we got to my fifteenth birthday and the family trip to Northampton.

'I was downstairs on the sofa bed,' I recalled. 'His wife left and everybody else was asleep upstairs. And then Mr Willson came into the room.'

I cannot imagine how it must have felt for my mum, listening to me describe how I lost my virginity while she and my father had been slumbering peacefully in the room upstairs, guests of a man who had betrayed them. To know that a 'friend' could do that to them – could do that to their own daughter. It is beyond words.

'Was this consensual?' the policewoman asked.

'Yes,' I replied. After all, even though I'd felt extremely uncomfortable about it, I didn't *say* no. I don't think I would have known *how* to say no to him. 'It was a relationship to me,' I explained to her. I could hear how innocent and foolish that sounded.

'And why now?' she asked. 'Why have you come forward now?'

So I explained how my life had basically fallen apart in the years since Mr Willson had swept me off my feet. How first my body had broken, and then my mind. I told her that I'd now got crippling depression and anxiety and that I'd seen a counsellor as a result – and that he was the one who had made me realise how wrong this all was.

'OK,' she said, and she scribbled down a final note. The whole room seemed to breathe a sigh of a relief now that my statement had been given; there was a palpable sense of the tension breaking. I'd been speaking for hours – it was gone 11 p.m. 'I'm going to go and process this and write it all up properly,' she told me. 'You'll get a phone call tomorrow to arrange your video interview. And I just want to say: don't worry, OK? You've been extremely brave, Hayley. Thank you very much.'

Mum and I stood up to see her off; my brother, Dad and Leroy came back in from the kitchen, where they'd been hiding out, to say goodbye too. She had a strong word for the men in my family as she took her leave: 'Fellas, don't go anywhere, don't do anything.' I think it's the sort of thing they do say in that situation, just to make sure that people don't take the law into their own hands. With emotions running so high, I guess it could easily happen.

After she left, my family prepared to make their departure too. It had been a long night. My parents wrapped me up in a hug. 'Well done,' my mum said. 'We love you.'

Leroy and I closed the door behind them and Leroy wrapped me up in his arms. It had felt strange telling the policewoman everything, as she'd questioned me and recorded every detail in her book – but it had also felt *good*. That night, I knew I'd done the right thing. That millstone around my neck loosened, and I felt as if a weight had been lifted. The secret was now free, like a helium balloon soaring into the sky. Only time would tell where it would come to land.

Chapter 25

Police Process

I wish I could tell you that that light, strong feeling carried me all the way through the police process to follow. I wish I could tell you that, in telling the authorities, the angel had won and the demon had been vanquished, never to rise again. But having depression – and having been groomed – is like fighting zombies in a way. You think you've conquered them, but the moment your back is turned, they rise up and attack you with even more vehemence than before.

It was a long night. 'What have I done?' I asked Leroy, almost wonderingly. We'd started off the evening planning to tell my family, and that was a big enough item on the agenda by itself. But by the time the door closed behind them, I'd told not only them, but the police as well, and I'd given a formal statement and started an official, legal process that I didn't understand and of whose repercussions I had no concept. '*Why* have I just done that?'

I'd been very self-assured while speaking to the policewoman because I was simply telling the truth. Leroy told me over and over that hearing me speak had been very powerful, but the depression demons soon poured scorn on that idea. *I shouldn't have done that,*

I shouldn't have done this, I thought as I reviewed and derided what I'd said. Because I'd found it difficult to recall minor details about the abuse, and had had to rack my brains at times to try to remember the colour of Mr Willson's car or where he had taken me when he'd picked me up from my dance classes, I thought the police would ultimately surmise that I was making it up and lying about the whole thing.

They're not going to believe me, not when that woman writes it all up, I told myself. *I'm going to be classed as a liar. They'll think I'm just a silly schoolgirl.*

I fretted about my parents too. God only knew what conversation they were having right now in their car: it was nearly an hour's journey back to theirs and I started to imagine them being so distraught that they crashed. 'What if they don't get home?' I said to Leroy. 'What if this is the last time I see them and then they die?'

It would be my fault, I told myself. *If they die, it's all my fault. And if they don't have a car crash, then Dad might have a heart attack from the stress. My fault, my fault, my fault…*

I took all the blame on myself, worrying about worst-case scenarios that had ultimately been caused by my breaking my silence.

Leroy and I sat on the counselling bench for hours, talking it all through. It was a good spot, in the kitchen, and with the back door open we could throw a ball for Biffy into the garden and help him to calm down: he was a very sensitive dog, attuned to emotions, and the heightened atmosphere in the house that night had clearly got him all worked up too. I only wished my internal big black dog could be so easily tamed.

Eventually, in the small hours, I finally managed to get some sleep. When I awoke, the previous night felt like a dream.

'Babe,' I said, tapping Leroy on the shoulder where he lay beside me. 'Did last night really happen? Did I do that?'

'Yes, you did,' he told me. He wore a proud smile. 'And you were brilliant!'

Despite my fears that the police wouldn't believe me in the cold light of day, they continued to be supportive and efficient. Just as the uniformed officer had promised the night before, I received a phone call the day after I'd given my statement in order to arrange my video interview for the day after that. I was in a system now, and the cogs were turning and spinning me unstoppably along.

The lady on the phone explained that the video interview needed to be done as soon as possible as it would be used in any forthcoming trial. Hearing that felt horrible – I didn't want there to be a trial; I'd spoken up for other girls, not for me. If I was honest, now I'd begun this process, I had a second wish beyond protecting people, but it was simply that Mr Willson would admit that he'd hurt me: that he'd simply agree the truth I'd told *was* the truth. I didn't want there to be a big legal circus and for the man I'd once loved to be hauled off in handcuffs. Hearing the police speak of trials and gathering evidence was frightening; I wasn't ready for all that.

I wasn't ready, either, to be video-interviewed if it was going to be such an important part of the process: I was tired and all over the place and I was very worried that I was going to mess up, or not be able to remember significant details. Yet the police told me that that was exactly why now *was* the right time for me to be filmed. In a year or so's time – which was likely to be how long it might take to build a case – I might be much more together than I was right now, able to fix not only my hair but also my inner confidence to present a poised version of myself, all shiny and new. But for the jury to see the me that I was at this moment – the me who couldn't sleep, and was anxious and afraid – was powerful evidence of how I'd suffered and been hurt, no matter how much I might heal over the months to come.

I asked my father to come with me to the interview. Not to watch – I wouldn't put him through that in a million years – but just to lend support before and after. Leroy was at work that day and I couldn't face going alone. He agreed at once to escort me.

We had to go to this little building at the side of the police station. There was a discreet sign at the entrance that made reference to the fact it was helping victims of child sexual assault. It felt so wrong walking in there, and the way it was set up was catered towards children, which made me feel even more out of place. I felt like I didn't deserve to be there – a feeling emphasised when we were followed in by a grandmother, mother and child. Their case was a hundred times more important than mine, I felt – I was still trying to belittle what I'd been through.

At the front desk, I was told that the woman I'd spoken to on the phone wasn't available. I'd hoped that I'd get some consistency in who I was dealing with now, but in fact I had to tell the story – admit the truth – to different people every time. That was rather unsettling. I'd rather have built a trust and a rapport with one person, but that wasn't the way the system worked.

The receptionist asked us to take a seat. The waiting area was rather like a doctor's waiting room; its populace similarly grim-faced and anxious. There were noticeboards on the walls that served as another unwelcome reminder of why we were there – the posters were all about abuse, abuse, abuse, with primary-coloured encouragement to tell, tell, tell. It had only been about a month since the counsellor had turned my world upside-down. I still felt a slight sense of unreality that those posters referred to me and my experiences.

It was a busy office. As we waited, various employees were coming in and out, picking up files and heading off to meetings, bustling through their day. They were all plain-clothed: no uniforms here, perhaps so as not to intimidate the children. Our appointment was first thing in the morning, so as well as people seizing paperwork and signing in and out, many more were grabbing brews and making toast in the kitchen. The juxtaposition for us was bizarre: such run-of-the-mill activities for us to be witnessing, when this day was so extraordinary for me and my dad.

We waited and waited – and waited. A good half an hour went by with no sign of anyone attending to our case. The waiting room was directly next to the automatic entrance doors, and every time someone came in or out we'd feel a rush of cold November air sweeping through the lobby. As the time passed I got cold feet, both literally and metaphorically. Sitting there, doing nothing but staring at these grim posters and making the connection that they now applied to me, I got more and more agitated. I wanted to go. I didn't want to stop the process, but I thought, *I don't want to do this now: I'm not ready. I'll do it another time, another day...*

My dad took charge of the situation, as dads are so good at doing. He went and found someone who could help us and finally we were taken to meet the officers who would be conducting my interview. One was an older lady not far off retirement, while the other was much younger, perhaps in her early twenties. The older lady spoke first, somewhat brusquely: 'My colleague will be running your interview today. She's never done it before but don't worry.'

And you know what? Her youthful colleague had such a gorgeous aura about her that I really didn't. She looked nervous, but I quite liked that – because I was nervous too. It meant we were in it together. She was quite old-fashioned given how young she was, and she spoke softly: 'Would you like to come with me?'

In my life, I had watched a lot of documentaries about the police; in recent years, even more so, as I'd specifically sought out information on Operation Yewtree and other historical abuse cases. As the officer ushered me into the interview room, I had the most peculiar feeling because it was as if I'd seen that room before. But I wasn't watching this on the telly: this was *my life*. If I hadn't felt so rooted to the spot, I might have legged it. *This can't be me*, I thought. Yet the pounding of my heart told me deftly that it was.

There was a nice comfy sofa in the centre of the room so I sat down on it; the officer faced me in a big counsellor-type chair. There were flowers and tissues on the table before me. I was pleasantly surprised that I couldn't see the cameras – they're very clever in the way they make them so discreet.

'Sit how you want, make yourself comfy,' the officer encouraged.

So I tried, but I felt incredibly on edge. I was wringing and rubbing my hands together anxiously; I had sweaty palms. I wiped them on my jeans; I was wearing blue skinny jeans and a jumper that day, with my Converse boots. What does one wear to one's video interview about one's historical sexual abuse? It wasn't a dress code I'd ever come across, so I'd decided to keep it simple.

My officer was calm and lovely, just like the uniformed policewoman had been two days before. 'Don't worry if you cry, Hayley, OK?' she said. 'And talk for as long as you want, it doesn't matter how long this takes.'

She took me through it all, just as the first policewoman had. Frustratingly, her colleague had to keep interrupting us because the video feed wasn't working properly and that was very unsettling, but I managed to keep going. I thought the young officer was incredible: it may have been the first time she'd ever done it, but she was really good. In fact, once the older lady stopped interrupting us, I almost forgot why I was there and what I was doing. She put me at ease so that I simply felt I was chatting to her – she was warm and empathetic in everything she did. As I relaxed, I became more self-assured that I *was* doing the right thing and that in turn gave me strength. I found the interview empowering. Each new time I told my story, I felt I could lift my head that little bit higher, sit a little bit straighter in my chair. The secret had been weighing me down, but the more officers I told, the lighter I felt inside.

I cried only once. It was when she asked me: 'How do you feel now?'

How could I explain it, what this had done to me? Can you put into words what it feels like when the ground beneath your feet is suddenly insecure; when there's no escape from the monsters because they're inside your own head? As a child, I'd always looked under the bed for them; it had never occurred to me that there could ever be a creature that was impossible to slay and impossible to run from. So I cried, then, trying to articulate my anxiety and my big black dog. But I didn't cry when I was reiterating the simple facts: he touched me here; I touched him there; he climbed into my bed and had sex.

When it was finally over, she escorted me back to the waiting room and my dad stood up to meet me.

'How did it go?' he asked.

'S'all right,' I said. I told him that I hadn't liked being interrupted by the older lady; there was something in her brusque manner that I'd been sensitive to – I felt like she'd been thinking, *Here we go again, another one of these has come forward*. To her, of course, she dealt with this kind of thing every day, but her manner left me feeling like she hadn't perhaps believed what I'd been saying. Wouldn't her interruptions have been more sensitively timed had she truly thought I was a victim of abuse?

'She was probably having a bad day about something else,' my dad reassured me. 'And you know what? You might come across people who don't believe you, Hayley. But it doesn't matter. Because you *are* telling the truth, and *we* believe you. The important people believe you.'

'Yes, Dad,' I said.

His pep talk lasted me all the way home, but by the time Leroy got back from work later that day I was a mess all over again. In the interview room I'd felt empowered, but I even agonised about that to Leroy: 'I probably looked too happy!' I exclaimed, cross with myself for the positive feelings. 'I was probably too together and I've probably ruined everything!'

'Hayley,' he said firmly, 'you don't have to be looking at death's door for someone to believe you. You can be in full make-up and a business suit and go in there and be confident when telling your story. It really doesn't matter. Because you can always see the truth in someone's eyes. And you *are* telling the truth.'

As it turned out, I had to keep telling that truth – over and over again. I was now informed by the authorities that a different police force would be taking over my case. All this while I'd been speaking to local officers, the ones who were closest to my current home, but because Mr Willson had abused me in Lancashire, it now had to be picked up by the Lancashire constabulary. I was fuming when I found out: if they'd told me that in the first place, I'd have simply gone to Lancashire and reported it there. As it was, I now had to tell my story all over again to a whole new group of officers, and all the nice policewomen I'd met so far would no longer be working on my case.

I was not in a good way while we waited for the paperwork to be sorted out and the case to be transferred to a new team, not least because I'd decided to stop seeing my counsellor. He'd done an amazing job in opening my eyes to the abuse, but in our sessions I now found myself clamming up. It was because he was a man, and with everything I'd been through – and was even now *realising* I'd been through – I just couldn't talk to him about it anymore. He was brilliant about my decision and totally understood. My name went on a new waiting list for a female counsellor, and in the meantime Leroy and I just had to go back to *Counselling Skills for Dummies* and the counselling bench at home.

It was early December 2014 before the police were in touch again. I had a phone call from a detective called Mick, who said he was now in charge of my case and would like to come over to meet me. He was a little awkward on the phone, but he was much better in person and, from the moment I met him, I knew I was in safe hands. In his mid-thirties, he had brown hair with salt and pepper going through it, and he was smartly dressed and clean-shaven. Calm, quiet and kind, he clearly knew what he was talking about, yet I didn't feel I was with anyone autocratic or up his own backside.

'I've read through your initial statement, Hayley,' he said, once we were seated in my front room and Leroy had made the tea. 'I've got to say, I don't think I've ever had a more watertight case. I always have to look at these statements and think horribly, and throw back at you what a perpetrator's defence team might throw back at me, but I can't see any loopholes.'

I found his words very reassuring. He talked on about the process moving forward. 'We hope, of course, that we're going to get justice for you. But I want you to know, Hayley, that even if this doesn't go anywhere – if it doesn't go to court or he doesn't get charged – that everything you've said remains on file. So, for example, if in two, or four, or five, or even twenty years' time someone else comes forward, your original statement will add weight to those new allegations.'

It was a lot to take in, but I nodded sagely. I was still not enamoured of the idea of a big legal case. 'OK,' I said reasonably, 'so I might not get justice for me, but at least it's still there.'

'That's right.' He gave me a quick smile. 'So,' he went on, 'now I've read your statement, we're going to need to talk to Nicola and all the other people you've mentioned in it.'

What? I hadn't been expecting that – and I was mortified when he said it. 'Why?' I said out loud. 'Surely they don't need to be brought into it?' I felt firmly that this was *my* sordid mess; I'd had no intention of dragging anyone else down with me. But Mick said he needed to interview them all to see if they corroborated my statement. I'd included mention of the dinner party at Mr Willson's, so Mick now said he would need to track down all the children who'd attended it with me – people I hadn't seen in two decades, who were now about to get a phone call from out of the blue. It was hardly how I might have chosen for them to be reminded of Hayley McGregor.

'And, of course,' Mick went on, 'we're going to speak to Andrew Willson.'

Funnily enough, it felt good when he said that. I felt good that Mr Willson was going to know that I'd gone to the police – that finally, after all these years, I had at last learned that what he'd done to me was wrong.

'We're heading down to Northamptonshire tomorrow to question him,' Mick informed me. 'I hope we'll be able to find him.'

The sole benefit of Andrew Willson's continued friendship with my family was that we'd at least been able to supply the police with his home address. But Mick didn't know if he'd be there when the police came to call, so he wasn't taking anything for granted.

'I'll keep you updated,' he promised as he took his leave.

My head was spinning after he left. Tomorrow, Mr Willson would be getting a visit from the police. I couldn't imagine how he might react. I thought he'd probably crumble right away, because with my new adult perspective I could see he was a bit of a wuss really, especially in comparison to my dad, who was a real man's man. Part of me even wondered if he might actually say, 'Well, yes, it did happen – but I was in love with her,' and use his romantic passion for me as a legal defence, but that was really just the demon talking. In truth, I could foresee only two possible options: he would admit it right away, or he would deny it, badly, until he was questioned, when he'd trip himself up because I was telling the truth and then he'd have to admit it anyway. Either way, by tomorrow everything should be neatly tied up, whether he confessed straight away or an hour or so later in an interview.

Just as he had promised, Mick phoned me the following day, a triumphant tone to his voice. 'We've got him, Hayley!' he reassured me. 'We've found him and arrested him, and we're going in to question him now. I will ring you as soon as we're done.'

As I hung up, I felt this enormous sense of excitement. 'They've got him!' I called out to Leroy. I was really up at that moment – Mick had given me so much confidence that I truly believed the end was in sight.

Leroy and I decided to go for a walk while we waited for Mick to conduct his interview. As we strolled along with Biffy trotting at our heels, I outlined to Leroy what I'd gleaned from Mick of the events so far. The police had gone to Mr Willson's house that morning, but in order to limit disturbance to the rest of the family they had waited until Mrs Willson had left for work before knocking. Yet by the time they did so, Mr Willson had also left for the day. A neighbour had told them which school he was working at, and Mick and his team had gone straight to the school to find him.

And that's how Mr Willson was arrested: on school property. At the scene of the crime, if you will. When he'd caught up with him, Mick had asked, 'Do you know Hayley McGregor?'

'Yes, I do,' Mr Willson had replied smoothly. And then, with what I imagined was a concerned and charming tone, he'd asked: 'Is she OK?'

The detectives hadn't answered him, saying simply, 'I wouldn't go any further if I were you.' They read him his rights and he was carted off to the local police station for questioning.

I didn't think it would last that long. Even if he initially denied it, surely soon he would have to confess the truth? Yet the time ticked on: one hour passed, then two, and still no call came from Mick.

Finally, about three hours after his first phone call, my mobile trilled again. I answered excitedly, but I could hear in Mick's voice that the triumphant tone of earlier had gone. He sounded frustrated now, instead.

'I've been in there for two and a half hours, Hayley,' he told me. 'All he's got is "no comment".'

Since Mr Willson had admitted knowing me, responding to the officers' first question, my former teacher had not said another word – no words at all except 'no comment'. In the interview room, from what Mick told me, it ran simply like this:

'Do you know Hayley McGregor?'

'No comment.'

'Did you teach Hayley McGregor?'

'No comment.'

'Have you ever been in this high school in Bacup?'

'No comment.'

'Have you ever taught at this high school in Bacup?'

'No comment.'

It was all he had to say: 'No comment, no comment, no comment.'

I could hear Mick's account of the interview, but his words did not make sense. I didn't understand. I had expected Mr Willson to confirm or deny it; I had half hoped he would confess his love; I hadn't *ever* anticipated 'no comment'. That was cold, that was calculated – that was like the criminals I saw in the police documentaries.

That was what Mick and Leroy thought too. I was left numb by Mick's phone call, shattered and heartbroken – *after all Mr Willson has done to me, he's not going to admit it and go quietly?* I thought desperately – but Leroy was buoyant.

'Babe!' he exclaimed. 'He's dug the first foot of his grave!'

To him, 'no comment' meant 'guilty'. If you couldn't even answer questions about where you had worked for fear of incriminating yourself, to Leroy it was apparent that this was a man with something to hide; it spoke volumes. Yet my big black dog and my own insecurity wouldn't allow me to see it that way.

No comment? I thought. *He's not admitting it? He's going to fight this? But then it's my word against his – and who's going to believe me? He's better than me, he's more powerful: he's always made me feel that way.* I could feel the panic rising within me, higher and higher, till it felt like a wave washing over me, drowning me, flooding my mouth with filthy water till I choked. *He's going to get off*, I realised. *He's going to get away with it.*

I had thought that going to the police would give me power, but I was still jerking and twitching on the end of my puppeteer's strings. I could picture him in the interview room, but he looked very different in my mind's eye to the twinkling man I remembered. There was no twinkle in his eye now as he stonewalled Mick.

'No comment.'

So cold.

'No comment.'

So heartless.

'No comment.'

So very unlike a handsome prince.

Chapter 26

Curtain Call

I'm standing on my own in the corner of the room. I'm lonely, but there are other people in the room with me: my family – and Andrew Willson.

They are laughing and joking together, their heads thrown back in amusement. Everything is moving in slow motion, so those movements of hilarity are extreme and exaggerated: my father's grin wide and tooth-filled, Andrew's casual hand on my mother's arm placed there like a claw.

From my corner, I am shouting and screaming at them. They don't turn around and they don't look at me: they stay focused on their circle of fun and they ignore me completely. I holler and yell, but no sound comes from my mouth and I can't be heard.

I feel a rippling feeling in my belly: seasickness, as I sometimes suffered on the cruise ship, the rolling of the sea mirrored in my stomach acid. I am out on deck, watching these petrifyingly huge waves that are tossing the ship about as though it is a child's toy. Then I am on a beach, everything nice and sunny and calm – except for the terrifying tidal wave that is about to sweep everything I know and love away. I am panicking and screaming but the wave comes and washes me away anyway.

I don't die; I don't drown. But the water picks me up as though I am nothing and it hurls me about, throwing me any which way against my will. I am gasping and screaming – but no one comes, no one comes to rescue me, no one comes to help…

With a start, I awoke with a frightened shriek still trapped voicelessly in my throat, drenched in sweat as though a wave had truly soaked me. In the darkness, I whimpered, and then suddenly I froze, barely daring to breathe.

There was a man there.

I was still thrown by my night terror, half in and half out of my scary dream world, and I didn't know what house I was in, what year it was, nor who this imposing figure could be. He crouched down beside my bed, reaching out his large hands towards me. I felt threatened and scared; I felt the panic of fight-or-flight. With a scream, I tried to push him away from me, hitting out at him with all my strength.

'It's all right, baby, it's just me.'

Through my terror, part of me recognised the voice: *Leroy.* Tears filled my eyes, and guilt flooded into my brain. I curled away from him, no longer scared, but ashamed and embarrassed that I'd lashed out at him, when he was the person least deserving of my hate.

Ever since Mr Willson had said 'no comment', I'd been in the grip of these nightmares that had left me shaken and scared. With hindsight, I think they started because my tortured brain simply couldn't process this latest stage of his betrayal, this latest revelation that showed the true character of the man I had so mistakenly adored. They were always terrifyingly vivid. Frequently when I awoke I didn't know where I was and Leroy's masculine presence antagonised me. I would gasp, or curl up in a ball to protect myself, or glare at him aggressively or violently push him away. Sometimes, the jagged realisation that it was him – and not Mr Willson – was so powerful that I would collapse in his arms in relief.

When I was a girl, one of the top horror movies was *A Nightmare on Elm Street*: a film in which dreams merge into reality. My night terrors were so intense that I found myself suffering that same phenomenon. I would wake, but I would still be trapped in the fog of my nightmare, my brain discombobulated and my emotions awry. I felt like I was moving in slow motion, trapped behind a sheet of Perspex glass: I could see the world moving around me, but I couldn't keep up or do or say anything. I could see Leroy talking to me and I wanted to answer, but I was often unable to. It was as if I was underwater, trapped in that Little Mermaid world, but there were no dancing crabs or brightly coloured fish in this place. Instead, there were demons who would whisper words in my ear: 'No one cares, no one's listening to you, no one would miss you if you died.' The demons willed me to 'do the right thing' and take myself out of the equation. 'Then everyone would be happy,' they breathed with persuasive skill. Sometimes, in order to get away from them, the only option was for me to try to go back to sleep – but then there were more terrors waiting for me there, just like Freddy Krueger himself.

Mick tried to reassure me that, despite Mr Willson's response to the formal investigation, the police were still doing all they could to bring him to justice. Sometimes the police attempts to put my mind at ease made things worse, however. With Mr Willson not admitting that he'd groomed and then abused me, the likelihood of my case ending up in court was massively increased.

'But you can do your evidence from a video room next door if you wish,' officers told me, 'so you don't have to come in contact with him. We can put up partitions so you can't be seen. There are ways and means, Hayley. Everything will be done to make sure you feel OK.'

If my parents were attending a meeting with me or we were talking about the ongoing case, I would always act hard in front of them, saying the words that I thought they'd want to hear: 'I don't mind seeing him and looking him in the eye!' I would bluster confidently. But that was a lie – another lie to add to all the others I had told them – and inside I admitted to myself that I really didn't want that. It was a horrible thought that I might be put on the stand. I'd never stepped foot in a courtroom before and I really wanted to keep it that way.

The whole process was a rollercoaster. Inspired by all the American TV shows and police documentaries I'd watched, I'd expected the police investigation into Mr Willson to be much more investigative in style than it turned out to be. I'd had visions of them raiding his home and going through files on his personal computer to see if there was anything dodgy on there that might back up my case, but to my knowledge that sort of thing never happened. I found that quite shocking. Instead, they seemed to focus a lot on my statement – I had to go over it again and again, a ridiculous amount of times. Each time I did, I hoped to God that I wouldn't say anything that contradicted anything I'd said earlier.

Pushed by the police for more details, I found I was remembering more and more. I started listening to Alanis

Morissette's *Jagged Little Pill* again; I found it helped with my memory. It was quite therapeutic in a way, for it helped me to recall where I was in the dark times and why I'd been listening to the album in the first place, all those years ago. Humans don't remember pain – we're physically programmed to forget it – but as I listened to 'You Oughta Know' on repeat, I felt once again the agony I'd experienced when Mr Willson had first betrayed me. I had built him up to be a prince, but in fact his true colours had been there all along. As in the story of 'The Emperor's New Clothes', I just hadn't seen him for what he was.

Though I was anxious every time I went over my statement with the police, Mick always gave me a gold star. No matter how many times we went through it, no matter what different questions the officers asked, I never veered from what I'd said had happened to me in that very first statement of 23 November 2014. I could colour in the details, but the bare facts always remained the same.

Because so much of the police focus was on my statement, I felt under an enormous amount of pressure. Yet I had no real release for it – because the police now advised me that I had to stop any professional counselling in case it impeded what I was saying in my statement. Just at the time I most needed expert care, I was advised that I wasn't allowed it. This happens to most if not all victims of abuse who pursue a police process, and it's a devastating loss of support.

I did feel incredibly lonely. Other than Leroy and my immediate family, very few people offered to help me. I wasn't surrounded by this army of people; I can count on one hand the friends who stepped up. Nicola was one of them: I'd get a card saying 'Thinking of you' or another time, knowing I had no money because I was too poorly to work, she unexpectedly ordered a £70 shop for me from the supermarket. Those gestures really helped to pick me up.

I appreciated them from Nicola in particular, because I think the police process was probably very disconcerting for her too, given she was questioned and had to give a statement of her own. Yet her support was unflagging. I think it very likely that she had to go through a stage of processing it herself; she probably had her own moments of her world turning on its head. For we'd both been manipulated; we had both been in that bubble where we'd loved Mr Willson and had believed his feelings for me were genuine. Until I went to the police, Nicola had never thought of what had happened as a crime. I can't speak for her, but I suspect she experienced her own feelings of guilt, too, both because we had encouraged each other and because she was older than me. But Mr Willson had seemed magical to us both and we'd both been under his spell. I don't blame her. In some ways, she too had been another puppet on his strings.

Months passed. Months and months in which Mr Willson continued to try to slip his way out of what he'd done. For me the uncertainty and the pressure were unbearable: my anxiety grew even more intense. I couldn't bear to go out on my own and I had a panic attack if I had to answer the door or the phone. My drinking grew more dependent; I got through at least two bottles of white wine a night easily. Biffy was just amazing: he used to do these little inspections of the front room and if he sensed the slightest bit of emotion from me, or saw me sobbing on the couch, he wouldn't only offer his own love but he'd go and harangue Leroy in the other room until my boyfriend realised something was up and he'd come to support me through my pain.

More and more often these days, though, Leroy was the last person I wanted. Although for a time I could endure his arms around me – I often desperately wanted a cuddle – there were too many things he could unwittingly do that could trigger a flashback for me and take me to a bad place. Such as his hand sliding down to the base of my back. Or his thumb wiping away my tears. Or a kiss on my forehead. *Or, or, or…*

I knew, now, exactly why I had once freaked out on that one-night stand and in bed with Bill. The movement and the touch of those men had taken me back to Mr Willson's abuse, to that uncomfortable, I'm-not-in-control helplessness, and I'd involuntarily reacted to protect myself from harm. Yet even though I now understood what was happening, I couldn't control the way I'd flinch at Leroy's touch or suddenly recoil from him. It must have hurt him, even though he said he understood.

Even his kind words could spark a shiver down my spine that would make me feel sick. On a rare happy day I might smile at him and he'd say, 'You've got a beautiful smile,' and the day would go dark. Mr Willson had been such a charmer that there wasn't a compliment under the sun he hadn't ruined for me. My eyes, my hair, my smile… If Leroy complimented me, I would scoff. To me they were just words. They were words that *he* had used to ensnare me; I didn't believe them now.

As time passed and my big black dog grew stronger and stronger, I started to believe that Leroy didn't love me, either. 'Why do you want me? Why do you love me? Why do you even want to be here?' I would say to him desperately. I thought I was used and abused and that nobody could love me ever again, but he'd tell me that he didn't see me that way – that other people didn't see me that way – it was only my demons who did.

I withdrew into myself. As had happened with Bill, Leroy and I started having rows. We had some real humdingers. Anything could spark a fight – it was usually me picking one. I'd just get a bee in my bonnet and I'd take it out on him. He might talk to Biffy in a way I didn't like, or he wasn't getting me what I wanted (usually more wine), or we had no money, or he'd used my car. I was like a prickly hedgehog: so small and soft and vulnerable inside, but covered all over with vicious spikes to stop anyone getting close to me.

And I found the police process harder and harder to endure. I started listening more and more to the whispering demons. With Mr Willson not confessing to his crimes, to me it felt as if he was still controlling my life. The ball was in his court: he still had hold of the strings. I started to fantasise about cutting them once and for all – to take control and take myself out of this horrible limbo. If I killed myself, this could all be over now. I was overwhelmed by what I was going through and I think sometimes I just wanted it to be over, one way or the other. Yet if I withdrew my statement, everyone would think I was a liar. The idea of taking my own life grew more attractive. *I'd prefer to die and stop this process, to take it to my grave*, I thought, *than to choose not to do it and back out because I can't cope.*

I started mulling over the options, giving detailed consideration as to how I could do it; I was trying to think of a way of killing myself without it affecting anyone else. So not jumping in front of a train, then. Not hurling myself from a bridge. My dad had once told me that jumping into water from a certain height was like jumping onto concrete. I suddenly wished that I lived on the coast where there were high cliffs from which I could fling myself.

Taking pills never crossed my mind; they hadn't worked when I'd been unhappy with Robert and I thought they were more a cry for help. I was beyond the point of wanting help now, I just wanted this to be over. But how? I didn't have the guts to slit my wrists…

Day after day I ran through all the options. Every day, my main preoccupation was with how I could take my own life. But I'd come to the end of my review of the choices without a leading contender so I'd think despondently, *I might as well stay here and deal with it.* Sometimes the thought of Leroy or my family or Biffy would pop into my head, and the angel would tell me that those people did love me and they would miss me, but other times the demon would speak louder – sometimes even speak through me.

'You don't need me,' I'd tell Leroy. 'You and Biffy will be all right. You'll get over me soon enough.'

'It's so far from the truth, Hayley,' he'd tell me, hurt shining in his eyes. 'We would be in a worse situation than you are right now.'

I'd smile distractedly at that answer, not believing him. I know now that he was incredibly concerned about me: if I took Biffy for a walk on the tops, a place I often went because I could scream into the landscape in an attempt to release my pain, he would worry that I wasn't coming home. But I always did. That was mostly thanks to Biffy: I owe him my life.

He saved it on so many occasions. There were so many times when I was about to do it, to take my leave of this life, and he'd look at me with those understanding eyes of his, or put a paw on my leg or his head in my lap, and I just couldn't do it. On those days when I'd pushed Leroy away and my boyfriend wasn't able to bring me out of the fog of my nightmare world, Biffy could. Biffy would make me come back to my life: he gave me the will to live one more day.

But he wasn't the only dog with a hold on my heart. The big black dog, egged on by my anxiety and by my loss of control in the police process, growled and snarled at my beloved Biffy. He encouraged me to write out my funeral plans, so that when he finally won my family would know what to do. I wanted 'Reach' by S Club 7 played; I wanted my folks to have a nice, fun party – I knew they'd be better off without me.

I had no concern for my personal safety anymore. With my spirits all scrambled by my night terrors, I became angry and aggressive. When I took Biffy for a walk one day, a man took objection to him – you find that sometimes with German Shepherd dogs, people don't fall in love with them like they do with Labradors. It wasn't a particularly nice part of town and this bloke was incredibly belligerent: he actually threatened to stab Biffy. When I saw him again, another time, and he repeated his threat, I went for him. The man was rough, and before I knew it, he had an iron bar in his hand and was threatening me with it. But I didn't care. I was right up in his face: 'Come on, then!'

I thought to myself, *Go on, mate, hit me with it. Do me a favour*. I was waiting for the heavy bar to fall on my head and end it all when Leroy suddenly dragged me off him; he had to hold me back as I was itching for a fight. I then had a go at Leroy, of course, for stopping me from putting myself in danger. Of course, he was only looking out for me, but to my darkened mind this was simply another man controlling me, as they always had.

The streets were a dangerous place for me – and not just because of psychos like that, but because everywhere and everyone now became a potential trigger. It wasn't only compliments or touches on the base of my back that could set me off and leave me trembling and scared. I might catch the scent of a stranger as he walked along the street, and if he was wearing Eternity for Men, I'd crumple and crash. Noises scared me too. The world suddenly seemed a frightening and hateful place. More and more often, I turned again to the lure of white wine to drown out my distress.

There came a day in the summer of 2015 when the white wine ran out. We had no money – because I was way too poorly to work and Leroy spent all his time caring for me – but I was desperate for more booze; I'd only had a glass or two and it wasn't enough to quieten my despair. It had been more than six months since Mr Willson had issued his cold 'no comment' and I was still no closer to getting justice, nor resolving the hard hurt lodged inside my brain; put there by his abuse all those years ago. Everything had sharp edges these days, and only alcohol could soften them.

I demanded Leroy go out and get more. We argued about it, with me screaming my head off – I was in a dark,

dark place. Eventually, even though he had no money, to keep the peace Leroy agreed to go out to try to beg a shopkeeper to give us a bottle to tide us over until we could pay him.

As soon as he had gone and I was left alone with Biffy in the house, the demons started whispering and sneering in my head, doing me down, berating me for shouting at Leroy, telling me he didn't love me – that no one did.

I listened and listened and listened to their words.

What is the point of me? I thought. *If I went now, who would really care? Leroy will get over it, Biffy will forget me, my parents have got my brother and he's the blue-eyed boy anyway.*

I was fed up of being passed from pillar to post by the police, of being at Mr Willson's mercy once again. I couldn't take it anymore. I was thirty-four years old – he'd been controlling me for more than twenty years and I was still no closer to cutting those strings. But I could do it, if I was brave enough.

I was sitting numbly in the front room, tears streaming down my cheeks. Quickly, before I could change my mind, I bent down on one knee next to Biffy. I gave him a hug and a kiss.

'Look after your daddy, Biffy,' I murmured softly.

I was trying not to look in his eyes, but I could tell he was confused. He'd seen me cry many times before, but I think he could tell that something felt different about me this time: a choice had been made. My lovely dog was cocking his head to one side, but I couldn't look at him – I knew that if I did he would stop me, and the time for Biffy to be saving my life was over now. I kissed his beautiful head and walked out without looking back, the car keys clutched in my hand.

I was shaking as I put them in the ignition and turned the key. I tried to take big deep breaths through my sobs to calm me, roughly wiping the tears from my eyes so I could see to drive. Then I drove up to the tops; I'd had an accident before now up there, quite a bad one on black ice when I'd ended up in a ditch, and it suddenly seemed the perfect choice.

Incongruously, it was a beautiful summer's evening, maybe nine o'clock at night, but the time of year when it was still light. A strange sense of calm settled over me as I drove, as though I was doing the right thing. I either wanted to end up dead or in hospital. *At least then people would care*, I thought. The hardest thing about depression is that, because people can't *see* you're ill, they dismiss it. I wanted to hurt myself, and badly, because at least then I might get flowers and grapes and cards and care. Blinded by the black dog, I felt no one cared about me, that no one was putting me back together like I needed to be put back together.

But it was too late for remedies and sticking plasters now. I'd had enough of this poisoned life I was living. I wanted it to be over.

Time for the curtain call.

The roads were completely deserted. I pressed my foot down and further down on the accelerator, and idly watched the dial on the speedometer rise: 50 mph, 60, 70... As the landscape flashed past in the windows, it could have been my life going by. I could have watched it like a movie. But it wasn't the rom-com I thought I'd been living in when I was a teenage girl, it was much, much darker than that.

There was a strange sense of freedom, flying through deserted roads with the setting sun in my eyes. I felt an odd sense of peace. It would all be over soon. No more police. No more terror. No more Mr Willson pulling on my strings.

I stared ahead at the empty road. The dial on the dashboard showed 80 mph. Simply, and without fuss, I let go of the steering wheel.

What will be, will be.

Chapter 27

Back and Forth

I think my angel must have been looking out for me that evening. Nothing happened when I took my hands off the wheel, I just kept going in a straight line. Eventually, I put my hands back on the steering wheel and slowed the car right down.

Ring, ring! Ring, ring!

My mobile phone was trilling; I ignored it. I had just been ready to leave this world and I wasn't yet ready to return to it.

Still numb, I turned around and drove to a nearby reservoir, where I parked up, staggered out of my car and sat down on a bench overlooking the water. I was sobbing; heaving, ugly sobs. My mobile kept ringing and ringing: it was Leroy calling me from home, over and over.

It's a peaceful place, the reservoir. I could hear birds singing, and the ducks and geese who lived on the lake gently quacking as they bedded down for the evening. The final dregs of summer sunshine were still lighting the sky; there were quite a few people about, enjoying an evening stroll beside the water. Slowly, my sobs subsided. I sat on that bench for a long, long time. Eventually, instead of letting the constant calls ring out, I picked up my mobile and answered.

'Hayley?' I heard Leroy's beautiful London voice on the line. He was in a panic and I could hear the tears lacing through his words. 'Where are you? Are you OK? I'm scared. Please come home, baby. Please come home. Don't do anything silly.'

He kept reassuring me: 'I love you. Your mum and dad love you. I'm here for you, Hayley. We care.'

Finally, I murmured, 'I know.' Admitting their love was half the battle: one demon that fell down dead.

I knew I needed to go home – the fresh air, the peaceful setting and Leroy's words had calmed me. Carefully, I got back in the car and slowly drove home. When I opened the front door, I was nearly knocked down by Biffy, who jumped all over me, licking my face and hands and passionately showing me how very much he loved me. Leroy wasn't far behind him; I think he knew how close he'd come to losing me that night. Both of us were crying and hugging, with Leroy taking such care in the placement of his hands, knowing at least some of my triggers by now and not wanting me to fall any lower than I had.

And I think my angel kept on watching over me, because, as summer edged into autumn 2015, the police finally had some good news for me. All this time, they'd been following up on various lines of enquiry: interviewing Nicola and other people mentioned in my statement, and other leads besides. Thank God for Facebook otherwise I'd have had no idea how to find half of these people. Everyone they spoke to corroborated my statement. Yes, we'd been invited to Mr Willson's house for dinner – a peculiar thing for a teacher to do, when you think about it. They couldn't necessarily say that they'd seen us do this or do that, but they could talk about the closeness between us, or the way Mr Willson would hug students, or the way he'd sit next to the girls on the coach on those late-night journeys on school trips. Each new statement was like a piece of the puzzle, building up a picture that the police could use to build their case against my teacher. And perhaps the final and most crucial jigsaw piece of all was when they tracked down Mr Willson's friend: the man who'd owned the house that we'd visited in that January of 1996, when Mr Willson had savoured my young body as though it was an ice-cream sundae.

As with all the others, the friend corroborated what I'd said. Officers asked him to describe the layout of his house and the décor. In an echo of my original statement, he recounted those brown wooden stairs leading straight up from the living room and talked about the rocking chair and the clock upon the wall. He told the police that he'd had no idea Mr Willson was taking a schoolgirl there; all he said, according to what I was told, was that Mr Willson took women there behind his wife's back.

Mick was pleased as punch to secure his statement. I'd been worried that there was no hard evidence after all these years, but he explained that it wasn't about that, it was about gaining the full story of what had gone on from lots of different witnesses – and we were all saying the same thing. That was why, in September 2015, Andrew Victor Willson was finally charged with seven counts of indecent assault and four counts of gross indecency.

It felt brilliant, knowing the decision had been made to charge him. I was still really struggling, every day, but when the charges happened it felt like we were finally getting somewhere. All these months his fate had been up in the air, but the decision to charge him was a massive endorsement of the fact that both the police and the Crown Prosecution Service (CPS) believed my statement and believed in me.

It was very, very strange seeing it written down in the official jargon though – 'indecent assault on a girl under the age of fourteen'; 'incite a girl under the age of sixteen to commit an act of gross indecency' – and to know that girl was *me*. It was strange, too, to think how my lengthy statement of multiple kisses and fondles and instances of oral sex boiled down to that handful of charges. I think that's due in part to the fact it was historical abuse. I don't fully understand it, but from what I've grasped from what I've been told, if Mr Willson had abused me today, each kiss and touch and grope would be an individual charge. But because he hurt me in the mid-nineties, a different law then applied, and in charging him for these historical offences, the CPS had to charge him according to the law as it stood in 1995. And in that instance, from my understanding, they sometimes group the offences together under one charge, which was partly why the number seemed so small compared to the number of times we had actually been intimate. I was a bit up and down about that – in my opinion there could have been a lot more charges – but the police knew what they were doing and I was simply happy that the process had finally moved on. Mr Willson was bailed for another month and told that he would have to give his formal response to the charges in October.

There was something key about those charges that I hadn't expected, though. As the *Lancashire Evening Post* reported it: 'Ex-teacher charged with "sex offences" against two teenage girls'.

Another girl had come forward with a complaint against Mr Willson.

That was a huge shock to me. I felt it almost as a body blow: the certain knowledge that I *wasn't* the only one. It was a bitter moment, too: *Well, he didn't love me, did he?* More proof, if ever I needed it.

Though Mr Willson was charged with two offences against her and nine against me, her case did not go forward from there. I don't know why; I'm not sure if the girl changed her mind or if she didn't have the same supporting statements that I had for my case. I don't know if Mr Willson even entered a plea against those charges – he was certainly not convicted of them. I believe he denied them. It could be they didn't happen. It could be that the girl subsequently decided to move on in her life: to package up her own cardboard box and forget all about it. After all, some people don't want to open that box. I had once been one of them, but in the end, with everything that happened to me, I didn't have a choice: the box opened anyway and completely messed me up. In fighting for justice, however, I was hoping now to find some peace.

There was a fair amount of coverage of Mr Willson being charged: local papers in both Lancashire and Northamptonshire covered the story, and he was named in the articles. I think there was a reason for that: I think the police were hoping that even more girls might come forward at that point and they wanted to give them some encouragement to do so. I certainly think there are other victims, and I will go to my grave 100 per cent sure that I'm not the only one he has hurt. That girl I saw in Northampton, for instance. I don't know where she is now, but I wonder if she's repeating those patterns I once did. Who knows?

Despite the police hopes, and my belief, however, no other girls have come forward to date. It could be that he hasn't done it to anyone else. He could possibly only be guilty of hurting me. Personally, though, I wonder if his victims simply haven't realised they're victims yet – if they're still treasuring Cinderella's slipper in their own cardboard box and their world has not yet shattered. It took me twenty years to see the light, after all. Other women might not have reached that fork in the road yet. They may not choose to walk down this path when they do.

In October, I had an email from Mick: Andrew Willson had responded to the nine charges against me. Finally, after almost a year of saying nothing, he was ready to move forward from 'no comment'. He was willing, he said, to plead guilty to three of the charges out of the nine.

I thought it was a joke, an absolute joke: Mr Willson *knew* he was guilty of *all* of the charges. I'll never know why he denied them, but I was standing by my story. I was getting more and more angry with him – and the police weren't happy either. They said they'd give him another month to go away and think about it, and suggested he came back with a more sensible plea next time. I think they'd known from his first 'no comment' that he was guilty and now it was simply a bartering process: how much would he admit to, and when?

I found it very interesting what he was willing to plead guilty to at that time. He admitted taking me to his friend's house and to the stuff we'd done there, and he admitted taking my virginity in Northampton. Those were actually the most serious charges in terms of their sexual nature – but crucially they had both taken place when Mr Willson was no longer my teacher. As such, they were arguably less serious charges because he wasn't necessarily abusing a position of trust when he took advantage of me. I could still remember how free he'd looked, that day he'd picked me up in his car on the way to his friend's house. His manner had been different – was this why?

The third charge he admitted was either a grope or a blow job I'd given him – but he refused to admit it had taken place in his office; he said it was only in the car. I think he was strenuously trying to avoid admitting to any abuse taking place on school premises: again, it probably cast him in a slightly better light if he wasn't confessing to getting sucked off in between classes by a child he'd had in his charge.

His machinations as he tried to wriggle out of what he'd done made me sick. *Why is he doing this?* I thought. *Why is he playing this game?* He could have just admitted it, from the very start: done and dusted. Instead, we were having this year of back and forth, and once again I found myself in limbo, playing a waiting game while we all waited for Mr Willson to make his next move.

At that point, I thought it almost certain we were going to trial. If he refused to admit any more than those three charges, then the police and I were prepared to go to court. In some ways I was so angry with him that I was quite fired up about doing so, but I was trying to get my head around it too.

I'll be honest, it scared me. My uncle was a copper and he was warning me that my character would be ripped apart. I anticipated that they'd use my mental health against me, to make me out to be an unreliable and untrustworthy witness. I feared they'd dig up my sexual past – the one-night stands I'd had when I was only looking for love, wanting to feel loved because I felt so worthless – and use it against me, making me out to be promiscuous. I imagined it would be like a courtroom drama on TV: I could picture Mr Willson's special son being wheeled out as a trump card; maybe having to face his wife *if* she stood by him in court. I was worried for my dad if they called him as a defence witness – because he'd have to say that he'd never seen anything awry between me and Mr Willson, that he'd trusted my teacher all these years, and that it was only my so-called 'secret' being told that had changed his view. I thought my whole family would be put through the wringer and I was absolutely *dreading* it, with every atom of my being – not least because I'd seen at first-hand how good a liar Mr Willson was. I feared he was going to be able to charm that jury like he'd charmed everyone his whole life long and that, ultimately, *he* would come out on top. I wasn't sure I could bear it if that happened – I wouldn't want to live in that world.

In November, as expected, I had another email from Mick to update me again: Mr Willson had gone away and thought about it, and it seems he'd had a change of heart. Now, Mick told me, my former teacher said he wanted to plead guilty to *five* of the nine charges.

It was over half, which was good. He had also admitted kissing me in his office at school. That was really important to the police; they thought it would significantly increase his sentence. To them, it showed the deliberate grooming of a child in his care and that I wasn't just a family friend or a crazy girl who'd met up with my teacher outside school. Mick explained to me that, if we chose to accept Mr Willson's 'offer', the remaining four charges to which he had not pleaded guilty would still remain on file and be taken into consideration. He felt that Mr Willson had admitted to the most serious charges and that the four outstanding ones would not significantly add time to his sentence.

It was a big decision to make. Was this enough? Would I accept? If I said no to this offer, it was very likely we would end up in court. Was I ready for that? The police process so far had very nearly broken me: would I even be able to survive a trial?

Part of me was railing and angry. 'Don't lie!' I wanted to say to Mr Willson. 'Tell the truth, be honest! Admit you did *all* those things!'

On the other hand, if I fought for him to do so, it came with the looming threat of a trial – and the very frightening and very real possibility that he might be found 'not guilty' at the end of it. I *really* didn't feel confident about testifying and being cross-examined in court by cut-throat lawyers who would be out for my blood. At present I couldn't even answer the door without getting a panic attack – I couldn't imagine enduring a court appearance without suffering a complete breakdown, both physical and mental. So I listened to what Mick was saying: that the other charges remained on file and that the other four wouldn't really add any more time to the sentence. As for that sentence, the police were talking about him maybe going down for four to five years. A worst-case scenario, they thought, was that he'd serve two to two and a half.

In truth, it had never been about the sentence for me and, as I weighed it all up, I reminded myself of that. I had simply wanted him to admit it – and five guilty pleas were at least a part-victory in that regard. I'd never been especially concerned about him being locked up in jail for what he'd done to me – what was more important by far was that others were protected. Now, his name had been in the newspaper. Thanks to my coming forward, he *wasn't* going to be doing this again – as long as he was convicted of his crimes. This whole process would stop him doing it to anyone else.

So I made my choice. With Mick's blessing, we told Mr Willson's lawyer we would accept. Because he'd pleaded guilty, there would be no trial; he *would* be convicted. The only question was how long he'd get.

I felt... happy. So happy. It was an elated feeling. Having given the nod to the police, Leroy and I looked at each other, barely able to believe that this nightmare was finally coming to an end; that the end was now in sight. I think Leroy was almost happier than I was for he had seen what this process had done to me. He knew how close I'd come to not making it this far. I very nearly didn't live to see it, but the day had come when justice, of sorts, had been done.

Guilty. Mr Willson was guilty. He would be held accountable for his crimes.

Perhaps my father summed it up best when I phoned to let him know.

'Hayley,' he said. 'You did it.'

Chapter 28

Judgement Day

With Mr Willson having pleaded guilty to his charges in November, I hoped that this nightmare would be over by Christmas. That was really important to me: it had been the worst year of my life, and I wanted to draw a line under it and start afresh in 2016. I didn't want to carry this with me into another year.

The sentencing was originally set for the end of November – and then it got pushed back. Then it got pushed back again. And then I had a phone call from Mick to say it had been postponed once more because the powers-that-be had decided that Mr Willson should get the opportunity to spend a final Christmas at home before his sentencing. It was great for him, because he could have fun over the festive period, but for me it was an absolute disaster: a real low point.

'How can they treat him better than me?' I asked Leroy angrily. 'I'm here getting no help and they're going to let him have one last Christmas at home before he goes to prison? It's ridiculous!'

I didn't care what the sentence was going to be, I just wanted this to be over. And though Mick kept reassuring me that the guilty pleas meant justice *would* be done, I was nervous about it still. Until Mr Willson actually stood up in court and confessed to his crimes, I was wary of believing he was actually going to do it. I still thought something could go wrong: one loophole, one mistake, one change of heart and the case could fall apart.

Christmas was horrible. I wasn't in the mood for celebrating. This cloud was still hanging over me – I was still in limbo, without any control over my own life. The police asked me to write a victim impact statement to be read out in court, but I found it really hard to do. Given the way Mr Willson had been put first by the system so far, I didn't think it was going to make any difference to anyone and I couldn't see the point in doing it. It wasn't empowering; I felt like I was moaning and I was sick of hearing myself go over and over the same ground. I was conscious of this huge pressure to deliver something compelling, but I was so angry and worked up that I found it almost impossible to find the words to describe the impact that his crimes had had on me. Nevertheless, I tried.

Going to the police and having to give detailed evidence of what happened to me was horrendous, I wrote,

> *I lived every emotion available and felt like I was a young girl again… I felt sick as I started to live through it all, bit by bit, exactly what he did to me. All the horrid lies, telling me he loved me, that I was his soulmate, that he was in a loveless marriage and was only staying because of his disabled son. All the secret meetings, the sexual 'teachings',*

the 'relationship' turned from my first love to a living and disgusting nightmare. He'd taken my teenage years and ruined them beyond repair. I was becoming a prisoner in my own mind and my own home, too scared to even leave the house anymore…

My nightmares got much worse. I was signed off work and lost out on a contract worth £8,000 due to this horrid man, this trauma. This has had a huge impact on me financially, emotionally, physically. I couldn't pay my mortgage so I nearly lost my home. I couldn't pay my household bills and was struggling to scrape money together to eat. This was the first time in my fifteen-year professional career and my ten years of running a home that I wasn't able to function at all. I nearly lost everything through the fears and anxieties brought about by what this man did to me. This affected me badly. I started to blame myself and thought I deserved all this. Those childhood memories had been completely snatched, lost, and I felt a burden to myself, my partner, my family, to the world.

There were a million and one thoughts running through my head and each day meant a new memory would pop up; the police may need more details of a certain instance… and then I'd hit rock bottom again. All those school performances he cast me in were all ruined. My whole existence in those performances was a lie. All just for him, to make it easier to manipulate me to be with him, to be alone with him, to fall for him, to love him, to do exactly as he pleased.

Due to being so consumed by these thoughts I began to push people away without even realising it. My family felt like it was being torn apart as he lied to them as well. I could see the pain in their eyes and hear it in their voices...

I have been in the acting profession for fifteen years and have ALWAYS worked. Now? I can't. I have lost every inch of my confidence, my self-belief, my self-worth. Going to an audition was something I may do a few times a year or a few times a week and now the thought of even leaving the house sets a panic attack off, let alone attending an audition.

I can't trust anyone, I even find it hard to trust myself or my own thoughts and mind sometimes. I'm living in a big, dark, all-consuming bubble of his lies and destroyed memories. I've been unable to get proper professional help as I'm told I need 'specialist counselling' which cannot start until this trial is over.

Every day is a battle. I'm always tired, exhausted, drained. Just having a shower is like running a marathon. I just want my life back. I want to laugh, smile and joke with my friends. I want to answer my phone or my front door with confidence and without fear. I want to be able to love and to trust again. This seems all too far for me to reach at the moment. I feel like I'm drowning, suffocating after every nightmare or every thought of my past abuse by this man.

I'm existing, not living, and all I want is my life back.

When Mick read it, he told me it was extremely powerful.

I could only hope that the judge would take it into account.

The sentencing date was finally set for 24 February 2016. I planned to go – I thought, if I didn't, it would send the message that I wasn't strong and I couldn't face him. But the truth was I *couldn't* face him. I didn't want to look into his eyes; I didn't want to see the fake pain that I thought would be there. It would be fake, but I knew it would still get to me. Mr Willson had been able to charm me all my life and I didn't want to give him the opportunity to pull my strings again.

Mick and I talked it through. He was very sympathetic. 'What's the point in you being there, Hayley?' he said reasonably. 'He's being sentenced, it's really boring – it's not what you see on the telly. There is really no point in you putting yourself through that. The strength you've shown in coming forward is the strength that matters. You've managed this far without having to step foot inside a court, which is what we wanted right from the start, so you didn't have to have that memory. I'd really rather you didn't come.'

Eventually, I realised I was only planning to go in order to please other people. I decided I wouldn't have my day in court, after all. In truth, I found some satisfaction in imagining that Mr Willson might look for me that day, maybe to twinkle those eyes of his at me, and he'd find I wasn't there. I preferred for him to think that I couldn't even be bothered to turn up – that he meant that little to me. I preferred for him to think I was out having fun that day.

Mick promised to keep me updated on everything that happened. He warned us that it was all out of his hands though – it was in the hands of the lawyers and the judge now. How the day went would all boil down to which judge was on the bench and how they felt on the day. Mick was hoping for one particular female judge to oversee the case, a strong woman who was known for handing out tough sentences.

I couldn't sleep the night before the hearing; I dozed on Leroy in the front room instead, as we talked round and round the conflicting thoughts in my head. I'd had a tense phone call with my parents and that played on my mind: they were going to go to court. I think they felt it was their right and they wanted to be there. But they didn't understand why I'd chosen not to go and I didn't understand why they were going, so we'd talked at cross purposes. Leroy and I only went up to bed at about 6 a.m. to try to catch a couple of hours' sleep before Mick called to let us know what happened.

The hearing was scheduled to be one of the first of the day. It was due to begin at 9.45 a.m. and I thought Mick would phone pretty quickly after that. Yet it wasn't until gone midday that my mobile trilled. *What's taken so long?* I wondered.

My hand was shaking as I picked up the phone. *This is it.*

Mick, as he always did on the phone, spoke quickly and to the point.

'I'm sorry, Hayley,' he said. 'It's not the sentence we would have wanted.'

My heart sank like a stone. The police had been hoping for four to five years' imprisonment. But Mick told me that the male judge had ordered Mr Willson to serve only twenty months in jail; he would be out in ten months on probation: home in time for Christmas.

I felt bitterly disappointed, but as Mick talked me through the hearing, I realised in some ways we were lucky to get even that. 'I have given consideration as to whether the sentence could be suspended,' the judge had said in court. 'It seems to me, given the pupil–teacher relationship, that it cannot.'

Maybe, if Mr Willson had managed only to admit the things we'd done after he'd *left* the school, he would have got away with it all.

In the judgment, my teacher was also ordered to sign the sex offenders' register for ten years. I was pleased, at least, with that, because it meant, as long as people did their jobs properly, that he would never be able to teach again nor come into contact with young people. In coming forward, I *had* managed to protect other girls.

But I did feel deflated at the short sentence, and angry too. In my mind, it diminished what he had done to me, sending the message that it wasn't *that* bad. I tried to remind myself that it had never been about the sentence for me; I was only disappointed because the police had mentioned four to five years – I simply had to forget anyone had ever told me that. At the end of the day, justice *had* been done.

Nevertheless, I did ask Mick: 'Why is it so short?'

It turned out Mr Willson's lawyer had done his job well. In defending his client, he'd said in court, 'He accepts full responsibility and does not seek to blame the victim.'

It's a funny old world, when that should get you brownie points in court.

'He feels ashamed,' the lawyer went on, 'and this has had a significant impact on his life. He has lost his job, his marriage, will shortly lose his home and probably his self-respect.'

One could almost hear the violins playing.

It was the first time I knew for sure that Mrs Willson had chosen not to stand by her husband. I was glad for her – that she had the strength to leave him and didn't stand by him and pretend it didn't happen. I'd always thought she was a strong, attractive and formidable woman; he had needed her, not the other way around. I felt guilty too, though, to know that my actions had caused this family to split. I still feel immense guilt about that.

I guess my world was not the only one that shattered.

In many ways, I wasn't all that surprised that Mr Willson's 'mitigating circumstances' resulted in a shorter sentence for him. I hadn't had much faith that my victim impact statement would be taken into consideration and now I knew for sure that the criminal's rights outweighed my own. And as I'd predicted when I'd been imagining the trial, Mr Willson's disabled son *had* been wheeled out as his trump card. 'He is anxious as he is the main carer for his severely disabled twenty-three-year-old son,' Mr Willson's lawyer had added.

It was a bit galling, to say the least. Mr Willson's parental responsibilities apparently meant he couldn't be jailed for years for what he'd done to me – but those same responsibilities hadn't stopped him from kissing me over that same child's cot, nor from having sex with me while his child slept upstairs, while I was still a child myself.

I could tell Mick was disappointed with the sentence too. We were both simply pleased that at least he would be incarcerated. I hoped it would give Mr Willson some time to reflect on his actions. And it wouldn't be a pleasant experience, being a child molester inside. I couldn't actually imagine what it would be like to be in jail, but I was sure I would hate every moment of it. As Leroy pointed out, though, in some ways I have been incarcerated for more than twenty years, living in my own prison of hurt and lies, unable to move on.

As my conversation with Mick drew to a close, he cleared his throat on the phone, and I could tell he had something else to say to me.

I wasn't prepared for what he said next. He told me that Mr Willson had pulled him to one side in the courtroom, before he got sent down.

And my former teacher had said smoothly: 'Can you please tell Hayley I'm really sorry.'

An apology.

A gift?

A happy ending?

But I didn't believe it was sincere, not for one split-second. I truly wished it was – but I knew too much about him now to fall for his lies again.

If he was genuinely sorry, he would have handed himself in many moons ago. Or admitted to all the charges. Or not 'no commented'. He wasn't sorry for what he'd done – he was only sorry he'd been caught.

His apology made me feel quite sick, truth be told. *He's still doing it*, I thought, *he's still trying to get to me. He's still trying to charm and manipulate me. He's still pulling on those same old strings.*

315

I guess some things never change – but others do. For I wasn't dancing to his tune anymore; I wasn't falling into line: this marionette was now her own master. I had broken free of his chains at last.

Chapter 29

Speaking Out

In a fairy tale, with the bad guy banished, there is always celebration and joy. Ding dong, the witch is dead, and just like that the dark days are over. I think people assume that, the moment a court case is done in situations like this, there's a neat conclusion and simple closure and all of a sudden the demons drop dead. My mum seemed to think so: 'It's done now,' she said to me after the sentencing. 'It's done now, so you can close that door and get on with your life.'

But it isn't – and wasn't – that simple. My night terrors actually became *more* vivid after the sentencing, and the Mr Willson in my nightmares took on a new face: the face he'd shown in the courtroom, which appeared in the newspaper accounts of the case. He was very clever; he 'acted' the part of the devastated sinner to perfection, and the photos I saw of him at his sentencing showed a man who was nothing like the cheeky charmer I'd known as a girl. In those pictures he had a close-shaven head and looked tired and grey. And that defeated man now appeared over and over in my nightmares, begging me not to betray him.

With the court case over, I was at least finally able to get some counselling again. My new female counsellor took me through my diagnoses – I was still suffering from severe depression and anxiety, and she now informed me that I'd also added a third condition to my bag of tricks: post-traumatic stress disorder (PTSD). That was why I was having those vivid flashbacks, why I didn't care about consequences, why I was so angry, and tortured by night terrors. So I was still locked in my prison, looking out at the scary outside world.

As Mr Willson's conviction was reported in the press, I came to appreciate that the outside world was actually even more nasty than I'd thought. The story of Mr Willson's case was shared widely among my friends on social media, with my old school mates agog that their former teacher had been convicted of sex crimes. As the victim, I was anonymous, so no one knew who the girl at the centre of the story was. As I read the comments under the article links on Facebook, I felt sick.

'She's probably lying,' one person wrote.

'I don't know why these so-called victims of historic sex abuse come forward,' wrote another, 'they probably can't even remember, they're just attention-seeking whores.'

'All the girls at our school were slags anyway. She probably deserved it.'

It hurt; it hurt *a lot*. I was sick of seeing myself described as a victim, and not having the power to speak up and defend myself. So when I was offered that chance, I grabbed it with both hands.

One evening Leroy and I were sitting in the front room when there was a knock at the door. Leroy went to answer it, in full-on protection mode, and found this bookish little fellow on our doorstep. He said he was a journalist from the *Daily Mail* and that he wanted to interview me.

'I think it's a powerful story,' he told Leroy. 'What she went through was terrible. We want to help her get her story out there – if she wants to tell it.'

I thought it was the strangest thing in the world; I was shocked people were interested. Mick had warned me that some of the local papers might cover the case, but this was a massive national newspaper with a circulation of millions. Nevertheless, I instantly wanted to do it; I wanted to waive my right to anonymity. I was sick of being a silent, faceless, nothingness victim that people were having a go at, I wanted to stand up and speak out, to say, 'No, I *didn't* deserve it.' I wanted them to see, to feel, to understand what I'd been through, and most of all I wanted to get some control back. I'd thought going to the police would give me control, but Mr Willson had manipulated the entire process from start to finish. This was my chance to take back the power over my own life.

And so I decided I would grant them a full interview.

I felt nervous speaking to the journalists, but also empowered. They were so lovely to me. The *Mail* sent round a stylist and a make-up artist to my house because there would be photographs to accompany the interview – it was probably the first time I'd worn make-up in several years, because I'd given up caring for my appearance long ago. It felt really nice, actually, and as if I was taking baby steps to rejoin the world.

The article was published on 30 April 2016. I could not believe the interest – the phone started ringing off the hook. I'd said to Leroy maybe it would spark some more media enquiries, and that if anyone asked me to do a TV interview I'd really like it to be *This Morning* – and then, boom, we had a girl on the phone from *This Morning* asking if I'd like to come on the show! It was as though the universe was finally listening to what I wanted – and delivering in spades.

Once again, the whole experience was extraordinary. I wasn't too nervous about appearing on TV – after all, I am an actress, and even though my confidence had been shot to pieces, I think there's something in me that was born to storytell and communicate, and my instincts kicked in as I sat on the sofa with Holly and Phil. I found I was able to speak clearly and confidently about what had happened.

In many ways the decision to go public with my story was my way of turning this whole negative process into a positive, so that I didn't end on the disappointment of the sentence or the powerlessness of the process, or even the vicious trolling online. I've always been inspired by people who somehow turn loss or grief into a positive and in speaking out I hoped to emulate them. After *This Morning*, I gave interviews to several magazines to help spread the message even further.

Each time I spoke out, it felt worthwhile. It helped give me confidence and helped me to move on – and to smile more. Waiving my right to anonymity stopped the negativity online and I was suddenly flooded with supportive messages. 'Wow, Hayley, well done!' Facebook friends wrote to me now. 'I'm so sorry you were going through this. You are inspiring, keep going, stay strong. You're so brave.' Many said things like, 'I always thought it was weird he had girls getting changed in his office' or 'I always thought he was a creep.' The messages were a real confidence boost to me – I appreciated them so much and many days they quietened down the big black dog inside me.

Other people reached out to me after my media appearances too – people I didn't know.

'I'm so sorry for getting in touch,' the messages frequently began. 'I hope you don't mind. It's just... I think my daughter's going through this at the moment. Can you give me any advice?'

Victims, too, got in contact with me – other historical cases as well as young girls with overly tactile teachers. *Wow*, I thought, *this is a heck of a responsibility.* I tried to reply as best I could. Many asked me about the police process, and I didn't lie: I said it was difficult. I told them what Mick had once told me – that even if you don't get justice for yourself, making a statement always stays on file. In two or twenty years' time, making that statement might well help another girl to get justice when she comes forward; or, equally, yours might be the statement that flags up someone else's complaint from thirty years ago. It is *always* worthwhile telling the truth, but you have to be prepared that it is challenging. While no other girls came forward about Mr Willson, I know that seeing me speak out has encouraged other women to report their own teacher/student 'affairs'. That makes me proud.

I felt something else, too, as I listened to all these stories: shock. The sheer number of people coming forward made me realise: this is an epidemic. I felt even more impassioned about sharing my story, getting the message out there that *this is wrong*. After all, no one had told *me* it was wrong for many years; I was sick of people thinking it was OK. I believe strongly that we have a responsibility as a society to see what is going on in our schools and to take charge of it, including teaching kids about the warning signs and how to spot when they're being manipulated.

As I grew stronger in the wake of my own police process, I wanted to be at the forefront of that movement: I wanted to become an advocate for all the other victims that I knew were out there. I wanted to go into schools with my message, to teach it through drama and drama therapy, to tell the world what had happened to me in the hope that it would stop it happening to anyone else.

That was why, when Penguin approached me to write this book, I said yes straight away. And I really, really hope this makes a difference. I would love to be able to go into schools and read it, speak about it, have Q&A sessions with students about it. If this book can make it *not* happen to just one person, then I've done something. I've achieved something. It's happened to too many people, and it needs to stop. Today. Right now. And if I can help stop it in whatever tiny way I can, then that will make me happy.

And happy is a place I want to be.

In the summer of 2016, Leroy and I decided to set up our own theatre company, YOLO Theatre – *You Only Live Once*. We're planning to concentrate on young people's confidence, self-esteem and mental health. In particular, we want to write a play that we can take into schools that is about this very issue. We will perform it and workshop it with the kids.

Many people have told me that schools won't want it. But if they don't, I think they have to take a good hard look at *why* they don't. I really hope I can make all the teachers out there who are still doing this feel extremely uncomfortable. I'm shining a spotlight on this issue and it is my hope that we'll start local and then go national – I would love to get a tour in place. Because this happens *everywhere*. It could be happening in your local school right now.

If you have a suspicion that anyone you love is going through this, please, I beg you, ask that question. No one asked it of me, and I wish to God they had. If it's happening to you, I hope this book has made you realise it's wrong. If there is a man or a woman doing any of these things, saying any of these things, or infiltrating your family in the way that Mr Willson did mine, I hope this book makes their mask fall for you. I beg you to see them for what they truly are: a manipulative older person crossing a line and taking your innocence – and who will eventually seize the happiness of your adult life too. Please speak out. Please pick an adult you trust implicitly and tell them what is happening. It might not be your mum or dad, you might not feel you can tell them, and that's OK. But please don't suffer in silence. If it's happening to you now, if you think you're in love and you've got this crush and an adult is responding, *it is not right and it will affect you later*. With a bit of hard work, with support and with your own personal strength, you'll find that through telling the truth about it you *will* get your justice in some way and you *will* come out of it stronger, better and a more positive, rounded person.

Because that's what's happened to me. I don't have to take this secret to my grave anymore, as I had once planned to do. I've spoken out and I've seen the light, and in doing so I *feel* lighter: that weight has gone. Mr Willson's abuse was a dark secret rotting inside me, but in fighting for justice I have excised it once and for all. It *has* helped. Without a shadow of a doubt, I am healing.

Admittedly, it's taking longer than I originally thought and hoped it would. I have good days and bad days. On the good days I try to do too much, so it's three steps forward and four steps back. But I'm trying, and I *am* moving forward, inch by inch and step by step.

I'm learning. Learning about myself, and learning how to change. Because some of the patterns I've lived with for all these years are hard to break. I still flinch if Leroy puts his hand on the base of my back or kisses my forehead in a tender, teacherly way, yet sometimes it's *him* who pulls away from *me*: when I'm desperately seeking love and to 'earn' it, I offer myself sexually. He's trying to teach me there's a difference between being intimate and being close with somebody: that sex and love are different. Slowly, I'm starting to get to grips with that, and I'm trying to find a new way forward that doesn't repeat any of my old mistakes.

The chains that Mr Willson welded still occasionally tighten around me: when I smell Eternity for Men on a stranger in the street, for example, or even when I hear my full name being called: 'Hayley McGregor!' There are just too many bad memories associated with it.

I do feel tarnished; I can't help it, in a way. I've pushed many people away – yet others have simply drifted on, leaving me behind in their wake. I feel like a wounded animal in the pack of humanity, and I think many people feel uncomfortable being around me now, tiptoeing around the elephant in the room. Invitations to social occasions have dried up, as though as a CSA survivor, I'm a natural party-pooper. I can understand, after everything I've been through, that maybe people feel it's too much for me to come to a party, but I'd like to have the opportunity to make that choice myself, to be given the option. After all, Mr Willson made all my choices for me when I was younger and I'm sick of people making *my* decisions; I'm strong enough to stand on my own two feet.

It's not all positive. I do have dark days – days when I even wonder if I did make the right decision in going to the police. Sometimes I feel like I ruined my family's lives when I told my secret for they too have to live with the shame that comes with sexual abuse – and the guilt and the endless questions. Why didn't I tell them? Why didn't they see it?

I think it's affected everyone's health, and my relationship with my parents is at times strained. For two whole decades I lied to them and that is difficult for us all to come to terms with. There is blame on both sides. On occasion, I've asked my father how he feels about it all, but he always goes quiet and won't talk about it – I guess it's not his way. And maybe, after everything that's happened, he's trying to protect me too. I'm the child, and he's the adult, and maybe he's looking out for me in the only way he knows how.

As for Mr Willson himself, at the time of writing this book I know he'll be getting out of prison in a very short while. I won't find out exactly when – I'll just get a phone call to say, 'He's out.' I don't ever want to see him again. If I saw him and he didn't see me, I'd swivel on my heels and go. But I'm worried our paths will cross. After all, he won't be living in Northamptonshire in that lovely family home of his anymore, and I'm concerned he might choose to return to live in the North. We work in the same industry, so it's not beyond the realms of possibility that we might run into each other at a casting call. I hope in that instance I'd have the strength to tell him to leave, that the audition should be my opportunity, but I think it would depend on how I felt on the day.

I want to forgive him, but I'm not there yet. Some of the strongest people I've ever seen in my life are those who have been able to forgive though. There is something so powerful about the mother who forgives her child's murderer, or the husband who forgives the man who slayed his wife. They seem stronger than those who harbour hate and resentment, who never seem at peace. And I want peace; I want peace more than anything. So I'm trying to forgive him and I hope, one day, I will reach the end of that journey. I just don't know at this stage how long the road might be.

In the meantime, I keep on walking. I'm getting a handle on my bad days, and my body is responding. My psoriasis has calmed down: the red spots faded to white patches on my legs. I even had the confidence to get them out this summer and wear a skirt, something I haven't done in years. And in September, I bravely visited the hairdressers and managed to sit chatting as they dyed the tips of my hair a candy-coloured pink. I liked it – as I liked the day that Leroy and I went and sat in a beer garden with Biffy and I was able to chat to the other people in the pub and even give them eye contact. That was a big day for me. There was no panic attack. There was only sunshine, and society, and an unfamiliar smile on my face.

I think the last thing to heal is going to be my confidence when it comes to drama: my life's work and my ultimate passion. Mr Willson was the one who first told me I was talented – but he was a liar, with an ulterior motive, so am I truly gifted? I find it very hard to know now if I'm any good at what I do, or if I've just been living a lie. It has massively affected my confidence, so much so that I can't audition – even now, to this day. I'm hoping that setting up YOLO is going to help me work again because my love of performing is still there, so I hope an oak tree might one day grow from that tiny seed.

On a good day, if I'm brave enough and feeling in the mood, I'll put on a record and slip on my old tap shoes, just as I used to do back in Rochdale when I was learning to dance as a girl. With a drumbeat pounding, I'll have a tap about on the smooth wooden floors in my small front room, my heels and toes tapping out a jaunty rhythm as I keep time. And when I'm dancing, I can feel joy. I can feel happiness. I can feel hope.

I think there's always hope; I think there always has been. Even on my darkest days, even when I've thought my life was over, in fact there was always a little bit of hope in the hope jar and it encouraged me to carry on – for one more minute, one more hour, one more day. I opened Pandora's box in letting out the secret of Mr Willson and me, but, just as in the Grecian myth, hope was what was left after the evils of the world flew out.

So I hope I continue to get better. I hope I can eventually learn to properly trust again. I hope I can run my own theatre company, and get married, and have kids. I want to live in a country farmhouse with loads of land, four or five dogs, cats and a few cheeky chickens. I hope to study psychology and counselling myself, once I'm better, and try to get a few certificates so that I can help other people.

Most of all, though, I hope I live a simple, happy life.

Because – despite everything – I still believe in happy endings.

Acknowledgments

Thank you to my rocks and my strength: my amazing parents. Your unconditional love and support have helped me more than you can know. I realise how difficult all this must have been for you, but your dignity in this process has been awe-inspiring. You have always been by my side, supporting me, believing in me – even when I'm at my worst. Sometimes your hugs are all I need or want, as I feel safer there than anywhere. We've truly been pushed to the limit during this shitty time, but we're still here, still living, still fighting on. You both inspire me more than anyone! I don't have one hero, I have two. You give me hope, laughter, fun and all a daughter could ever wish for! We are stronger than ever now and I love you beyond all words. Thank you for everything mum and dad. My heroes!

To my baby brother. What a beacon of strong and silent hope you are. Thank you for looking after our parents and being there when I physically and mentally couldn't. Here's to more gigs and laughter in our future. Love you bro!

To Mandy, the kind lady who took my original 101 call. I don't know where you are or if you'll ever see this, but you were wonderfully professional and empathetic. It was exactly what I needed at that time. Thank you.

A huge thank you to all at GMP and Lancashire Police for dealing with my case. It was a tough and difficult process but you were kind and professional. But, most of all, I felt believed and safe. A special thank you to Mick Smith of Lancashire Police who looked after me from beginning to end of the process. Your door was always open and your phone always on. You took care of a very vulnerable woman through the worst time of her life. I'll never forget that. Thank you.

To Nicola. My best friend then, now and always. Well, what a couple of years this has been! We never did make things easy for ourselves did we? Thank you for the laughs, for the normality, for always being my shoulder to lean on. You're one of the strongest women I know. Love you, lady.

To my Grandad. You'll probably never read this and I actually hope you don't. You're the quiet solid strength behind us all. Always listening and never judging. You've helped me so much in my life and I love you so much. Thank you and God bless.

Thank you to the online trolls and the haters. You made me stronger every day. It helped me to never give up this fight.

Thank you to all of Leroy's family. You supported me and never judged me through my illness or when my secret came out. You welcomed me, along with all my baggage, with open arms. What stars you are! Thank you.

A special thank you to Kate Moore. Without you this book wouldn't have been possible. Thank you for your guidance, your kindness, your patience, your understanding and your amazing talent.

Thank you also to Anna from Penguin, and Diana. You have both made me feel safe, welcome, informed and have given me the confidence to believe in this process. Truly appreciated.

Finally – hopefully you will all know who you are. Thank you to Kate, Cat, Krissy, Helen, Kimberley, Siara, Sian, Cleo, Wesley, Kirsty, Paula, Jordan, Loren, Gina, Daisy, Rachel, Alexandra, Rusty, Jodie, Dancing Debs, Paul, Trina, Jodie, John, Emma, Donna, Annette, Tee, Jo and Barry, Diarmuid, Martin, Malik and last but not least Biffy and Bella! Some of you were at school with me, some of you lived near me, some of you have met me along the way through my many years treading the boards, travelling the world and having fun! What you all have in common are your kind words of support and strength, your openness and honesty, throughout this process. You've all helped in your own individual way. Thank you! Woof Woof to the two Bs! (That's thank you in doggy language.) Your walks, wagging tails and puppy eyes kept me alive!